CLARK HOWARD'S

LIVING LARGE FOR THE LONG HAUL

CLARK HOWARD'S

LIVING LARGE FOR THE LONG HAUL

*Consumer-Tested Ways to
Overhaul Your Finances, Increase Your Savings,
and Get Your Life Back on Track*

CLARK HOWARD

with Mark Meltzer and Theo Thimou

AVERY
a member of Penguin Group (USA)
New York

AVERY

Published by the Penguin Group
Penguin Group (USA), 375 Hudson Street,
New York, New York 10014, USA

USA · Canada · UK · Ireland · Australia
New Zealand · India · South Africa · China

Penguin Books Ltd, Registered Offices:
80 Strand, London WC2R 0RL, England
For more information about the Penguin Group visit penguin.com

Most Avery books are available at special quantity discounts for bulk purchase for sales promotions, premiums, fund-raising, and educational needs. Special books or book excerpts also can be created to fit specific needs. For details, write: Special.Markets@us.penguingroup.com.

Library of Congress Cataloging-in-Publication Data

Howard, Clark, date.
Clark Howard's living large for the long haul : consumer-tested ways to overhaul your finances,
increase your savings, and get your life back on track / Clark Howard ; with Mark Meltzer and Theo Thimou.
p.   cm.
ISBN 978-1-58333-525-3
1. Finance, Personal—United States.   2. Consumer education—United States.
I. Meltzer, Mark.   II. Thimou, Theo.   III. Title.   IV. Title: Living large for the long haul.
HG179.H6852   2013   2013016854
332.02400973—dc23

Printed in the United States of America
1   3   5   7   9   10   8   6   4   2

BOOK DESIGN BY TANYA MAIBORODA

Nothing in this book is intended as an express or implied warranty of the suitability or fitness of any product, service, or design. The reader wishing to use a product, service, or design discussed in this book should first consult a specialist or professional to ensure suitability and fitness for the reader's particular lifestyle and environmental needs.

While the authors have made every effort to provide accurate telephone numbers, Internet addresses, and other contact information at the time of publication, neither the publisher nor the authors assume any responsibility for errors or for changes that occur after publication. Further, the publisher does not have any control over and does not assume any responsibility for author or third-party websites or their content.

Some names and identifying characteristics have been changed to protect the privacy of individuals involved. Interview subjects have been quoted with permission.

To my wife, Lane, and my three kids.
And to Christa DiBiase, who pushes me to do my best.
—Clark

For my dear sister Barbara, who left us way too soon, and my dad, Morty.
I wish they could have seen this, and hope they would have been proud.
—Mark

To Cynthia, Mason, and Sierra—the newest member of the pack—
for all your enthusiasm. And to Mom and Dad, of course!
—Theo

CONTENTS

WORKING AND LEARNING 263

THE EMPOWERED CONSUMER 285

CLARK HOWARD'S

LIVING LARGE FOR THE LONG HAUL

INTRODUCTION

··

WE ALL HAVE WHAT I like to call "pivotal moments" in our lives. Something happens that alters the way we think and perhaps even changes the course of our entire lives. For me, it happened when I was a teenager.

I was born in 1955 and grew up on what I like to call the "silver spoon plan" in Atlanta; it seemed our family wanted for nothing. When I was a teen, I went to American University in Washington, D.C., and my parents were footing the bill.

One Thanksgiving, I came home from college and there was something like an air of death around our house. We had a solemn dinner and everyone was quiet. I kept thinking, "There's something wrong. I just know it." Sure enough, we finished dinner and my dad asked me to wait at the table after saying, "I've got something to tell you."

I thought for sure he was going to tell me he was dying. Then he looked at me with this pained face and said, "I lost my job." Suddenly, I started smiling from ear to ear.

"Why are you smiling?" he asked me.

I had to explain how relieved I was because I thought he was dying! He relaxed at that point because he probably saw that things could be a lot worse than a job loss.

But the next thing out of his mouth was a stunner. "There's no money to pay for your next semester at college."

Now, I thought my folks were loaded with dough. But they lived a high-voltage lifestyle, where everything they earned, they also spent.

I was eighteen or nineteen at this point. So I went back to school and started looking around for work. I wound up working during the day full-time and going to school at night. After I finished my bachelor's degree in urban government, I got a job with IBM as a bill collector because I knew they would pay for my master's degree.

The deal was that I had to pay for my own books and get a B or better in a course in order to be reimbursed. I hate to say it, but I was never the best student. But you better believe I got a 3.9 GPA in my first quarter in grad school! And I never got less than a B during the rest of the time there, because I wanted IBM to pay the tuition for my master's in business management. Thanks, IBM!

I spent the first part of my twenties working as a social worker for almost four years out of grad school. But at twenty-five, I decided I wanted my own business. The airline industry had just been deregulated and I thought the free market would help travel explode in popularity. This was before the Internet. Turns out I was right; every eighteen months I would open a new office.

In 1987, I got a buyout offer for my chain of travel agencies. The buyers wanted my locations and my employees but not me. So I moved to the beach and had a grand old time living the retired life at thirty-one.

For some complicated family reasons, I soon had to leave the beach and go back to my birth home. I was doing nothing, just watching reruns on TV and training for biathlons. Out of the blue, I got a call from a local radio station that had a Sunday travel show and they asked me to be a guest.

From that one appearance, everything else in my career happened. Over time, I went from being an occasional guest to a regular guest to a host on my own travel talk show. I ultimately ended up as host of a weekday call-in advice show about money called *Cover Your Assets* in 1989.

Ever since then, I have been giving advice on the air. The show eventually morphed into *The Clark Howard Show*. I became a newspaper columnist in 1990 and started doing TV work in 1991.

In 1993, I saw there was a need for people who were too shy to talk with me on the air to have their questions answered off the air. So we started taking phone calls forty-five hours a week off the air with the help of more than one hundred trained volunteers at the Consumer Action Center (later rechristened simply as "Team Clark").

In 1997, we launched ClarkHoward.com. The following year my radio show went into syndication. And over the years, I've written nine books. I'm also the cohost of HLN's *Evening Express* every weekday evening.

The other things in my life involve investing on two different fronts. I've been in real estate since I was twenty-two, as a buyer of distressed property and as a landlord. And I've been investing in the stock market since I was very young.

My dad worked on the floor of the New York Stock Exchange as a young man, and he taught me in elementary school how to read stock tables while most kids were trading baseball cards. I've always had a fascination with it, based on his enthusiasm. I also had an investment company with my dad, which invested in everything from privately held to publicly traded companies of all sizes.

For me, what happened when I was a teen was great. It made a huge difference in my life by getting me to work at a very young age. That meant I missed a lot of the fun that people have in college, but the result of it and the benefit in my lifetime has been great. So when you hear me talk about how to save, that's not a theory. That's the truth. It's the reality of my life.

I don't want you to be or feel powerless, to feel as if you don't have options. Sometimes things happen that are out of our control. Most of the time, though, it's the choices we make, both little and big, that make the difference in what control we have over our lives and over our future.

I want you to take charge and take control. One dime at a time, one dollar at a time, and one day at a time. The end game is not to pinch a buck; it's to have the freedom to make choices—freedom to save, invest, and do as you wish. You'll notice that's a strong theme throughout this book.

In my last book, *Living Large in Lean Times*, I offered hundreds of great tips on how to save money. Since then, it's become clear that not only do we need to save for the short term, we need to think of lean times as something that might be with us for years.

So how do you prosper at a time when our country is not prospering as much as it did in the past? How do you thrive with the new rules of the game?

Living Large for the Long Haul introduces you to some Americans who are thriving and shares their fascinating stories with you.

At the end of each person's story, I offer commentary and takeaways that wrap up their story and explain what you can learn from them—what they're doing right and what they could be doing better. After you read just one story, you'll know how you can put my financial advice to work in your own life today.

Because I live in Atlanta, a number of people you'll meet in this book are also from Atlanta. That just makes sense. But you'll also meet many others from across the country, from the Great Lakes region to the Pacific Northwest, from New England to the heartland, and from the Southwest to the mid-Atlantic and everywhere in between.

—Clark Howard

CREDIT

Your credit score—it seems like the whole country is obsessed with those three little digits that hold the key to unlocking better interest rates for borrowers, lower premiums from insurance companies, and even job offers from many employers.

In this chapter, we meet three people who are recovering from shaky credit, one family who maintained rock-solid credit during the recession, and one person who went from having no credit to having great credit. I'll also show you why credit scores fall, how to make them go back up, how to challenge errors on a credit report, and how to get credit if you've never had it before.

THE RISING STAR

Anthony raised his credit score by 300 points
while earning under $30,000

ANTHONY EARL IS A STAR. Not a rock star or a star of stage and screen, but a rising credit star.

He's among an estimated 1.5 percent of Americans who took the necessary steps, sometimes against all odds, to boost their credit score during the Great Recession.

In Anthony's case, he actually raised his score by nearly 300 points at a time when we as a country were in the deepest trough of recession.

And he did it, in part, by paying down more than $30,000 in credit card debt while earning, as he told me, "below $30,000 annually" working for the government delivering mail to state facilities in Salt Lake City, Utah.

Now normally when someone's consumer debt exceeds more than 50 percent of their annual income, it becomes very difficult to dig out. But Anthony refused to accept poor credit and mounting credit card bills as a fact of life. And that's why I want to share his story with you.

Every day the fortysomething state employee's mail delivery route takes him from Layton to Sandy straight through the heart of his downtown metro area. A breathtaking view of the snowcapped Wasatch mountain range is his constant companion. But life wasn't so picture-perfect for Anthony when he was digging his way out of debt for nearly five years.

His problems with credit card debt and low credit scores started for perhaps the noblest reason of all: because he chose to help a family member when she needed it most. People end up in debt for all different reasons, and helping a loved one is one of the best I can think of, though the consequences are no less dire just because your heart is in the right place.

"My sister was separated from her husband and he was not providing financial support. Every time the state found him and garnished his wages, he would just switch to another job," Anthony says. "I stepped in to help, and ended up in a bad way. When my sister's husband finally started supporting her and their children, I had accrued just over $30,000 in credit card debt on a half-dozen cards."

Being unmarried with no children himself allowed Anthony to swing the financial commitment to his sister from April 2006 to March 2008, paying for her groceries and utilities. But during that time, the former army and navy man who served during Operation Desert Storm was racking up more and more late payments on his own bills.

When he checked his credit scores from Equifax, Experian, and TransUnion, he discovered they averaged out to 512—firmly in the subprime credit category.

"All of my friends had scores that were in the high 600s to 700s, and they were telling me that I needed a score in the 600s to get a loan for a vehicle," Anthony says. "The situation was depressing because I did not know exactly how to improve my credit score, so I could not get a new vehicle loan." (Anthony continues to drive his "old, beat-up" 1998 Ford Ranger with 121,000 miles on it and a rebuilt transmission.)

After listening to my radio show, he quickly formulated a plan that he put into action starting in May 2008. He began throwing the bulk of his money at the credit cards with the highest interest rates first, while still making more than the minimum payment on his other cards.

But he made a few critical errors along the way.

"When I had one card paid off, I would then cancel that card, and then proceed in the same pattern with the next card," Anthony says. "Ouch. I was stabbing myself in the back by doing this! My debt-to-credit ratio would jump to about 90 percent after I canceled the paid-off card."

This is a classic mistake and twofer that's really easy for most people to correct. Thirty percent of your credit score is keeping a low credit utilization rate. So each time Anthony canceled a card, he reduced his available credit and actually *raised* the percentage of the credit he was using. Meanwhile, another 15 percent of a credit score is keeping lines of credit open. Between the two, that's almost half of your credit score right there.

That's why I always tell people to resist the temptation to cancel a credit card when they've paid the balance down to zero. It's better to keep it open and use it for small charges twice a year.

Anthony also had some sporadic late payments that were dragging his score down. So he came up with a very old-school solution to address that problem.

"I started sending all of my payments USPS Priority Mail so I could track when they arrived, and I changed myself so that I was positively sending every payment in early. Paying $5 was much better than paying a $25 or $35 late fee," Anthony told me. "Whenever I got a late fee charge, I would call the company and challenge it, and then send in a written statement saying the same thing, accompanied with copies of my proof."

With those problems under control, Anthony had to find a way to build his credit score back up. The quickest way for him to do that was to apply for more credit.

Applying for credit is the kind of move that pinches your score by 10 or 15 points in the short term because the risk you pose to a lender rises when you have more credit that you could potentially charge up and default on. But, ultimately, it raises your score in the long run when you demonstrate that you can responsibly manage having a higher available credit limit.

So Anthony got two additional major credit cards—not store cards that don't really help your score at all—and practically guarded them with his life.

"These extra cards were locked away and I would use them only for small purchases under $50, so they could be paid off when the next card statement came," he says.

I encourage people to get a calendar and mark a date—maybe your birthday or the first of the year—and then another date six months later. When those days arrive, get your credit cards out of the dresser or from the back of your wallet and use them. Then pay the bill when it arrives in the mail. This keeps them active in your credit mix.

After four years of paying down his debt in a timely manner, Anthony made his final payment in May 2012 on the debt he had accumulated helping his sister. And at last check, the blended average of his credit scores had climbed from a below-sea-level low of 512 to a Wasatch mountain high of 805.

Reducing debt in his life has made so much more possible. In early 2013, Anthony bumped his 401(k) contributions up from 3 percent to 6 percent to pick up his employer's full matching contribution, and he also started a rainy day account. Next on the horizon is saving for some college evening classes. Even having to self-finance a bathroom remodel that he's doing himself is easier now that he has the experience of paying down $30,000 under his belt.

Know that there is no magic bullet to fix your credit.

- Credit repair companies say they'll remove bad credit marks from your record for a price. But what these firms typically do is use a technique to temporarily raise your score by a significant number of points for a few weeks before it plummets back down again. Anyone who says they can magically eliminate bad items on your credit report is telling you a big lie. Use the money you would pay them to pay the debts you owe and that will improve your credit score on its own.

Find out what's in your credit report.

- You have a credit file at each of the three main credit bureaus—Equifax, Experian, and TransUnion. Once each year, you're allowed by law to see your credit file.
- AnnualCreditReport.com is the only legitimate site to do this for free. I advise people to pull one report every four months. That way you're never more than 120 days away from knowing if there's funny business going on with your files.

Challenge errors with the credit bureaus.

- Errors on credit reports are common. Maybe your credit file is "married" to somebody else's who has the same or a similar name, or maybe there's a false lien supposedly filed against you. It could be anything; those are just two of the most common examples.
- When there's something wrong on your credit file, you need to file a dispute with both the credit issuer and the credit bureau simultaneously. Send all your documents by certified mail, return receipt requested, which means you have to use the manual form, not the automated system.
- If the problem is not fixed, redispute it with the bureau. If that fails, you must sue both the credit issuer and the credit bureau in small claims court. Most of the time, both parties will cave before the court date and remove the black mark from your report.
- Should all this fail to get the job done, there's a new cop on the beat overseeing the credit reporting industry.
- The Consumer Financial Protection Bureau (CFPB) is now accepting complaints if you've been ignored by Experian, Equifax, and TransUnion over errors on your credit

report. Make a visit to ConsumerFinance.gov/Complaint your last resort; you want to give the bureaus a chance to mend their ways first!

Don't apply for in-store credit.

- "Would you like to save 20 percent on your purchase today by opening a store credit card?" Not me! Store cards don't build your credit the way major credit cards from banks or other lenders do. In fact, they actively hurt your score. Opening a single store card will ding your score by up to 30 points for twenty-four months. Plus, store cards have historically had a much higher interest rate than most other regular cards. If you're going to run a balance, the upfront benefit of a one-time discount doesn't work out for you.

THE FALLEN ANGEL

Joyce and Don killed $40,000 of debt in twenty-four months

LIKE SO MANY OTHER PEOPLE I talked to through the Great Recession, Joyce Fondren knew she was in serious financial trouble.

In 2008, Joyce, then sixty-five, and her husband, Don, sixty-seven, owed $30,000 on an assortment of credit cards and had refinanced their mortgage to get a lower monthly payment. By July 2010, they owed $90,000 on fifteen credit cards, and most of it came from interest charges.

"I was making payments of $300 to $500, of which only $100 or so was going to pay down the debt," said Joyce. "In addition, I was still charging for food [and] gas. It finally got to the point that there was no money left after bills were paid. I would make a $350 payment, which would give me available credit of maybe $100, which I would use. I was robbing Peter to pay Paul—juggling credit cards."

Then one night, Joyce and Don had a bit of an epiphany. They were driving their 2000 Ford F-150 pickup from their home in rural Chandler, Oklahoma, to Cimarron Casino near Stillwater, where they went on occasion to forget about their troubles. It was a cool fall night, and Joyce was watching for deer. She saw three cross the road on the forty-five-minute drive.

Joyce and Don turned on their radio to listen to my show, and heard me mention one of my favorite organizations, the National Foundation for Credit Counseling (NFCC.org). Joyce opened her purse, got a pen and paper, and wrote down the website.

At first, she looked at the website for the organization but took no action. But later she made contact with the local affiliate, Consumer Credit Counseling Service (CCCS).

"CCCS contacted all our cards and negotiated very low [6 percent or less] interest and arranged for the debt to be paid off in five years or less. In return we had to contact all our accounts and tell them what we were doing, which was very humbling, and close accounts. We could not incur new debt."

Joyce and Don had to cut up all their credit cards, not an easy thing to do for a couple who was relying on credit to buy essentials like food and gasoline.

So they decided to make a major ceremony out of it, and on July 14, 2010, one by one, each card went into the shredder.

"My grandson, who was twelve at the time, [manned] the shredder," Joyce said. "If you have ever watched *Survivor* on TV, at the end of the show when only two contestants are left, they talk about and remember those who are gone. We did that with each card. For example: 'This card was used on the trip to Indiana to see our son and all the casinos in between. This one was used to buy our mattress set.' We would make a comment about the card and then our grandson would send it to shredder heaven."

Joyce said the last card was the hardest of all to shred.

"It was the first card I ever had in my own name. We owed $15,000 on it. It was the card we used to go to casinos in Tunica, Mississippi."

And, oddly, there was a problem sending it to its fate.

"It seemed the shredder was worn out with the previous fourteen. We could also imagine my last card hanging on for dear life to not go down the shredder. But, alas, it also succumbed."

With no more active credit, Joyce and Don, with the help of CCCS, set about paying down their pile of debt. They began sending $1,897 a month to CCCS, which after a fee of $35 per month, would then make payments to each of their creditors at a discounted negotiated rate.

Joyce said the CCCS plan was to pay off the smallest balances first. A little more than two years after they began their plan, Joyce and her husband had paid off five of their fifteen credit cards and expected five more to be paid off within five months.

Their total debt had fallen from $90,000 to $50,000.

Believe it or not, Joyce and Don were a frugal couple whose once tidy financial life spun out of control from a combination of medical bills and their love of the aforementioned casinos.

"I knew all about the dangers of credit cards," Joyce said. "In fact, I am a math teacher, and one of the classes I teach is Math/Finance. My only defense is that we were victims of excellent credit just a few years ago and so came a deluge of cards."

The couple raised five children on one income. Then came a series of illnesses.

"It seemed we developed the attitude of 'Eat, drink, and be merry, for tomorrow we die,'" Joyce said. "The problem is we did not die and we found ourselves saddled with unsecured debt."

It started when Don felt compelled to retire from his downsizing company at age fifty-three in 1994. It was the second downsizing for the company, and the retirement package was not as good as the first. Future downsizings were expected, and they were worried about benefits for the next group to be downsized.

"Our lives changed more drastically than we realized at the time. Our two older children were ages twenty-eight and twenty-six and on their own. We still had three, ages eighteen, sixteen, and fourteen, at home. College expenses loomed. In addition, I was attending college," explained Joyce.

Don's income from his company pension plan was less than a third of his salary. Joyce had assumed he would get a part-time job to supplement their income, but she didn't realize what a blow it was for him to have lost his full-time job.

In 1998, he went to work as a maintenance supervisor for a college. But between 1994 and 1998, he only had some sporadic temporary work. During this time, Joyce was working on getting a degree to become a math teacher.

They lived off the $100,000 in his 401(k) and went through it all.

Then things started to improve. By August 1999, Joyce had a full-time teaching position and Don was working and receiving a pension from his old company. Her health insurance was covered at work and his was covered by his pension plan.

That's when the health problems started. He had two strokes, developed diabetes, and had to quit work. He accrued high medical bills despite his insurance. Later he suffered a blood clot in his leg and a second stroke.

"He was actually quite lucky. No serious debilitating side effects from the two strokes. However, we did have serious, debilitating medical bills even with good insurance," said Joyce.

Joyce had her own medical problems that caused the couple to accumulate bills. But they're still pushing through. Her health has been pretty good, except for being plagued by kidney stones for forty years. In April 2009, she was hospitalized with renal failure due to blockage of the kidneys by numerous stones. This was followed by quite a few outpatient procedures to get rid of the stones, creating some big-time medical bills.

The couple did not buy things or splurge at restaurants. They drove their cars until they could run no more. They paid their bills on time.

"Casinos were our downfall," Joyce said. "They enable you to forget your worries."

After they paid their bills, they would spend their extra cash on casinos.

"At first we had to travel out of state for the casinos. At that time we were not addicted. Then about six years ago, Indian casinos started popping up everywhere. If we spent all our cash on casinos, then we used credit cards for gas, food, whatever."

Now there is little to spend on casinos.

"We still go, but now we can only spend a little. We cannot borrow money to get us out of a tight spot."

As for me, I don't understand casinos. A couple of years ago when I was in Las Vegas, my executive producer Christa DiBiase asked me to play one dollar for her in a Tabasco slot machine on her behalf. Well, I promptly lost it and, boy, did that foul up my mood for the rest of the day!

But with Joyce and Don's debt clearing, there is reason to celebrate. Joyce's credit score on CreditKarma.com was up to 720 and on TransUnion it was 679, up from the 500s in 2010, and it showed her paying on time.

And every July 14, on Bastille Day, Joyce and Don remember the day they shredded their credit cards and took a big step toward a better financial future and hopefully many more happy days together.

What can you take away from the couple's story?

Get legitimate professional help with your debt.
- Whenever people get into trouble with their bills, I recommend they go talk to a local chapter of the National Foundation for Credit Counseling. The NFCC offers free or very low cost credit and debt counseling through affiliates around the country that are branded locally under different names. Consumer Credit Counseling Service was the local affiliate in Joyce and Don's area.

- One in three people seen at an NFCC affiliate needs simple budgeting help to get their debt under control. I usually find setting a goal of paying down debt in sixty months or less works best for people. Anything greater than sixty months and people tend to lose their focus.

- Joyce and Don, however, needed something more—a hardship debt management plan. With this kind of plan, the NFCC affiliate charges a nominal fee to negotiate a reduced interest rate and lower your payments if you qualify. Visit NFCC.org or call 1-800-388-2227 for more details.

Or do it yourself!

- Did you know that you can negotiate down debt on your own? Begin by figuring out what you owe and what you can afford to pay. Then call up your various creditors and say, "My total debt is X number of dollars and I can afford to pay you X amount every month."

- Make sure all your creditors agree to your terms *in writing* or tell them no one will get anything at all. They're all scared that you'll bankrupt out and leave them high and dry, so you have the power in this situation.

- When you do agree on a negotiated payoff for all your creditors, make your payments by money order only. Don't give any creditor access to your checking account or they might help themselves to your funds.

- I should note that this approach will foul up your credit and you'll get a tax bill from the IRS for each settlement. But if you've reached this point in your financial life, your credit is most likely fouled up already and the end result of this attempt can actually improve your situation over time.

- Regarding the tax bill that you'll get, say you owe $10,000 to one creditor and they take $2,000 to settle up. In that case, the $8,000 that's written off is considered taxable income for you. Expect to get a 1099 form in the mail that's considered "phantom income" by the IRS.

Make a credit card payment every fourteen days.

- The method of paying down debt recommended to Joyce and Don by the NFCC affiliate—paying off the smallest balance and then working your way up to your biggest balance—is called the "debt snowball plan." It's an idea that's been popularized by my friend and fellow radio host Dave Ramsey.

- That's a great way to get the job done, but far from the only approach. I'd like to suggest one other approach that I learned about in the book *Invest in Yourself: Six Secrets to a Rich Life* by Marc Eisenson.

- Begin by targeting the card with the highest interest rate. Pay more money toward that credit card and slightly less toward the other cards, until the card with highest-interest debt has a zero balance. Then you move on to the next card, and so on and so on.
- Eisenson specifically suggests that you make a separate payment every fourteen days to the credit card company. Work these payments around your statement cycle to avoid paying late fees. Credit card interest is typically compounded daily, so this can get you paid off a whole lot faster.

Stop the pre-approved credit applications in your mailbox.

- In the final summation, Joyce and Don got into trouble partly because they had too much credit at their disposal. If you're worried about following in their footsteps, there's a simple fix I can recommend.
- Dial 1-888-5-OPT-OUT (1-888-567-8688) or visit OptOutPrescreen.com and you can have your info removed from marketing lists for preapproved credit and insurance offers from the three major U.S. credit bureaus. It's OK to enter your Social Security number when prompted for it by the computer system. That's how they verify your identity and remove you from the lists.
- However, calling the number will not stop your bank, credit union, or brokerage company from selling your information. For that, you must respond individually to the privacy policy statements you receive from each financial institution in the mail. Or you must call the institution or company yourself.

Watch your discretionary spending.

- Joyce and Don still go to the casinos, but they've learned to control their spending. Other Americans might not regularly hit the casinos, but there are other gambling threats draining their wallets and they're going on unchecked.
- There's a convenience store gas station down near my house that every Friday night is swarmed with people buying lottery tickets. I see people drop $20 at a time on scratch-offs and lottery tickets—and we're talking about people who absolutely need that money to pay bills and take care of their families.
- But there's the lure posted on those big billboards on highways pushing that huge jackpot of $140 million or whatever it is. Yet have you ever actually stopped to think about the odds that you'll hit the Mega Millions jackpot?

- Physicist John Swain (aka Dr. Knowledge) of Northeastern University ran the numbers for the *Boston Globe*. His findings show that you have a 1 in 175,711,536 chance of winning. Meanwhile, Swain says there's a 1 in 10,000,000 chance you'll be struck and killed by lightning.
- To quote Jim Carrey in 1994's *Dumb & Dumber*: "So, you're telling me there's a chance?!"

Have a positive mental attitude.

- Keep the spirit and don't give up, or these tips I've laid out here and elsewhere in the book won't work for you. Everybody has problems, but some people choose to make a bump in the road into a molehill, while other people let it loom as large as Mount Everest.
- My late father used to tell me that life is like a boxing match with ninety-nine rounds, and sometimes you get knocked down, get back up, and go on to have a good round. You might be in your eightieth round, but you've got to get back up.
- Winston Churchill said it best when he said, "Never give in. Never give in. Never, never, never, never—in nothing, great or small, large or petty—never give in except to convictions of honor and good sense." You might be deep in credit card debt today, but don't throw in the towel. You probably didn't get into debt overnight and you won't get out immediately, either. But you've got to keep working your way out, day by day and piece by piece.

GOLDEN

Melinda and Doug's income dropped by 80 percent,
but they kept their credit rock solid

LET ME LAY MY CARDS on the table: My credit score was 776 at last check, not exactly "golden" in the industry of the credit lingo. In order to be golden, you need a credit score that's 800 or above on the 850-point FICO scale. At 776, I have a patriotic number, but it's more silver than gold!

So I took notice when Melinda Smith of Hillsboro, Oregon, wrote to me saying that she and her husband, Doug, both forty-two, have maintained golden scores for decades despite falling on hard times during the Great Recession.

"Mine is 805, my husband, 809. Had those scores or higher since our twenties. Even after one or the other being unemployed for about three of the past five years," Melinda noted on my Facebook page.

Having great credit scores during both good and bad times has helped the Smiths when they needed it most with low interest rates on home loans, auto loans, and credit card debt, plus it allowed them to refinance mortgages easily.

"I remember when I was twenty-eight and wanted to refinance my house and I called a lender to get a quote," Melinda says. "The gentleman who I spoke with seemed very condescending and didn't seem interested in dealing with me until he pulled my credit score. He was shocked and said that I had 'gold balls' credit and he was impressed. The refinance went much smoother after that and he was much more helpful."

Fast-forward to the Great Recession, and like many Americans, the Smiths have wrestled with having their work hours scaled back over the last five years.

Beginning in 2007, Melinda went from a $25-an-hour position doing administrative work at a small environmental consulting firm to $10 an hour for the same job at a dentist's office. She's now working as an office manager at Allstate for $14 an hour, with a schedule that can vary from ten hours a week to as many as thirty-six hours.

Meanwhile, Doug has held four jobs since 2007, all in the service departments of Portland-area car dealerships. He's now the full-time service manager at a dealership specializing in Volvos and other vehicles, and is paid mostly on commission, with biweekly checks that range from $1,867 to $3,387 per check.

But during the worst stretch, their household income dropped from $100,000 to $20,000 between unemployment compensation and part-time work.

That put the Smiths into an uncomfortable position. They had to wipe out a $20,000 emergency fund in order to keep up with their monthly bills. They also had to pay for COBRA when they didn't have steady work. (Melinda is diabetic.)

So the couple, who has a nine-year-old daughter named Olivia, went from paying their credit card bill in full each month to being partial payers still making well above the minimum payments.

By prioritizing their obligations even when money got tight, the Smiths did the single best thing anyone can do for their credit score: Always pay each and every bill on time.

"We have always paid more than the minimum payment even when money has been tight and always on time," Melinda says. "I'm not going to say that we haven't had to utilize some credit to get through the past five years or so, but we are making great strides in getting it paid back down while trying to build up our emergency fund again."

Doug adds, "My parents taught me a long time ago, for the most part you pay cash for things. If you can't afford it, you can stretch it, but no more than several months. I figure it's part of my duty as an American to have good credit."

Another key to the Smiths' maintaining a high credit rating through thick and thin has been keeping their credit utilization low. Currently, Melinda and Doug have charges of $16,000 against their total available credit of $120,600 across four different credit cards. So they're using 13 percent of their credit.

The Smiths also have unusual ways of staying afloat when times get tough.

For starters, Doug told me he's perfected the art of car flipping. Last year, he bought a beat-up 1999 VW Cross Country with 138,000 miles on it for $1,000 cash. With his dealer discount, Doug got the necessary parts for $800 and did the repairs himself. He later sold the car for $4,900 on Craigslist, and that's roughly the tenth time he's flipped a car over the years.

Doug's entrepreneurial spirit carries over into one other area of the family's life too: birthday party entertainment.

If you want a real fire engine to come to your kid's birthday party in Portland, the Smiths are the only game in town. Doug owns and operates Engine 51, a 1987 Spartan FMC Type 1 fire truck with a Hale water pump that holds 750 gallons of water. Basically, every seven-year-old boy's dream ride!

Doug was a volunteer firefighter in Cornelius, Oregon, from 1998 to 2000, but he had one gripe during his service. "They never let me drive the fire engine. It got to the point where I was still probationary and I was kind of like, 'Now, wait a second. Here I am risking my life and you won't let me play with your toy,'" he told me.

In 2009, he saw Engine 51 on eBay for $3,500. He watched the auction for weeks, but it never garnered a bid. Finally, with just seconds left, he bid the asking price. The Spartan is valued at roughly $250,000. (Yes, you read that right!)

Melinda was initially aghast at the buy.

"When I actually saw that he had just purchased a modern full-sized fire engine, I promptly announced that he would need to figure out a way for it to make us money," she says. "I then thought about birthday parties and found that no one was offering them in our area. It has been a nice part-time job and really helped us out financially during periods of unemployment."

The Smiths charge $175 to bring Engine 51 to parades, restaurant openings, weddings, and other events. Doug even rented out the truck for a season finale of the TNT drama *Leverage*, earning $1,500 for the two days of filming along with $90 to appear as an extra. For the birthday parties, the family rolls up with sirens blazing in firemen's turnout coats and helmets and lets all partygoers spray the hose, even adults!

Always pay your bills on time.

- This goes for credit card bills, doctor bills, utility bills, cable bills, and every other kind of bill. You can use a free budgeting tool like Mint.com to automatically send yourself simple reminders when your bills are due. Or if you're not high-tech, just mark your bill due dates down on a calendar. Whatever it takes to get the job done. Making timely payments alone accounts for 35 percent of your credit score.

Don't use too much available credit.

- Let's say you have one credit card and it has a $5,000 limit. If you're carrying a $1,500 monthly balance, you're using 30 percent of the total limit. For a solid credit score, don't use more than 30 percent of your available credit. For a top-tier score, stay below 10 percent. This factor accounts for another 30 percent of your credit score.

When you pay off a credit card, don't close the account.

- People get so excited to close their cards when they pay the balance down to zero. Don't do it! It will only reduce your available credit and lower your score. You want to have four to six lines of credit. Use them twice a year for small purchases to keep them active and pay them off right away. Fifteen percent of your credit score is having open lines of credit that are responsibly managed.

Know your credit score.

- Your true score is the FICO score, but you have one FICO score from each credit bureau.
- The one most lenders use is the Equifax FICO score. The question is, do you really need to know your real credit score? It's only really necessary when you're getting ready to take out a home or auto loan. In that case, you can pay a small fee at myFICO.com to learn your true score. Otherwise, if you just want a credit checkup, you can get a free non-FICO credit score from Credit.com, CreditKarma.com, or Quizzle.com.

Have alternate streams of income.

- Melinda and Doug found clever ways to make money, pay their bills, and maintain good credit even when the income from their day jobs dwindled. You've probably seen ads by the side of the road promising you can make hundreds in your spare time working at home. I get calls every day on my radio show from people who have been duped out of money that was supposed to get them insider info on the track to wealth.

- In reality, the best work at home is almost always drawing on your life experience, skills, training, and prior work experience to do something better, cheaper, or more conveniently for someone else based on what you already know. Anybody who promises you an insta-business for your cash is only going to make you insta-poor.

CREDIT NEWBIES

Patricia navigated the American credit system as an immigrant

TRYING TO GET YOUR FIRST CREDIT card or car loan isn't easy when you're starting out. But imagine how hard it would be if you came to the United States from another country and had no credit record and no understanding of the American financial situation.

That's exactly what Patricia Jimenez-Ronka faced when she came to the United States as a thirty-eight-year-old from Mexico in 1990.

"At that time there wasn't any recording of your credit transactions in Mexico," said Patricia, now sixty-one. "You could go from one institution to another and ask for credit and they would not have any idea, besides your word, of your financial status. There was no credit score. Getting a bank loan was very difficult unless you had money in the bank, and credit cards were not easy to get, [though] credit in stores was."

Patricia came to the United States after sending her daughter, also named Patricia, here to learn English.

"Even when she was attending a bilingual school in Mexico, she decided not to learn it. My sister was living here in Atlanta, and I sent my daughter to be with her for a school year. She was thirteen years old. After that year in school, she was bilingual, but she did not want to go back to Mexico."

Patricia's daughter had liked sports, and there weren't too many sports opportunities for girls in Mexican schools, except gymnastics and swimming. In the United States, she got involved in basketball, volleyball, and track, among other activities.

"The company for which I was working—Nacobre, which makes copper, brass, and aluminum products—had a branch here in Atlanta; I asked for a transfer, and because my job involved managing the import/export side of the organization, and it was possible for me to do it from Atlanta, I got the transfer and I came to the United States."

Not knowing how the financial system worked here was hard for Patricia.

"You can make costly mistakes without even knowing it. I did. I remember working in a company for a couple of years, and after I left it, they sent me a notification asking for instructions about my 401(k)—would I like a check or should they send a deposit directly to a retirement account? Not knowing anything about it, I asked for a check in my name! I lost some money there."

Getting a check in her name meant she was taking a withdrawal and had to pay taxes and penalties on the money. But she didn't know any better at the time.

Friends and family back home, she said, were equally puzzled by the U.S. system.

"They were horrified that 'everyone' should know about my salary and my personal financial situation. They did not understand the credit system. On the other hand, they said that with the system it would still be difficult to establish credit. If you don't have a history, you won't get credit. If you don't get credit, you won't have a history."

Patricia was turned down the first time she applied for credit because she had no credit history. She opened the door to the American credit system by buying a used car at a dealership. She bought a 1986 Toyota Camry for about $3,500.

"I was charged high interest, 18 percent, and the price of the car was too expensive," she said. "It took me a while to pay it. It was a hard learning experience."

Patricia was able to buy her first house in 1995, and she said the feeling was terrific.

"I felt secure and stable, on my way to a better future. I felt that I was part of this country."

Patricia has built a successful financial life, but she had some hurdles to clear.

After one of the Mexican peso devaluations, her company closed its Atlanta branch. She had to decide whether to stay in the United States or go back to Mexico.

"I decided to stay in Atlanta, and I had to do some work I was not used to doing. I had a business cooking Mexican food at people's homes. At the same time, I had a part-time job as a waitress in a hotel. I was always running from one job to the other. Sometimes I was working until two o'clock in the morning and getting up again early the next morning."

For a time Patricia decided to deliver phone books to get additional income, and her daughter had to help because she could not go up and down the stairs at an apartment complex.

"While I was working two part-time jobs with crazy hours, I volunteered in my spare time as an interpreter at St. Joseph's Hospital. They offered me a job and I fell in love with nonprofits."

After that she worked at United Way with the Hispanic community for ten years, and then at Consumer Credit Counseling Service for almost ten years. Now she is starting her own consulting business.

As she found success in work, she learned more about personal finance.

"Once I understood the system, I was careful managing my credit. I understood that the only way to have a stable financial situation was not to spend more than what I made."

At the beginning it was hard to save, but Patricia, whom friends describe as passionate and determined, began to learn how to buy things at lower prices. And she opened a savings account.

"Then I applied for a credit card and paid it in full each month. Little by little my credit improved. My savings went to investments. I contributed to a 403(b) plan up to the amount that the company matched. It wasn't easy, but now it is very rewarding."

Patricia loves to use her knowledge to help other immigrants. In fact, after talking to "anyone who would listen," she was asked by a local radio station to host a program about personal finance. The Spanish-language station focuses on the needs of immigrants.

"I had been in their shoes, so I can talk to them about my experience and also let them know about the steps they need to take to be financially successful."

First, she tells callers that the most important tool they can have is a monthly budget. Once they know how much they make, they know how much they can spend each month, Patricia said, and where they stand financially.

Then she suggests they apply for a secured credit card, which requires a deposit equal to the amount of the credit line. In a year, she says, customers should ask the bank to convert the card into a standard unsecured credit card.

"I stress the importance of making all their payments on time; this is one of the main points to having a good credit standing. I also ask them not to get carried away by the notion that they have to buy what their family or friends have. Some people have the idea that having credit is having debts. I explain to them that they do not have to be in debt, but they need to have a good credit history if they want to get lower interest on a house or a car, and to use a credit card as an intermediary between their money and the business where they normally buy."

Having a good credit score is more important now than when Patricia came to the United States more than twenty years ago.

"In 1990, you needed a good credit history to get credit; now even employers, insurance companies, and other type of businesses are using the credit report to screen potential employee or clients, and even when they do not use the credit report in the same way as the lenders do, they use it as a way to determine how responsible a person is."

What can you learn from Patricia's efforts to get credit when she had none?

Open up a secured credit card.
- If you've never had any kind of credit before, you'll probably find no one wants to give you a credit card when you apply! That's because lenders have no point of reference on you. Will you pay on time? Will you pay late but steadily? Will you charge up your card and then just walk away from the unsecured debt? They have no idea.
- The basic way a secured credit card works is you deposit money with a credit union (or bank) and they issue you a credit card, knowing they have your money as collateral. You can charge only as much as you have on deposit. This allows you to build a credit history where you previously had none.
- It's like training wheels for credit. Look for a card with a reasonable annual fee of no more than $60; no application fee; and be sure that after twelve to eighteen months of paying on time, the issuer will upgrade you to a traditional credit card. It's a slow process, but an important one to build credit.

Or get a "fresh start."
- My preferred way for you to get credit is more of a fast track: Join a credit union that has a "fresh start" program and apply for their credit card. The fresh start program is an informal name for any of a number of initiatives at credit unions that are geared toward people who have never had credit before.
- As with a secured card, the fresh start program will have you put money on deposit with the credit union. Then the credit union will write you a small loan or issue you a

Visa or MasterCard with a small limit against the money you put in savings. But unlike a secured card, the credit card from a fresh start program reports as regular credit from day one. And that's why it's better.

Rely on a spouse's credit.

- It used to be that you could make your spouse an authorized user on a credit card and that that alone would build his or her credit when they had none of their own. But today, you've got to go one step further and make your spouse a joint account holder, not just an authorized user.

- The distinction is that a joint account holder is responsible for the debt that you jointly incur in a marriage; an authorized user generally is not. Along with that added risk comes added reward. The joint account will appear on the credit report of the spouse who started with no credit, and it can go a long way to helping them qualify for credit in their own name.

HOMES AND REAL ESTATE

During the Great Recession, the American Dream of home ownership became a nightmare for some because of declining home values. Yet with extreme hazard comes extreme opportunity. It was the best time I'd ever seen for anyone to buy a home. Even today's homes are still a relative deal because of depressed values and artificially low interest rates.

In this chapter, we meet five people whose lives and housing choices highlight the ups and downs of the real estate market. I'll also explain how to find the best rents if you're involuntarily forced to become a renter because of a foreclosure, how to steal a deal on distressed real estate, how to get out from underneath an upside-down mortgage, and more.

THE HAPPY RENTERS

Foreclosure leads Rowena and Rodolfo to a less stressful life

(WHILE ALL THE PEOPLE *in this book are real, several did not want me to use their real names. That's the case here. However, every other detail of this story is factual.*)

The bonds of a neighborhood die hard—and not even foreclosure, bankruptcy, or a storm as severe as Hurricane Sandy can sever them.

After Sandy ravaged the New Jersey coastline in October 2012, Rowena Santos would drive back to the street in Cliffwood Beach, New Jersey, where she and her husband, Rodolfo, spent eleven years raising three children before they chose to walk away from their mortgage in November 2010.

"Every once in a while we would go and visit, just to check [our old] house, and mostly to check on our old neighbor who lived across from us," Rowena says. "She was like an Italian grandmother to our kids. I don't know how many blankets she had crocheted for them."

Today Rowena and Rodolfo—both of Filipino descent—still live in Cliffwood Beach with their teenage kids, but they're in a different neighborhood as renters.

Cliffwood Beach is a working-class town of three thousand with a gorgeous view of the Raritan Bay. With its blue-collar roots, it's the kind of town that represents the true Jersey Shore. The hardscrabble streets make the glitzy "GTL" lifestyle (gym, tan, laundry) of a particular reality TV show seem a million miles away—even though Seaside Heights is only about thirty-five miles south on the Garden State Parkway.

Rodolfo, forty-one, works for a major cable operator, and Rowena, thirty-seven, does part-time administrative work at a company that sells high-tech equipment to government and private companies. Their kids, Marcus, Lucas, and Lea, are fifteen, thirteen, and twelve, respectively.

Like a lot of Americans who were rendered renters by the Great Recession, a perfect storm of factors conspired to bring Rowena and Rodolfo to where they are today—including a cash-out refinance for home improvements and to pay down some bills, a slew of unexpected medical expenses, and a change on the job front.

"The hours I worked dwindled where I was working before [my current job]. The health insurance my job provided didn't cover what was needed for Marcus, who has had many medical issues since he was born," Rodolfo says. "It all started coming at us at once. I found another job which cut my pay in half but provided better health insurance. The bills started to pile up from there, and the house started to fall around us."

"The house in which we offered our blood, sweat, and tears for eleven years was slowly killing us physically, emotionally, mentally, and spiritually. Rodolfo and I were fighting more and more about money, about time," Rowena says. "Rodolfo was working more hours [at the new job]. I was trying to work more than the hours my company could give me, but all the money that we worked so hard for was all going to the house and some bills that we could afford to pay."

Rowena jokes that they "couldn't even afford to buy pizza"—only it's closer to truth than jest, and that becomes painfully apparent when she reveals, "It was like Jesus' cross [to bear] this house."

Still, the couple filed for Chapter 13 bankruptcy hoping to stay in their home. But their mortgage lender was not willing to work with them.

"I had actually made it a career to call them almost every day and got the runaround each time," Rowena says. "They would always tell me that they didn't receive whatever paperwork that I had snail mailed or faxed or whatever the excuse was at the time. For almost a month, I was trying my best to work out the best deal for us to stay in the house. Even though it was such a burden for us, it was still our house."

Rodolfo credits their lawyer with helping them navigate the difficult situation the best way they could.

"We were just going to leave our house and get all our stuff because our mortgage company wasn't working with us, but our lawyer advised us to go the bankruptcy route," he says. "[But] I was concerned with more legal fees. He then told us to pay them whenever we got back on our feet."

With their back against the wall, Rowena and Rodolfo were forced to file for Chapter 7, which will stay on their credit report for ten years. They finally left their home at the end of 2010.

When someone has a foreclosure, they typically move back in with family for two reasons. First, that's the cheapest option. And second, their ailing finances could prevent them from easily getting into an apartment.

But damaged credit was not a problem for the Santos family as it might be for others in their situation; they wound up renting a split-level single family home that had been on the market for almost two years. They had an "in" because the landlord was a friend of Rodolfo's brother-in-law and they had met him a few times in the past.

The property had become available for rent almost immediately, right after their future landlord turned down an offer from a buyer for his house. The owner and his wife felt the property would be better off with Rowena and Rodolfo living in it and caring for it.

"[Our landlord] and his wife are a godsend. He checks up on us a lot, especially during Sandy, but he knows that any repairs that the house needs, we're able to do and he [doesn't] worry," Rowena says. "He sets up appointments for the care of the house like the HVAC and the roofing. He even drops off Christmas gifts for the kids, and whenever we need anything in regards to the town, he is on top of it."

Certain things softened the blow of having to lose their home. For example, the kids didn't have to change schools since the family moved within the same school district. That alone was a huge weight off Rowena and Rodolfo's mind.

And the neighborhood they left behind was going downhill.

"The area where we are now is a better location in Cliffwood Beach. Our old neighborhood was going down the crapper—there was a crack house on our street, and the playground where the kids used to play and where I walked the dog was being overrun by drunks, addicts, and other not very pleasant people," Rowena says. "It made moving much easier."

Now Rowena and Rodolfo pay $1,525 in rent each month instead of a mortgage that was $2,100 before taxes and insurance. They're also no longer responsible for $3,600 annually ($300 a month) to pay New Jersey's notoriously high property taxes.

Is the Santos family scared off from home ownership in the future?

"To put it plainly, yes," Rodolfo says. "With all the lessons that we learned, though, I still would love to be able to call something my own, provided that we are ready financially, emotionally, mentally, and physically."

Most Americans measure their wealth by the equity in their home, which is what makes building wealth a problem with renting long-term. But Rodolfo says he's more concerned with rebuilding his and Rowena's credit right now than with building long-term wealth through being a homeowner.

Meanwhile, they'll keep checking on their "grandmother" in the old neighborhood. The last time they went by after Sandy, "the entire street was in her house to check on how she was doing. There may be a crack house on the street, but we cared about one another."

What tips can you learn from Rowena and Rodolfo's story if you have to make the jump from homeowner to renter?

Buy renters insurance.

- You know that if you own a home, you need to insure it. If you have a car, you need to insure that. But when you're a renter, you don't always think about having renters insurance!
- Renters insurance is cheap, typically less than $20 a month. You might think it's just in case somebody breaks in and steals your belongings. But it's for many other reasons too.
- Maybe it could be water that comes in and damages your stuff. Without renters insurance, you're out of luck. And often during the winter, there are apartment fires because of space heaters, and when the word comes that no one had renters insurance, the Red Cross has to find a place for people to live.
- Some landlords will require that you have renters insurance, though that's very rare. The policy you get must have replacement value coverage for your belongings and relocation assistance should your place become uninhabitable. Don't leave yourself unprotected!

Know how to shop for a better deal on rent.

- If you're looking for an apartment, it's possible to go to a rental complex on three different days and get three different rents on the same apartment thanks to the affordable dynamic demand pricing software being used by even small property management companies. The value of an apartment can change as often as every twenty-four hours based on market conditions in the area and what's going on in that complex.
- So shop methodically and keep a list of quotes. Checking back several times for new quotes will make a big difference in what you have to pay for rent. Know too that rents might even be different for apartments with the same floor plan, depending on the loca-

tion in a given complex. One strategy might be to look for a less desirable floor plan that meets your square footage needs to save money.

Be careful what you post on Facebook and Twitter.

- Landlords are reportedly checking out would-be tenants on their Facebook pages, according to what I have read in the *Chicago Tribune*'s article "Beware of Screening Tenants via Facebook."
- If a landlord sees photos of somebody partying it up big time, they might not rent to that person. What you show on your picture wall can create an image of you that's not necessarily flattering for somebody looking to do business with you.
- The thing you need to know is that what is posted by you and about you can come back to hurt you in so many ways. Your reputation follows you in ways it never did before the era of social media.

Beware of bogus landlords renting foreclosures.

- There's a fast-growing scam where fake landlords pretend to rent a property that's not even theirs. Here's how it works: They go onto legit listings where real estate agents list homes for sale and they screen-scrape all the pictures and text. Then they put them out there on something like Craigslist, start communicating with potential tenants, and even con people into paying deposits. In many cases, people never even see the inside of the property or the scammer, according to the *Baltimore Sun*.
- Here are a few rules to protect yourself: First, make sure you see the place you're going to be renting and that you go through it room by room. Second, search the county's property records to see who the owner is. If it doesn't match up with the owner who wants to rent to you, be extra careful and suspicious. Finally, have the landlord show you a copy of the deed on the property.

WELCOME TO THE FORECLOSURE JUNGLE

Janet buys homes for up to 75 percent off—critters and all

THE REAL ESTATE COLLAPSE that began in 2007 led to misery for many Americans, who either lost their homes to foreclosure or saw the values of their homes plunge, erasing tens of thousands of dollars in home equity, and in many cases trapping people in houses that were worth less than what they owed on them.

But for some people, the drop in property values and wave of foreclosures created opportunities. One of those people is Janet Boyd of Berwick, Maine, a town of about 7,200 residents that sits beside the Salmon Falls River, about six miles from the New Hampshire state line.

Janet's son Dan, twenty-eight, was living at home and working at a bank, and fifty-four-year-old Janet was thinking a foreclosure might be just the right thing for him.

"I was watching [HLN's] *The Clark Howard Show* on Fannie Mae foreclosures on September 25, 2010," Janet recalls. "Right after the show aired, I searched online and found a property for $40,000."

Janet immediately made an appointment to look at it two days later. It was a small three-bedroom home in nearby Sanford, Maine, with about 1,020 square feet of space on a good-sized lot. Fannie Mae listed it as built in 1950, but Janet said the house, a former post office for Sanford, is older than that.

It had previously sold for $165,000 in 2007.

Janet and Dan offered $35,000 in cash, got a $38,000 counteroffer, and settled at $36,000.

They closed on December 8, 2010.

Dan was prequalified for a mortgage up to $40,000.

"This sale had to be a cash-only sale so I decided to help him out," said Janet. "We purchased this house together, and Dan will eventually get a mortgage to buy me out. I would say it is his house done by my deal."

As with most foreclosures, Dan's house needed some work, as a home inspection determined. Oddly, it had no insulation, despite its location in wintry Maine.

"Dan spent that first winter living with us until we got all of the cosmetic repairs and insulating done," Janet said. "We painted all the ceilings and walls, replaced all the carpeting, put in a new kitchen floor, reinforced the sagging floors up from the basement, and installed a new hot water heater. It cost about $5,000."

So all told, they spent $41,000 for the house, 75 percent less than it had sold for three years earlier at the height of the housing boom.

Dan got married on December 30, 2011. He and his new bride love the house. It still needs a new furnace, but it is a work in progress.

Actually, this house wasn't Janet's first foreclosure, and that one too was a product of the housing bust.

"I had helped my oldest son, Dennis, buy a foreclosed house in 2008," she said. "We paid $72,000 for a house valued at $140,000."

That house, about a mile away from brother Dan's house, needed $20,000 in repairs, and just taking possession of it was a bit of a challenge.

Janet first saw the property in April and didn't get a good look at it except for noticing a lot of boxes that looked to her like "an organized mess." When they bought the house in September, she learned that the previous owner had a boa constrictor for a pet and raised rats to feed the snake.

Dennis gave the guy a few extra weekends after the closing to get his stuff out of the house, but Janet was in there trying to fix things up, and she could see and hear the caged rats. It reminded her of the 1971 movie about a social misfit who leads a rampage using an army of rats.

"I was in there painting and it was like *Willard*," she said.

The boxes the previous owner had were way more abundant than she thought, Janet recalled.

"The upstairs and downstairs looked like an episode of *Hoarders*."

Dennis actually bought an old refrigerator from the previous owner and found a dead boa constrictor inside it, wrapped in a plastic bag.

"In a million years, who would have thought there'd be a dead thirteen-foot boa constrictor inside?" she said.

Janet learned from Dennis's purchase that you have to see the inside of a foreclosure before buying because you never know what surprises await. Dennis, thirty, still owns the house.

Janet says she'd definitely buy a foreclosure again. In fact, she was looking at another property the weekend before we did this interview, a $65,000 house in her own town of Berwick.

She missed the open house, and when she went back to see it with the Realtor, she noticed water. Since there hadn't been a lot of rain in the area, that probably meant mold and the possibility that the house would need to be torn down. And $65,000 would be a lot in that area for two acres of land. So this house was a no-go.

Her daughter Jennifer, twenty-three, who works at a local hospital, might be in the market soon for a house.

"I'm thinking if I can buy them all a house, they won't land back here." Janet laughed.

Janet, who's originally from Rhode Island, came by her frugality from her parents, who grew up during the Great Depression.

"I learned at a young age the value of saving up my money," she said. "We never went without, but we never took things for granted. I had a paper route for ten years as a kid. Towards the end of it I drove because I had saved enough money to buy an old clunker!"

Janet's husband, Dennis Sr., fifty-five, recently hit a deer on a rural road near her house, and the accident damaged the hood of his Chevy Prizm. Did Janet and Dennis go to a body shop and pay hundreds of dollars for the repair? Heck, no. They found a similar hood, the same dark green color, at a junkyard, and asked the junkyard owner who might be able to install it.

That led them to Little Freddy's Auto Repair in nearby Barrington, New Hampshire, and to Janet's delight, Little Freddy had the Prizm up and running for less than $200.

Search for foreclosures the Clark Smart way.

- When Janet tuned in to my TV show a few years ago, she heard me talking about HomePath.com and quickly logged on to find the foreclosure she would buy for Dan. HomePath.com is a site designed to unload the foreclosure inventory of Fannie Mae, a large government-chartered organization that helps underwrite mortgages behind the scenes. There's a similar organization called Freddie Mac and they operate a similar website called HomeSteps.com to get their foreclosures off their books. Both are free to use. But don't just rely on Internet listings; you need to get out there and see the houses you're interested in!

Hire a home inspector.

- As Janet found out, homes can have a lot of hidden problems. That's why I've always recommended that you hire a home inspector anytime you buy a used home. Make sure the inspector you hire has experience inspecting foreclosures. I prefer inspectors that are certified by the American Society of Home Inspectors (ASHI.org). And let's not even mention the snakes and hoarders and rats that your home inspector can't exactly do anything about!

Buy owner's title insurance.

- Most foreclosures are bought outright with cash. It's very important to protect yourself from the possibility that someone might come along and contest your ownership of a foreclosure. How do you do that? By purchasing a little-known policy called "owner's title insurance" (aka simultaneous title insurance).

- There's a big misconception that when you buy a home, you're paying a premium for title insurance and that protects you. No! That insurance just protects the bank. Don't rely on the title insurance the lender buys; you need to buy your own. EntitleDirect.com sells title insurance directly and can save you up to 35 percent, though that figure varies widely by state.

Cash is king.

- Cash is king right now in the real estate market. As Janet's story shows, the scenario of paying cash for real estate isn't entirely unrealistic. According to research firm Crane Data LLC, Americans had $2.6 trillion in money just sitting on the sidelines in money-market funds earning almost nothing at the end of 2012. So if you're among the millions of Americans who have money—but are clueless about what to do with it—let Janet's story be food for thought.

- One additional word of caution: You need to have the right personality to buy distressed property. You need to be willing to put up with the grime and the gross and see the potential in a house if, as they say in the real estate industry, the bones are good.

THE WANNABE HOTELIER

Samantha turns an underwater property into a cash cow

(WHILE ALL THE PEOPLE *in this book are real, several did not want me to use their real names. That's the case here. But while Samantha isn't her real name, her story is terrific.*)

The plunge in real estate values that followed the Great Recession made it impossible for some people to sell their homes. They can't get enough for them to pay off their mortgages.

The problem is the same for condominium owners, who sometimes choose to rent out their condos and then buy a home.

But that solution wasn't going to work for Samantha Taylor, a thirty-six-year-old professional in Atlanta whose condo association had a 25 percent cap on how many owners can rent out their unit at a time—and there was a three-year waiting list.

Samantha had been seeing her boyfriend, Erik, for about two years, and she was spending most nights at his place.

"We started talking about getting a place together and I started researching my condo value and thinking of selling. Since I love my condo and my neighborhood, the housing market tanking really didn't affect me until I started thinking about getting rid of the condo. I was shocked at how little it was worth."

Samantha had purchased the condo in July 2007 for $133,000. It had previously sold for $140,000, so she thought she was getting a deal.

Enter the Great Recession. She found out that a one-bedroom condo in her area was selling for an average of $85,000.

"My boyfriend and I were pretty bummed. It seemed silly to pay for two places when we were only using one."

Since selling wasn't an option, and neither was renting, Samantha got an idea.

"I started reading the details of my condo association rules, and in the section that covered having renters, it discussed the penalties of having a renter without permission. The rules state that a renter is considered to be a nonowner paying rent for more than fourteen days. I decided to quietly test that fourteen-day idea by listing my condo as a vacation rental with a fourteen-day maximum stay."

Samantha found a company called Airbnb.com in January 2012, which works like an unofficial bed-and-breakfast booking site that puts you in the action as an independent hotelier.

"We chose Airbnb because they do everything for you. They handle the money, give you an insurance policy, keep your calendar, take professional pictures for [your online listing]—it was incredibly easy to get started."

Airbnb takes a 3 percent cut of the money as its fee.

"Once I got the pictures up and put my listing as 'live,' it was immediately rented for the very next weekend, and has been rented at least twenty days a month—never more than fourteen for the same guest—every month since."

Samantha's mortgage payment on the condo is $710 a month, and she pays a $190 a month condo association fee. She needs $900 a month in rental income to completely offset the cost of her condo. On average, Samantha earns about $1,500 per month from her apartment. (In her slowest month ever, she brought in $1,100, while her best month yielded $2,100.)

"I try and price the condo about 20 percent lower than nearby hotels. Depending on season and demand, I've had it priced from $60 to $100 per night."

Samantha has a unique sense of style. Her condo, in a hip section of Atlanta called Little Five Points, reflects that. The look is vintage/midcentury modern, with lots of collections, lots of records, antique radios, and 1960s art.

"I like pretty goofy stuff, and since I love to travel there are knickknacks from around the world," Samantha said.

Fortunately, she didn't have to "de-Samantha" it for renters.

"Quite the opposite. The only things I removed were jewelry, financial records, my photo albums, and my computer. I left all my furnishings and decorations and knickknacks and made sure my place still has my personality. Not everyone on Airbnb does this, but it was a no-brainer for me. I like the idea of people sharing my home—not renting a bland hotel room."

Samantha pitches her place as artistic and fun and she's had incredibly positive feedback from guests, who often leave kind notes and thank her for sharing her home with them.

She's had renters from all over the world. Her first guests were from France, and there have been Italians, Saudi Arabians, Egyptians, South Americans, Canadians, Germans, and folks from all over the United States.

"I had to get zen with the idea of something breaking—but in the end it's just stuff, and I think people treat my place with amazing care . . . perhaps partly because it does have so much personality. They feel connected to me, and I do to them. We e-mail a lot before I let them book, and I usually go to meet them for check-in. It's really an amazing travel community."

She did have one guest damage her vintage dresser, accidentally leaving a large water mark.

"They felt so terrible. The wife cried, and the husband bought me a piece of art that they thought would go with my place, and they offered to pay for the damage. They weren't from the States, and their English wasn't great, but they were so genuine that I didn't take them up on their offer to pay for the damage."

Samantha considers it travel karma. She's used Airbnb herself while visiting Chicago, Paris, Florence, and Sedona, Arizona, and always respects the homes she stays in.

"I've had consistently great experiences. I like it so much more than staying in a hotel because you get a very local feel for a city. The neighborhoods we've gotten to stay in have been places that suited our personality to a tee.

There was one notable mishap. In Paris, Samantha and Erik locked themselves out of their apartment.

"The owners were out of town and had a friend—who spoke very little English—helping and he did not have a key for the specific lock that we had accidentally flipped. We ended up having to call a locksmith and it cost us 190 euros."

They were hoping the owners would split the cost with them, but they did not.

"We decided to chalk it up to bad luck and not pursue a refund, because as an owner myself, I understood where they were coming from and I just didn't want to put out any bad travel karma. That's one of the amazing things about Airbnb, people really try and be good to each other and care for each other's places. The entire process is based on reviews and no one wants to be the jerk."

While the company handles the heavy lifting, Samantha stays very involved. She considers herself a nontraditional hotelier.

"I leave bagels and coffee for my guests and check on them throughout their stay to make sure they are happy. It's like running a bed-and-breakfast without me having to be there to cook them anything," she joked.

She still stays there occasionally, like when she and Erik want to see a concert nearby.

"When a guest comes, I make sure the place is spotless for them, and if they have any problems along the way they can text or call me. My boyfriend's place is only ten minutes from the condo."

Running a kind of bed-and-breakfast is a natural for Samantha, a thrift shop girl with entrepreneurial flair.

"My dad lost his job when I was fourteen and had to do some pretty creative things to keep us afloat, including working at a gas station down the street from my snobby high school. My folks were never very great with money and neither was I."

She got through college on student loans and credit cards, but she adopted a more sensible financial approach at twenty-five, and got out of debt by twenty-nine.

"Since then I have never carried a credit card balance, but I'm not a huge saver, either. I have a very carpe diem attitude about money. I don't buy more than I can afford, I save a little for the future, and I travel with every extra penny I have. I don't spend much money on clothes or a big house or a fancy car, but I will throw down some cash for life experience."

She started thrift shopping in high school, and now can't bear to pay retail prices for clothes.

"A dress from a thrift store is 80 percent cheaper than in a department store, and I can use that savings to wear my gently used dress on a beach trip."

Samantha became a hotelier sort of by accident. But she loves the experience.

"It's a very warm, fuzzy way to make some extra money," she said.

What can you learn from Samantha's story?

Determine if you're legally able to rent.

- Particularly if you live in a covenant community that has a homeowners association, the first thing to do if you're considering renting your property is to read your governing documents carefully like Samantha did. She found a loophole that allowed her to rent out her condo for less than two weeks at a time to a tenant.

- There probably won't be any documentation to restrict you if you own your own home. In that case, you should check with local ordinances in your municipality to see if Airbnb is legal where you live. For example, the Airbnb business model is not permitted in cities like San Francisco, New Orleans, and New York.

- As *The New York Times* wrote on the topic, "Local laws may prohibit most or all short-term rentals under many circumstances, though enforcement can be sporadic and you have no way of knowing how tough your local authorities will be."

- Know before you rent.

Check with your insurer.

- The insurance issue is what's been the great unknown with Airbnb. But the service now offers $1 million in insurance coverage if you make your home or second home or a single room available for rent to travelers. That should go a long way to addressing concerns about what happens if you rent your home and the renter damages it.

- Your own home insurer might become a problem and kick you to the curb if they find out about what you're doing! In this respect, the insurance industry has a lot of catching up to do with the realities of what's going on in the marketplace. Again, you've got to know before you rent if being a wannabe hotelier like Samantha makes sense for your life.

Remove all valuables.

- If you decide to go ahead and rent your place on Airbnb, you'll probably want to take some things out of your space before a temporary tenant shows up. As Samantha noted, she took out her jewelry, financial records, personal photos, and computer before renting out her condo. I would add any old cell phones or other mobile devices to that list. It's too easy for somebody to seize sensitive financial info you might have on an unloved smartphone that's sitting in a drawer or closet somewhere.

Consider the tax issues.

- Like with anything else in life, Uncle Sam will want his share of whatever money you earn on Airbnb. "I'll be getting a Form 1099-Misc from Airbnb and I have to declare all of the revenue I make from them," Samantha says. "I can subtract out my expenses and I need to pay the state sales tax as though [I am] a hotel."
- Visit IRS.gov and search keyword "Topic 415" for more info about this important tax issue. Publication 527, Residential Rental Property (Including Rental of Vacation Homes), also has more info. Consult your tax adviser if you have additional questions.

THE
TWENTY-EIGHT-YEAR-OLD
LANDLORD

Joel is a real estate mogul in the making

AFTER BUYING HIS FIRST HOME IN 2009, Joel Larsgaard considered it his goal in life to acquire and manage a second property as a rental. His love of the neighborhood that he bought in and the economics of the real estate market sealed the deal for him.

Joel is the twenty-eight-year-old associate producer on my radio show and the youngest member of my crew. I admire greatly the way he and his wife, Emily, have chosen to handle money in their life.

They drive a 2000 Nissan Altima that Joel bought with 150,000 miles on it for $3,200 in cash several years ago. They purchased a $40 couch for their living room at a scratch-and-dent furniture store. And even the $20 wedding ring Emily gave Joel is made of hammered copper. No gold or platinum for this boy!

Like other urban pioneers his age, Joel bought his first home in a slightly run-down but promising part of a metropolitan area. In his case, he and Emily reside in Atlanta's historic Grant Park neighborhood.

"I wouldn't have even purchased a home were it not for the Great Recession. The result of that economic catastrophe for so many was incredibly reduced prices and incomprehensibly low interest rates," Joel tells me.

"These in combination with the [now expired] first-time homebuyer's tax credit made it a no-brainer. I purchased a single-family home for $89,000 on a fifteen-year note. Even on a fifteen-year loan my payment was much lower than the cost of renting."

His mortgage, including taxes and insurance, is around $570 a month. For his money, Joel got a postwar 1940s home that still has original features like the beautiful hardwood floors. It's 1,050 square feet with two bedrooms and one bathroom.

When he and Emily married in late 2010, they spent time putting in new windows and a new bathroom. They also decided to save like crazy in order to make a down payment on another home in their neighborhood.

"We needed to put 20 percent down to avoid PMI [private mortgage insurance] and in order to make it an intelligent purchase. This meant that we had to forgo other purchases that others place a priority on. I continue to drive my 'beater' car with almost two hundred thousand miles on it," Joel says.

They spent months looking for the right place at the right price. In late 2012, they found it—a 1925 bungalow of about 1,250 square feet with two bedrooms and two bathrooms that they bought for $163,000. Their monthly mortgage, with taxes and insurance, is $825.

They had to owner-occupy to get the low 3.25 percent interest rate on a thirty-year mortgage that they had been quoted. So rather than renting out the new property, they moved into it and rented out their first home.

"Our neighborhood is full of these turn-of-the-century to 1920s bungalows. They are our favorite style," Joel says. "Since I'm almost six feet six, the taller ceilings are my favorite!"

Joel says he and Emily will have to replace the old HVAC system in the next couple of years and lay down some new coats of paint around the house. Their goal is to do what's cost effective and most necessary in order to enjoy the home now but also to invest in it for the future—because they want it to become a money-making rental down the road.

"Our houses are almost a half mile apart and we really like it that way. We believe in our neighborhood and love the architecture and community. We have also decided to do the upkeep ourselves. It makes it an even smarter move when you don't turn those responsibilities over to a real estate management company. If we didn't have a deeper connection to our properties that meant more than money, it wouldn't be worth it."

As a landlord, Joel's had to deal with requests from his tenant for new curtains, a couple of paint touch-ups, and a fix to an electrical outlet. He charges his renter $1,225 a month.

"I really like being a landlord so far. It certainly isn't for everyone, but it appeals to me. You have to be ready to roll your sleeves up and spend some time getting things in proper shape. Emily and I could probably start a professional painting service at this point, as our skills are getting very good!" he says.

"We haven't set up an LLC [limited liability company] or anything yet. Maybe that will come as we continue to save up and purchase another place. We aren't set on it, but if conditions continue to be favorable and we continue to enjoy the process, we hope to find something that works well for us."

Joel doesn't exactly come from the thriftiest family, but seeing his folks grapple with money issues when he was growing up strengthened his resolve to better handle his own fiscal affairs.

"My inspiration for frugality all stems from my childhood. There comes a point in time when every kid realizes the monetary struggles inherent in a middle-class upbringing. Both of my parents worked extremely hard to provide for my two sisters and I. We were really fortunate to learn that skill well.

"As with most families, though, money was tight and was sometimes a source of tension. . . . The tension that money can cause in a family is something that I really wanted to avoid. This is why I have such an outside-of-the-box view towards money today. I view it as a tool, not as the end goal."

What lessons can you learn from Joel's story?

Follow the 90 percent rule.
- People ask me all the time if a particular property they have their eye on would be a smart move as a rental. You should only buy a rental property if the rent will cover at least 90 percent of the monthly mortgage, taxes, and insurance.
- In Joel's case, his monthly mortgage on his first home, which he now rents out, is $570. That means he would need to charge no less than $513 in rent to meet the 90 percent metric. At a monthly rent of $1,225, his property pays for itself twice over every month! (That's only possible because Joel and Emily saved money by doing a lot of the improvement work themselves rather than hiring a contractor.)
- Many people start thinking about buying another rental property once their cash flow is positive in their first rental. I say slow down and don't rush things. We went through an unusual cycle where real estate was an amazing deal. But for most people, spacing out

your acquisitions of rentals every five years during normal market conditions is the way to go. I call it the get-rich-slow plan!

Be sure that rentals are allowed.

- More and more homeowners associations (HOAs)—not just in condominiums but in neighborhoods with mandatory HOAs—are banning or highly restricting rentals. You don't want to be in a situation where you get a bargain on a piece of real estate only to have to leave it sitting empty because you're not allowed to rent it out.
- This is fair warning anytime you're looking, especially at a condo; you've got to know if the odds of your being able to rent it out as a landlord are low. Do your homework before the fact so you don't get burned.

Screen your tenants.

- The key to being a smart landlord is to get a good tenant and keep them happy. If you have a great tenant, you want them to stay for years, if at all possible, because turnover costs you money. You'll need to run a background check and a credit check. Ask for your potential tenant for references and call them. I especially like to check with former landlords and a current or past employer. Visit Landlord.com for more help and advice on becoming a landlord.

Consider giving an early-pay discount.

- As a landlord, you're running a business and you expect to be paid in a timely manner. I've often given discounts of $50 off the rent if a tenant pays before the first of the month at my rental properties. Tenants are happy because they get a deal and you're happy because you don't have to hound them for the money each month. It's a win-win.

Protect yourself.

- Joel and Emily's goal is to acquire more rental properties down the road. If you have a great deal of assets to protect, as they will, you need to make sure you have a good liability policy with separate LLCs for each of your properties.
- As an alternative to setting up an LLC for each property, you could instead buy an umbrella insurance policy that gives you blanket liability protection for each of your properties. Umbrella policies are cheap and effective; for each million in coverage, you usually pay a few hundred dollars a year.

- I talk to a lot of people who are miserable being landlords and don't feel the joy that Joel might feel in being a landlord. Generally, if you have trouble acting like a collection agency and kicking out a nonpaying tenant, then being a landlord won't be suitable to your personality. Likewise, if calls about an overflowing toilet on a Saturday night at 10 p.m. sound like a nightmare to you, then being a landlord will probably be a nightmare for you too.

CARS

What you pay for transportation is probably the second largest expense you face after housing. But there are ways to lessen the bite your car takes out of your budget.

In this chapter, we meet four very different kinds of car buyers, each with a lesson for your wallet. I'll also tell you how to get the most car for your dollar, how to get the most life out of the car you already have, and how transportation alternatives can make you a richer man or woman.

"CAN'T GET ANY MORE AMERICAN THAN THAT"

Robert and Cia dumped their cars for bikes and saved more than $90,000

HAVE YOU EVER SAID, "I wish I had a nickel for every time I . . . ?" Well, imagine if you had 60 cents instead. AAA says that's the cost of driving a vehicle per mile in America today. What would your life be like if you had that 60 cents back in your pocket for every mile you drove to work, school, or church?

Robert Johnson and his wife, Cia, do. They have no car. And no, they don't live in the heart of an urban area with extensive public transit like New York, Denver, or Boston.

They willingly went carless six years ago in Columbia, Missouri—right in the heart of the heartland—and continue that lifestyle today in Barrington, Illinois, about twenty miles west of Lake Michigan.

"My financial reality is far different than most others' because of it," Robert told me. "Imagine taking every dollar that you spend on car payments, repair, maintenance, gasoline, insurance, and registration and instead saving and investing that money. You not only stay in great shape bicycling and walking, but you become wealthy very quickly."

That "different" financial reality includes having paid $18,000 in cash for the final year of Cia's postgraduate studies, plus having eliminated $72,000 in other accumulated student debt in just twelve months. And it will continue until late 2014, when they expect to pay off their mortgage.

Robert, thirty-two, is the director of consulting at PedNet Coalition, a pedestrian advocacy group. He splits his time between telecommuting and traveling the country to meet with clients from cities and school systems interested in more pedestrian and pedaling options for their communities. (He does rent cars that are paid for by his employer while on the road.)

Cia, twenty-eight, works as the assistant director of animal welfare at the American Veterinary Medical Association. Her commute to work entails a train ride every day and eleven miles of round-trip biking.

The Johnsons married in 2005 and knew they both enjoyed the pedaling lifestyle. But the idea of going carless wasn't an automatic no-brainer for the like-minded newlyweds. The real aha moment came when they watched how they bulked up their budget as they drove less and less.

At the time, Robert had a $280 monthly truck payment for his Ford Ranger and paid around $60 in monthly insurance premiums. While that might be no big deal to some people, it was a lot to the young couple, who were living on his $11 per hour wage ($22,000 annually) while Cia was a full-time student.

By 2007, the couple had sold both Robert's Ford Ranger and Cia's Dodge Dakota, with the goal of trying out the carless lifestyle for a couple of months. They were met with laughter from friends and fear from Cia's parents, who worried about them being three and a half hours away with no wheels while Cia's dad lived with Parkinson's disease. (When Cia and Robert visit their families, they go by plane, train, bus, or rental car, depending on which option is cheapest at the time.)

"People really have this sort of knee-jerk reaction, they just don't feel like it's possible to live in the United States in modern times without an automobile, but we've never looked back," Robert says.

Their new "wheels" are now Robert's $700 Trek 7.3 bike with a special $1,500 gearing system called a Rohloff hub and Cia's $2,500 Brompton folding bicycle. Going without an automobile has impacted everything from how they get groceries (on foot, with backpacks) to their choice of a side business.

In 2008, Robert and Cia ran a human-powered lawn cutting business called Green Team Lawn Care on the weekends. The Johnsons used an old-fashioned reel mower instead of a gas-engine lawn mower, long-handled clippers instead of a weed whacker, and a broom instead of a noisy leaf blower to remove the clipped grass from sidewalks and driveways.

All the low-tech gear was, of course, hauled to job sites in an 8-foot-by-3-foot cargo trailer behind a bicycle!

"There were many Saturday mornings when we would be standing at the first [client's] lawn just waiting for the sun to come up high enough so that we could get started," Robert recalls. "We didn't have to worry at all about waking anybody up. I don't think even the people that lived in the home knew that we were out there most of the time. We were just able to quietly roll up on the bikes and get going."

After clipping more than five hundred lawns at just north of $30 a property, the Johnsons took the $18,000 they earned and paid the final year of Cia's veterinary medicine doctoral studies in cash. They have since retired their garden shears and no longer run the business.

When it came time to move from Missouri in 2010, the couple handpicked the Chicago suburb of Barrington because it was bike and pedestrian friendly. Cia could also ride her bike to the train line before hopping on to get to her office at the American Veterinary Medical Association. (Upon arriving at work, she simply closes her office door and takes a few minutes to freshen up and change clothes.)

Things have gotten a lot better financially for the Johnsons since moving to Barrington. They now pull in a combined household income of $135,000. And thanks to their thrift, they were able to put a 20 percent down payment on a $137,000 one-bedroom/one-bathroom condo four years ago. The couple even managed to grab the $8,000 tax credit that was then being offered to first-time homebuyers.

In July 2012, the Johnsons made the final student loan payment that knocked out $72,000 of Cia's lingering educational debt. After that, the couple built a year's worth of expenses in an emergency fund. Right now they're targeting their mortgage, which Robert and Cia expect to pay off in December 2014, when he's thirty-four and she's thirty. Not bad!

For those of you who are wondering, Robert and Cia don't have any children. But before you dismiss their story because of that, I want to introduce you to Gina Overshiner, bicycle program manager at PedNet in Columbia and one of Robert's coworkers.

Gina is a forty-six-year-old mother of a twelve-year-old girl and a fourteen-year-old boy. She and her husband, Tim, thirty-six, are a "low car" family because they have one vehicle that's primarily used for emergencies and longer trips. The bulk of their daily life—going to school, going to the store, going for nonemergency doctor appointments—is lived by bike.

Gina started biking the kids around before their first birthdays. As they become toddlers, she started using a bike trailer to haul around "normal mommy minivan detritus," including sporting goods, backpacks, snacks, and toys while staying home to care for her kids during the early baby years.

As the trio rode around, she soon realized that "for every super-busy highway, there are usually a lot of smaller neighborhood roads that run pretty much parallel and have very little traffic. Because of the lower traffic on these 'parallel' roads, biking can actually be safer than driving." Gina also discovered that the roads that jam up during rush hour are almost empty during midday, "when most mommies of small children are going to play dates at the park."

The kind of lifestyle the Johnsons and the Overshiners have adopted is not for everyone. In fact, it's almost culturally renegade to live in America—the land that practically invented the automobile—without a car. But that doesn't deter them.

"I really think the future is Americans owning fewer cars," Robert told me. "It just doesn't make sense to own a $30,000 piece of capital that you use thirty or forty-five minutes a day, something that depreciates by thousands of dollars in a year. I think more people are going to figure that out."

For Robert, he and Cia have figured out a way to have carless living make sense. "It's a very American thing," he says. "It's being self-sufficient, it's a little bit of hard work, and it's trying to become wealthy. And I don't even think you can get more American than that."

What lessons can you draw from the story of Robert and Cia?

It doesn't have to be all or nothing.

- Obviously, the Johnsons sold both vehicles and are heavily invested in this lifestyle. But there are all sorts of people out there with three cars that could go to two cars, or two that could go to one. If you're like the average American and you can find a way to replace even a part of your trips by biking and walking, you've just increased your income by what's likely to be a meaningful amount. Visit the Association of Pedestrian and Bicycle Professionals at APBP.org for tips on bike safety and how to get started integrating pedal power into your lifestyle.

Try a scooter or motorcycle.

- I like to think of scooters as a "step down" program from car ownership. Scooters are fuel efficient and cheap to buy. A slew of Chinese imports on the market price out below $1,000 for a 50cc model with a top speed of forty-five miles per hour. Check Craigslist for gently used scooters at half that price. If motorcycles are more your style, be sure to pay for a safety course through the Motorcycle Safety Foundation at MSF-USA.org before riding.

Use cheap interstate bus service for travel.

- Robert told me he and Cia often use bus or rail for leisure travel. For the first time in forty-five years, the bus is becoming a real option for more people. Bus lines including MegaBus.com, BoltBus.com, and Greyhound.com/GreyhoundExpress offer travel between metro areas with a limited number of fares starting at $1.
- Services like these were originally designed to attract the young and broke, but they're now branching out and crossing economic and age lines. Women traveling alone are a particularly booming client base for some of these players. Free Wi-Fi and luxury seats are among the amenities most of these bus lines offer.
- My associate producer Joel Larsgaard, his wife, and another couple used MegaBus to go from Atlanta to New Orleans last year. They paid $46 round-trip in total for four people!

Try sharing a vehicle.

- Shared car services, where you rent a car by the hour, are gaining in popularity, particularly on college campuses. ZipCar.com is probably the leader in the industry, though Enterprise Rent-A-Car and Hertz are trying to elbow their way into the market too.
- Once you sign up with ZipCar for $50, you receive a ZipCard that allows you to access the vehicles that are parked at easy-to-reach locations. You typically pay an hourly charge of $6 to $12 to rent a car, and that price includes comprehensive insurance, gas, and roadside assistance/maintenance.
- When you're done with the vehicle, just return it to the same location where you picked it up. It's kind of like "public transit, private driving," and it's much cheaper than adding another car to the family fleet.

CONFESSIONS OF A RETIRED AUTO SALESMAN

Gerry sold new cars for forty years but drove one that cost him $300

GERRY SCHRAM HAD A VERY GOOD LIFE selling cars. After four decades on dealer lots, the sixty-five-year-old former salesman from Becker County, Minnesota, was able to retire in 2006 with no debt at all.

He did that, in part, by owning his cars for a long time, unlike many of his customers who would get eaten alive by the cost of continually buying a new car every few years.

In some of his best times as an auto salesman, Gerry sold three hundred or more cars a year. "I had so many good years: '75 was a good year, '86 [too], and there were so many more," Gerry recalls. "In my early days, we sold the car and filled out the contracts by hand, so it took longer. But there were lots of twenty-five-to-thirty-car months."

Many of the sales were to customers trading in cars just a couple of years old. While they opted for new wheels, Gerry was holding on to his old ones.

For example, he enjoys the '69 Dodge Super Bee coupe he bought when he was twenty-three and still has to this day. Or the Dodge Power Wagon that he purchased in 1974—the same year he put a $10,000 down payment on his $28,000 home. Gerry held on to the Power Wagon for eight years before selling it at a modest profit, right around the same time he paid off his mortgage in full.

Early in his career, the salesman saw the folly of people getting into a new car every few years, often before they'd even paid off the old one.

When you roll the outstanding balance on an original loan into a new vehicle loan, you create a much higher monthly payment for yourself than if you'd just waited until the original note was paid off.

It's like "paying for July's hamburger in January," Gerry says, sounding like a modern-day version of the Wimpy character from *Popeye*.

"It is automatically a warning signal about your finances. It tells you you're using the car up faster than you can pay for it and you are using too long of a term on the contract," Gerry says. "Sometimes, two or three financial institutions turn down a contract, however [another one] may take it. This is a signal to the consumer *not* to be buying. The financiers are telling the consumer, 'Whoa there, big boy. Think it over!'"

In one extreme example of the mistakes people make, Gerry had one repeat customer with a constant case of new car-itis. In fact, the man bought from him so much over the years that he eventually became Gerry's friend.

Let's call him "John" because that's what Gerry used for a pseudonym when discussing his friend's incurable new-car fever.

By Gerry's telling, John typically went through one truck a year. During one particular year, though, he bought and traded no less than two Dodge trucks and two Ford trucks in rapid succession.

"When John's coworkers or pals traded, he was also knocking on the showroom window. Somewhere along the line he went on his own as a plumber and bankruptcy ensued," Gerry says. "He always told me he got stiffed on a plumbing construction job, but I think his foolishness caught up with him or was a contributing factor.

"[Another time] I sold John's wife a new 2000 Buick [Regal] she loved. He tried to trade that, but she put her foot down. Yay for her! Well [in 2010], he traded that Regal for a Subaru Impreza and she is not happy one bit about that," Gerry told me. "As a young person, I remember guys who had a nice car, married, [and] then would come to 'trade down' or sell. Now it's spend till the well is dry."

But you'd be wrong if you think Gerry never let passion sway his usually cool-headed approach to buying and owning cars. During the golden era of American muscle cars, Gerry was guilty of at least one self-confessed "frivolous" car buy. Yet he still found a way to make it work financially.

"As a young fellow, I ordered a new '69 Dodge Super Bee coupe . . . and saved every last cent to pay for it. This meant frugally selecting options right down to the last penny; I even had to order it without a radio to make the car meet [my] money," Gerry says. "The car was probably a frivolous expenditure. But at twenty-three, things appear differently. I was never in over my head, [and] I could have sold my Super Bee easily, but I suppose it was a statement of who I was."

Muscle car purchases aside, living within his budget and making sensible car purchases go hand-in-hand in the Schram home.

"My wife drives a very rusty '88 Olds I bought five or six years ago for $300. I drive a '97 Dodge Ram Laramie 1500 with 214,000 miles. These cars just go down the road, never ever leaving us stranded."

That '88 Oldsmobile had 140,000 miles on it when Gerry bought it from a friend, and he put less than $100 into it to replace a water pump.

"This was not a glamorous car but did have a 'like new' interior. Some relatives and friends said, 'Why don't you get your wife a decent car?'" he says. "Well, my wife is not a princess; she just appreciates dependability as well as affordability. Many folks in any income bracket would not consider this car!"

My favorite part of the Olds story? After putting about 20,000 miles on it, Gerry later sold the car to his cousin for $388—so he pretty much broke even!

"Upon making a one-hundred-eighty-mile trip at thirty-one miles per gallon, [my cousin] told me it was apparently quieter than his 2008 Chrysler Pacifica. Go figure!" Gerry says. "He now wants to find two blue doors to replace the rusty ones."

Meanwhile, Gerry's wife is now driving a '94 Pontiac Bonneville with 197,000 miles and a 2004 Ford Taurus with 130,000 miles.

The message of Gerry's story is to hold on to your cars until the wheels fall off or risk the undesirable financial consequences—if not now, then later in life.

"I had supper with a fellow recently who paid $10,000 for a ten-year-old Toyota van," Gerry told me. "He probably could have bought a [used Dodge] Caravan for half the price. But maybe that's why my friend is still making house payments at sixty-five. My wife and I have everything paid for and have for years."

Independent car repair shops are preferable to dealers.

- Developing a relationship with a mechanic is one of those important intangibles of car ownership. I like single-brand shops that only service one brand of car because they have in-depth experience and are usually familiar with older out-of-warranty cars. Contrast that with the experience of bringing your car to a traditional dealer's service facility: You typically don't get to see the mechanic who works on your car and instead have to deal with a commissioned service representative.

- Yet not all single-brand shops are good. You need to get referrals from trusted friends and family. The time to find an independent mechanic is not when your car is broken down on the side of road, either. If you're new to an area, use an online review site like Yelp.com to vet shops or use an AAA-approved shop. Then build a relationship with one by first trying them out for routine maintenance.

Keep up with routine maintenance.

- Following the factory-scheduled maintenance gives your vehicle a longer life span and eliminates problems that could otherwise occur. The most basic thing to do is change your oil as often as recommended in the owner's manual. There is, however, one caveat: If you're having the work done at a dealership, the dealer will often run up your bill by doing unscheduled work. Make sure you authorize only the scheduled work that's required at the time you have your vehicle in the shop.

Beware of auto repair service plans for older vehicles.

- Auto repair service plans can be enticing in an era when the average car on the road is now eleven years old. But I say they're a waste of your money. These third-party extended warranties cost up to $3,000, according to *Real Simple* magazine. Worse still, the contract for that supposedly "bumper to bumper" coverage is so riddled with holes you can drive a couple of ten-year-old minivans through it. If you are worried about extreme out-of-pocket expenses from repair bills for old cars, I recommend you buy the auto manufacturer's own extended warranty.

- When you have an older vehicle, you've got to know when it runs out of useful life and be wary of the point at which the cost of repairs outpaces the value of the car itself. I've long said that when the annual cost of repairs exceeds 50 percent of your old car's value, then that's the time to get rid of it. But *Consumer Reports* says it's OK for repairs to equal an older car's value dollar for dollar at 100 percent each year. So we're of two different minds, but the point is: Don't hang on just to hang on.

Beware of bandit tow scams.

- If you're stranded on the side of the road, be careful which repair shop your tow truck driver steers you to. The shop might overinflate its prices and give the driver a cut for each stranded motorist they bring them. Allstate cites one example of somebody being charged $1,600 for a flat tire in a bandit tow scam—*$1,600 for a flat tire!* That's an extreme scenario just to get your attention, but it actually happened.

- If you're out of town and don't know where to go or what to do, find the closest AAA-approved repair facility and request to be towed there. Have AAA do the tow if you are a member. And if you break down near home, it's often better to be towed to your home and then pay a second fee to be towed again to a repair shop after you've had a chance to do some research about which ones won't rip you off.

THAT NEW CAR SMELL

John proves that leasing isn't a lemon

JOHN MILLER WAS BORN IN VIOLA, ILLINOIS, a quaint village of less than one thousand people.

"Except for being in the North, it was a lot like Mayberry. Seriously," the seventy-year-old says. "People were your typical down-to-earth, shirt-off-their-back types, who looked out for each other—good and bad. The land was quite flat, with rich black dirt. Great farmland."

His parents were typical Depression-era types. "Frugal to a fault," John tells me. "You would have loved them!

"They maintained a monthly budget, and by 'maintained,' I mean they stuck to it. They accounted for every penny they spent. If we ate out, Dad would write down the total on a slip of paper and stick it in his pocket, to be recorded later."

John originally intended to teach guitar at the college level, but he went into the navy, got out in 1970, and went into broadcasting to work his way through graduate school. That ultimately led to a public relations career, and in 1984 he transitioned to computers, doing IT work.

He's had stints at big companies like Georgia-Pacific and the Coca-Cola Company. Now in retirement, he's back to music while living in Fayetteville, Georgia.

John is also a big fan of car leasing.

"In retrospect, I may have been a leasing trendsetter," he tells me. "In 1978, I almost had to arm-wrestle the dealership to get them to lease a car to an individual."

That was thirty-five years ago at a Pontiac dealership in Jacksonville, Florida. His first hurdle to the lease was overcoming the dealership bias that "leases are for businesses, not people." Of course, there was no valid business reason why they couldn't lease to an individual, so John was soon on his way in his new white Grand Prix with a dark red interior.

At the time, he was working as a regional PR manager for the St. Regis Paper Company and being paid mileage for business use of his privately owned vehicle. He needed a nice reliable car for image reasons. But he also wanted to keep the bare minimum of money invested in it, knowing that he'd walk away from it in a few years.

"I ended up leasing . . . for considerably less than car payments would have been. In '81, I happily turned it in. I would have just as happily bought it for what turned out to be a nominal residual value, but I'd just bought a new replacement for less than invoice price."

Over the many subsequent years, John has gone on to buy or lease nice late-model used cars, beaters, and even a couple of new cars for the use of himself, his wife, and his daughter.

"For me, the buy-or-lease decision boils down to whatever will best leverage my funds," he says.

I've long been an outspoken critic of leasing. Sure, you might get a low monthly payment, but you have to come to the table with a big nonrefundable fee called "capital cost reduction" or "capital acquisition fee." This can often be between $2,000 and $4,000. It's like you're prepaying a portion of the lease in advance; that's what artificially makes that monthly payment seem so low.

Unfortunately, too many people use leasing to get more car than they can afford.

Let's say that upfront fee I just talked about is on the low end at $2,299, and you get a lease payment of $249 a month for thirty-six months. The thing you've got to know is the effective price is more like $313 a month, not $249. You've got to consider that $2,299 over thirty-six months works out to about $64 a month. Add that to the $249 and you're now at $313.

And that's just why it stinks before you drive off the lot!

On the flip side of leasing, when you're getting ready to turn the vehicle in, you could face more fees if the car's condition has degenerated beyond normal wear and tear, or if you've gone over the typical allowance of 12,000 miles annually.

Plus, after three or four years of making payments, you own nothing—unless you buy the car for its residual value.

Not a good deal in my book.

But, as I mentioned, John loves it. His rationale is that he knows cars rapidly lose value during their first years of ownership—so he'd rather not be an owner.

"There's a fundamental issue here. How much do you want to be invested in a depreciating asset?" John challenges me. "A guiding principle of mine has always been to minimize equity in depreciating assets. I have always wished for car payments to be approximately equal to interest plus depreciation, with the result that at the end of the term, there would be no equity in the car."

In fact, John can't get his head around why I would even worry about the question of building equity in a vehicle when he could so easily sidestep that question with leasing.

"I think we all agree that term [life] insurance is better than whole life or 'permanent' insurance, because using an insurance policy as a savings account is not the best use of funds," John tells me. "Why, then, would we want to use automobiles as savings accounts?"

John and I don't disagree on everything, though. It seems he's really taken my advice about ways to cut the cord from pay TV.

"Sitting here watching a *M*A*S*H* rerun, smiling warmly at having gotten rid of the cable company," he wrote in a recent post on his Facebook page. "In addition to [local] broadcast stations, some of which are HDTV, I've got Amazon Prime, Hulu Plus, and Crackle for a total outlay of less than $16 a month. Variously using Roku player and PC to deliver the signal to TVs."

What tips can you glean from John's story if you're looking to lease?

Know when leasing can work.

- As I've long said, there are really just two times when leasing makes sense. The first situation is if you know that you like to have new wheels every three years and you don't want to worry about disposing of your old ride. Then it's ideal for you.
- The second scenario is when there are special factory-subsidized leases (primarily on luxury vehicles and electric vehicles) or a manufacturing oversupply that leads to great deals at the dealership. Luxury automakers hate to cheapen their brands with a bona fide sale, so they often offer such leases to help move extra product.

- How do you know it's a factory-subsidized lease? Look at the advertising. When it pushes the brand rather than your local dealership, you've got a pretty good indication that's a factory-subsidized lease.

Know your usage patterns.

- Most leases give you strict mileage allowances. That typically means you can drive an average of 12,000 miles per year with no penalty. If you go over that cap, you have to pay a penalty of 15 or so cents per mile when you turn the car back in.
- A lease might not work for you if you're a super-commuter with a daily ride of ninety minutes or more each way—unless it's for a company car where the lease is subsidized. But even then, the amount your company is paying could change without notice, or you could leave the job or get fired. Be careful.

Return the car in good condition.

- When you return your leased car, the dealership will be looking carefully at the condition of the vehicle. That's why I recommend hiring an auto detailing service to make the car look spick-and-span. If you damaged something on the car, like maybe there's a busted mirror or a minor dent in the body, pay to have the repair done yourself before you turn the car in. Be sure to save your receipts and take plenty of pictures to document that you turned in the car in perfect condition.

To buy or not to buy at the end of your lease?

- So you've reached the end of your lease and you're unsure what to do. If you liked the experience of driving the car, it makes the most sense to consider buying the vehicle for its residual value. That's the best way to turn a not-so-good financial decision into a good one. Just be sure you have some cash on hand for this. Banks might not want to lend you the money for a car with a lot of miles on it.

Buy formerly leased vehicles.

- Finally, you can get a real deal on a vehicle that someone else leased. In fact, it's not uncommon to pay half the retail price or even less when you're buying a previously leased ride. John told me the following story about his experience: "In 2008, I bought a 2004 Jeep Grand Cherokee [with] one hundred thousand miles that was just coming off a corporate lease [at] Georgia-Pacific from a former colleague of mine. Got it for $7,000 cash, which was 20 cents on the dollar compared with the sticker price." And he tells me he's still happily driving it today!

TECHNOLOGY

If Horace Greeley were alive today, he'd probably say, "Go wireless, young man," not "Go West, young man." Technology brings so much to our lives and has become the land of opportunity for the young and the young at heart.

In this chapter, we meet three different kinds of consumers who underscore the dos and don'ts of buying gadgets and tech services. I want to show you how to do a surgical strike on what can be a real budget killer, with an emphasis on the freshest and most updated info since my last book, Living Large in Lean Times, *came out.*

THE GADGETEERS

Betsy and Scott slash their technology budget by $2,000
annually without suffering

BETSY AND SCOTT ARE RAISING three kids without traditional pay TV and loving every minute of it.

The urge to save a buck runs deep in Betsy, thirty-nine, and she credits her parents for that. "I was raised in a military family and my parents taught me to think through purchases, evaluate needs versus wants, and save rather than go into debt."

By her telling, forty-three-year-old Scott's family lived paycheck to paycheck when he was growing up.

Such different financial backgrounds could cause friction in a marriage, but it didn't for Betsy and Scott. They quickly got on the same page financially after tying the knot.

I often tell male callers to my radio show that knowing their wife or bride-to-be is always right is key to a successful marriage. As I like to say, "Happy wife, happy life." Good job, Scott!

For Betsy and Scott, the first thing they tackled after marrying was about $60,000 in debt, which included two car notes, Scott's student loans, and some miscellaneous consumer loans.

"We attacked that and paid it off within the first four years of our marriage, then started budgeting and collecting all the information we could on using money wisely. At that point, my biggest resource was *The Tightwad Gazette* by Amy Dacyczyn," Betsy recalls.

"I read and reread that book and not only used many of the ideas, but also bought into her idea of frugality as a creative and fun endeavor. . . . It really is a creative expression—instead of just buying the newest and greatest thing, we determine what about it appeals to us or would meet a need, then think of alternate ways we can achieve the same result. It's kind of a fun hobby now."

As I noted, one hobby Betsy and Scott *don't* obsess over is watching pay TV. In fact, they fired their cable provider way back in 1998.

At the time, they both were going to graduate school and didn't have the time or money for cable. They wound up switching to satellite four years later, but the romance with traditional TV providers didn't last long.

"We were pretty much weaned off TV by then and cut it off in 2002. So we bought a DVD player and signed up with Netflix. It was pretty new then," Betsy recalls. "I don't know how my husband found out about Netflix, but he told me about it and we decided to give it a try—we were definitely early adopters. Between the library's selection of DVDs, Netflix, our antenna, and the Internet, we have plenty available to watch."

Because Scott isn't a huge sports fan, he didn't have to worry about giving up ESPN. "We catch some SEC [Southeastern Conference] football games over the antenna. The boys are more into football than he is," Betsy says. "We watch a lot of classic movies, documentaries, and miniseries—Netflix has plenty!"

Other than that, the programming they recently watched when I spoke to them included the original *Planet of the Apes* movie, British TV miniseries such as *Downton Abbey* and *Cranford*, the History Channel, and PBS documentaries such as *The Shakers*.

As Betsy remembers it, firing the pay TV providers put between $30 and $40 back in their budget every month. But that was more than ten years ago and the typical cable or satellite bill is now twice as much as it was back then.

Of course, pay TV is just one piece of the technology budget in anybody's life.

Telephone, cell phone, Internet, and telephone services cost the average American household an estimated $2,160 in 2011, according to the most recent data available from the U.S. Bureau of Labor Statistics.

When it comes to their cell phone bill, I'm happy to report that Betsy and Scott are definitely not your typical data-hungry, smartphone-loving American family.

"We both have TracFones and spend about $10 a month to keep both going. We don't use cell phones much—my husband just for emergencies and traveling, and I mostly use mine to text, which only costs about 5 cents [per text message]."

Meanwhile, they cut the cord on their landline in 2011 and now get their phone service through an Internet calling company called VOIPo. Instead of paying $35 a month to their monopoly phone company, they now pay a little more than $6 a month with a twenty-four-month contract.

The funny thing is, while Betsy and Scott skip the fancy smartphones, they don't deny themselves other hot gadgets. But as you might imagine, they've found ways to get their gadgets on discount and to reduce the costs of ownership once they have them.

Scott has an iPod Touch that he loads only with free podcasts, and Betsy has a Kindle Fire that she keeps packed with (mostly) free e-books.

"I bought the Kindle refurbished for $30 less [than list price] and . . . I've spent $7 on books in the six or eight months I have had it," she says. "I have hundreds of books loaded up on there to read. I'm on a mailing list for EreaderNewsToday.com and they send me a daily e-mail with books available free for the Kindle. They are independently published books for the most part, but mainstream ones come through sometimes."

Saving money on technology is second nature in their household and it's a key piece of their overall financial strategy. But they're not just saving money for the sake of saving it; they do it with a higher goal in mind.

They have decided to live on Scott's roughly $80,000 income working in the field of electrical power while Betsy homeschools the couple's children—ten-year-old Nicholas, eight-year-old Todd, and four-year-old Elijah.

Homeschooling draws on Betsy's early career experience as a teacher of everything from seventh-grade math to AP calculus.

"We were interested in a solid education for our children and looked into private religious schools," Betsy says. "We have a very good public school system in our area, but having taught school, I know a lot of time is wasted and I know children do better with individualized instruction and smaller teacher-student ratios."

When I spoke to Betsy, she was doing a yearlong focus on American history with her kids. There were also planned forays into astronomy and Mesoamerican Indian tribes.

"A few days a week, we get together with other homeschooling families [in our area] for classes in music, science, and history, as well as [to] have social interaction. The other days, we stay home and spend four or five hours doing our school subjects and then run errands as needed. It has been a great choice for us to be able to spend quality time together, use our learning time very efficiently, and choose the best learning materials for our family."

By homeschooling, the family can avoid cumbersome homework, spend more time together, and even save money on meals.

"I know exactly where my children are in every subject, and we can move on quickly or spend more time on a subject as needed rather than having them go at the pace of an entire classroom of children."

Betsy and Scott's approach to life has definitely rubbed off on the kids.

"My boys like to come thrift shopping with me. My oldest is always excited when he finds a name-brand shirt in mint condition for $2 or $3. It blew his mind when I told him that they often cost over $30 if you buy them new. He looked at me like I was insane.

"We're all content with what we have and feel very blessed, and that's rubbed off on them—they seem to 'get it' that money is a tool but doesn't bring happiness, and we are having more fun together than a lot of people who spend a lot more money."

What lessons can you learn from the story of Betsy, Scott, and their three boys?

Cut the TV cord.
- More than 5 million households have cut the cord from pay TV as Betsy and Scott did. Today's modern TVs make it a cinch to get Internet programming on your screen. Here's my strategy for giving your cable or satellite bill the one-two punch and getting it out of your life.
- First, you're going to need an over-the-air antenna for getting your local networks. Visit AntennaWeb.org and search your home by address to see what kind of reception you'll get and what type of antenna you'll need. Then you can visit your favorite retailer or shop online for their recommendation.
- Second, you're going to want to supplement local programming with some level of Internet-delivered pay programming. An "all you can watch" monthly subscription to Netflix or competitors like Hulu Plus and Amazon Prime is about $8 or less.
- For the sports fans among you, you can watch free live programming on the ESPN3 channel of ESPN.go.com/WatchESPN if you're with a participating high-speed Internet service provider. Visit the website to see participating providers.

Cut the phone cord.

- Still stuck paying $35 or more for a home phone that you can't or don't want to give up? I have a new option that could lower your cost for the same service, starting at $15 a month. Straight Talk has a wireless home phone at that price with unlimited nationwide calling, voice mail, caller ID, and three-way calling—all with no contract!
- This home phone service does not require an Internet connection. You basically purchase a $99 wireless base station that you put wherever you happen to get a good signal in your home. It's compatible with your existing corded or cordless phone. You can even port your number over from the local monopoly phone company.
- One word of caution: This is *not* compatible with home security systems, fax machines, DVR services, credit card images, or medical alert systems. (This is true for many home phone systems now, and so each of these industries has adjusted to allow you to connect in different ways, such as with medical alert systems and burglar alarms that work free of a home phone line.)
- But if this works for your life, it will allow you to fire the local monopoly phone company and stop paying $35 or more for their service, which doesn't include any special features! Visit StraightTalk.com/wps/portal/home/shop/ShopHomePhones for more details.

Rethink what you're paying for cell phone service.

- Betsy and Scott are unusual in their pattern of low-volume cell phone usage. That translates to a super-cheap cell phone bill each month on a noncontract carrier like TracFone.
- On the other hand, many Americans are data-obsessed, card-carrying members of the smartphone revolution—and they pay the big bucks for buckets of data in twenty-four-month contracts to prove it.
- Fortunately, there is a middle ground between the two extremes. As I write this, Republic Wireless has again opened a beta test for $19 a month unlimited smartphone service. With this innovative service, you get unlimited calling, texting, e-mail, and Web on a Motorola DEFY XT—all with no contract. Since they're not subsidizing the phone under a contract, you have to pay the full retail price of $249 for the DEFY, plus a $29 activation fee.
- The big idea behind Republic Wireless is that most of the time we're using our phones, we are near or in a place with Wi-Fi. So with this service, all your activity is routed over Wi-Fi. It's an automatic and seamless process that's done entirely by your handset; you aren't required to manually do anything to get on Wi-Fi.

Know the risk of going with smaller technology players.

- While Betsy likes VOIPo for her home-phone replacement service, I love a similar provider called Ooma for cheap Internet phone calling. Ooma was selected two years in a row by *Consumer Reports* as the best home phone service.
- But if VOIPo and Ooma go out of business tomorrow, the money Betsy and I spent to buy those devices from the respective companies goes down the drain.
- I've been burned in the past on another VoIP service called Sunrocket. With that particular one, I laid out $200 for a year of service back in 2007 and the company went bust four months later. So I paid about $50 a month for something I expected to cost $17 a month. I was not a happy camper.
- But that's the risk when you're an early adopter of technology start-ups.

THE NEGOTIATOR

Krista wheels and deals to save big bucks on monthly bills

KRISTA DAS SAYS SHE'S the girl every cable and Internet company hates.

Krista, thirty-three, makes a good living in health care communications, and lives in a beautiful brick high-rise condominium in the historic Mount Vernon section of Baltimore, Maryland, a mile north of the Inner Harbor. Her building has a twenty-four-hour front desk person, a doorman, and a valet.

But that doesn't mean Krista is willing to accept high prices, either as a consumer or at work.

Every six months, Krista has a little chat with her cable company, and the result is always the same—she ends up with a lower rate.

"My cable company was trying to charge me $109 a month for two hundred channels plus HBO and Showtime, but I got it down to $72 a month for the same package," Krista told me. "I go through a separate company for Internet because their rates are better even with my cable provider's 'special discount' for a bundled package—$206 for cable, Internet, and phone combined per month for the first six months. Then the rate goes up after that. Ridiculous! Plus it gives me better leverage by having two companies that don't want to lose a customer."

One thing Krista has learned is not to select "billing" on the phone tree when she has her semiannual conversation with her cable company. When she did that, she got no for an answer.

"The representative was very rude and said that a $5 monthly discount was the best he could do. He told me that if I didn't agree at that moment, then the deal was off. So I hung up and called back, but this time connected to the cancellation department."

Krista had no intention of canceling her cable service. That wasn't a good option because her building prohibits satellite TV and she didn't have any other pay-TV choices. But she didn't tell her cable company that.

"I simply explained that while I was happy with their service, my rates had become too high and asked if there was anything they could do to retain me as a customer. The representative was more than willing to assist and that is when he knocked $37 a month off my bill."

Negotiating lower prices is pretty much the norm for Krista.

Not long ago, she was overseeing a complex print/direct-mail job on a tight time line. She received five bids, ranging from $11,000 to $16,000.

"The lower bids looked really enticing, but no one was familiar with their work or ability to deliver within the time frame," Krista said. "If we didn't meet the deadline for this direct-mail campaign, the company would end up losing a lot of money on product sales for that year."

The high bidder was an outstanding printer, one that Krista knew would do a great job and do it within her tight time frame.

So did she pay the higher price for the top company? Nope.

"I went back to my top pick and asked for a price match. The printer wasn't sure at first, but after some research, came back to me with a bid for $10,000, which was now lower than the lowest original bid . . . not only was the project completed on time, but the quality of the paper and assembly was better than we had ever seen in years past. Additionally, the printer saved the company over $2,000 in postage by suggesting that we make the height of the piece one inch shorter."

Krista says she's always had to negotiate with vendors at work, and whether it's for herself or her employer, she wants to make sure no one takes advantage of her and she gets the best possible deal.

"A former boss heard me negotiating a contract once and said, 'I am changing your title to chief negotiator. Can you talk to our CEO and renegotiate my salary for me?'"

Krista put her skills to work when she was looking for a good-quality point-and-shoot digital camera.

"When I went to the store, I had narrowed it down to two choices—one was a Samsung on sale for $212 and the other was a Sony on sale for $218. Against my better judgment, I ended up going with the one for $212 because I liked some of its features."

Krista had the camera for two weeks and was not only dissatisfied with some of its features, but the lens jammed. So she took it back to get the Sony Cyber-shot HX10V for $218, but it was now $249.

"I explained why I was returning the Samsung and that I wanted to purchase the Sony for the price that it was listed at two weeks earlier. The salesperson couldn't find any record of the lower price in the system and called the manager over, who also couldn't find any record of it in the system."

The manager told her that it could have been a rebate that the manufacturer was offering, but that there was nothing that the store could do about the rebate offer now.

"I asked them what they could do to discount the item, and the manager said that if they sold me the Sony for $218, the store would only be making 94 cents off the camera. I replied, 'I understand. Well, I'm happy to pay $218. If not, I will just return the Samsung.' He knew that I would take my business elsewhere and he caved in, selling me the camera for $218."

Krista grew up in a small country town a half hour north of Baltimore and went to an all-girls prep school. She comes from a long line of savers, including her grandmother, who kept a spiral notebook of things she purchased, including french fries from Wendy's and aspirin from the drugstore.

Her parents live in the same house they bought in the 1970s.

"My father, in particular, has always avoided debt like the plague. So for two years, my parents scrimped and saved, allowing each other to have only $5 each in spending money per week so that they could pay off their mortgage . . . and they did it. It only took them two years to pay off their mortgage."

Krista started babysitting at twelve, and her parents made her open a savings account. At sixteen, her parents told her she had to get a summer job, so she became a lifeguard—and her parents told her she needed to start investing.

She opened her first retirement account at twenty-two after working in a nursing home and seeing how expensive end-of-life care is.

She bought her first condo on her twenty-fifth birthday, and sold it two years later for a 152 percent profit.

One area Krista likes to splurge on is travel.

"By taking control of my finances and keeping a close watch on where the dollars go, I am able to put that money towards things that I really want to do, like diving the Great Barrier Reef in Australia, seeing the pyramids in Egypt, and sailing the Greek isles—all things that I have done when most of my peers said they couldn't afford to. But better than those nice vacations, I have peace of mind with the nest egg I've grown. When those rainy days come, I won't be stressed, because I'm prepared."

Friends always react favorably to Krista's exceptional frugality.

"Everyone's reactions are pretty much the same when I tell them about how I negotiate lower rates; they chuckle and then say, 'I didn't know it was possible to negotiate lower prices. Can you teach me how?'"

What can you learn from Krista's story?

Pit the pay-TV providers against one another to lower your bill.

- When it comes to pay TV, many people now have access to four providers—two satellite companies, one cable company, and a monopoly phone company. Having all those choices makes comparison shopping pretty easy.
- Call each provider up and see if you can get their best offer in writing, or just watch the mailers with advertised deals that come to your home. Then pit them against one another and let them slug it out so you can get the best deal.
- As Krista found, you'll get better results if you connect to the cancellation department rather than the billing department when you're working the phone tree. Not making any progress with the phone rep you initially get on the line? Ask to speak to their supervisor and make your case.

Being unbundled offers a better position for negotiating.

- Bundling of pay TV, home phone, and Internet is not pushed as heavily as it once was, but I still want to warn you about the dangers of these package deals for your wallet.
- The practice of bundling handcuffs you to the phone and cable companies, usually with a minimum twelve-month contract. That makes you a prisoner when technology moves on in the marketplace. Plus, if you dump any one service in the bundle, the price on the other services can go crazy.

- As for whom bundling is actually good for, well, I'm sure there's somebody out there. But my general advice is to run away from those bundle offers! As Krista pointed out, she gets more leverage for negotiation when she's not in a bundle package.

Give Roku a try.

- A lot of my ultra-cheap readers might balk at Krista's revelation of paying $72 for TV each month. But that does represent a savings of more than 30 percent just because she asked for it. Not bad.
- For the truly frugal among you, I'd like to recommend a little box called Roku. It's an easy-to-use streaming player that makes it simple to access a massive choice in online programming.
- Roku devices sell for anywhere from $50 to $80. They hook up to virtually any TV in just a few minutes and connect to the Internet either wirelessly or via a hard wire to your high-speed connection. (Today, roughly four in ten of us have an Internet-enabled TV.)
- I was stunned by how easy Roku was to hook up and use. I tried it out and bam! Just like that I was up and running with simple access to my existing Netflix and Hulu Plus subscriptions. It truly is Internet TV for dummies like me who just want things to be easy.
- Paired with an antenna to pick up your local channels, this magic box will give you more TV to consume than you could possibly want or need. Visit Roku.com for more details.

Use artificial intelligence to find real deals.

- When it comes to buying electronics, I love Krista's story of getting her camera for less than a dollar over what the retailer paid for it.
- If you want an easy way to see if a quoted online price for electronics is a deal or not, try websites like Decide.com that use price-analysis algorithms to alert you when a deal is really a deal based on historical pricing models.
- Another alternative would be to install a browser plug-in like GetInvisibleHand.com that automatically pops up an alert while you're shopping if a better price is available on another website.
- Finally, Amazon customers can typically get a better deal on many items if they put something in their cart and then abandon it before the final purchase. That usually signals to Amazon that you're willing to walk away and triggers a lower price the next time you put it in your cart to check out.

REQUIEM FOR A DEAL

Martin has made sacrifices to stay on top of technology

LONGTIME FANS KNOW THAT, while I love my gadgets, I don't think it's a good idea to buy the latest, greatest technology. Early adopters pay the highest prices for technology, and I think it's better to let manufacturers work the bugs out first, make improvements, and bring the price down.

But that's definitely not the approach of Martin Smentczak, who thinks cutting-edge technology is the way to go. And he's a big fan of Apple products.

Martin, twenty-five, owns or has owned an iMac (2008) with most of the upgrades they offered back then, iPad (first generation), iPad Mini, iPod Touch, Apple TV, iPhone 1, iPhone 4, and iPhone 5. He has an "air-print" compatible HP printer that lets him print directly from any iDevice, and he has preordered a Lockitron, which will make it possible to have your front door unlock automatically when it senses your iPhone via Bluetooth. He also had an iPod/iPhone compatible stereo installed in his Toyota Prius.

Martin would like to buy the Nest, the thermostat that was created by one of the inventors of the iPod.

"I also have a Dyson vacuum, if that counts."

Martin makes about $33,000 a year working in the operations department for a bank called BB&T (Branch Banking and Trust). He lives with his boyfriend, Josh, in an $800 a month apartment in Concord, North Carolina, near Charlotte. He balances out the amount of money he spends on technology by cutting back on his spending in other areas.

"My wardrobe could use some updating once in a while, but I get more excitement from buying a new gadget versus some new shoes or a button-up shirt," Martin said. "Also, I keep a limited social life, because that can get really expensive! But again, it's just who I am—gadgets versus a night out with friends? I would rather have the tangible item."

So why is it so important for Martin to own the newest stuff?

"I try to justify it to myself like this," Martin said. "The world is moving into a 'technology only' society. You will not be able to function without the knowledge of how to work the stuff and what it does or can do."

For example, Martin explained, a man in the early 1900s who refused to learn how to drive a car and instead stayed with his horse might not seem that odd at first. But thirty-five years later, it would be bizarre.

And technology is evolving much faster than it did one hundred years ago.

"Taking just a year off from technology will set you back further than it would have last century. This is the reason I might tell a friend—to make my spending sound a little smarter. But it really boils down to being a hobby. It's like asking a coffee mug collector why they do it. They'll come up with their own little reasons, but it's simply a hobby. [I love] the excitement of opening the package, tracking the item on UPS/FedEx, and then getting to play with the gadgets, of course."

Martin is not, however, a collector when it comes to technology that is no longer cutting-edge. He sells his old gadgets early, before they lose too much of their value.

"With Apple products, they hold their value a lot better than Android products. But even if it's not an Apple product, I find it better to keep the clutter down when it comes to old gadgets. Sell now and get 40 percent of the original price, or sell later and get 20 percent."

Why does he prefer Apple products to the cheaper Android products? First, he likes the way Apple products work so well with one another. And in addition to that compatibility, he likes their reliability, durability, and usability.

"Before the iPod era, you would have never seen me with Apple items," said Martin. "I thought it was a failing business and technology that I didn't understand. Now it's all I will buy! The reason I point this out is because Apple has made it so all your gadgets play well together. And now they have such a market share that it's 'safe' to buy their gadgets because you know that they will be compatible with anything you buy."

Martin likes the fact that Apple designs and manufactures its own products, and creates both the hardware and software.

"If something goes wrong, there is only one company to go to versus a Samsung phone running Android software. If ever I've had a problem with an Apple product, I've taken it in, and they have simply given me a brand-new one."

In 2007, Martin said he spent $1,200 on Dell's top-of-the-line laptop, and it didn't last him two years.

"I have had the same iMac for over four years and I never saw the decline in speed like you do with PCs. You can't beat the materials, either!"

The same thing goes for the tablet market, Martin said.

"In short, I don't buy Apple just because it's Apple."

Martin's boyfriend of four years doesn't share his enthusiasm for new technology.

"Josh typically just rolls his eyes or fakes his excitement with a forced smile, but all of it is playful and it has never escalated to the point where we would argue or it would threaten our relationship," said Martin. "His spending habits are so much different than mine. He feels almost guilty spending money on himself."

Martin does plan his spending carefully. He has a financial plan in place before he makes a purchase, and if he finances it with a credit card, he makes sure it gets paid for in a reasonable amount of time. For anything that costs more than $750, he delays his desire to be an early adopter and waits to make sure he has the money to make the purchase.

He also thoroughly researches the products he buys so he knows what he'll get out of it and, more important, when it would be better to wait for the next generation. (For my money, I like to check *Consumer Reports* and CNET.com for tech and gadget reviews.)

When Martin was a teenager, he learned what happens when you're irresponsible with your money.

"I was reckless with credit lines and loans right out of the gate when I was eighteen, nineteen. Now I am twenty-five and I recognize the importance of staying ahead of the game, because I'm still paying for my recklessness when I was younger."

It's taken him several years to get his credit score back to a high level, and now he keeps his credit card balances very low.

And working for a bank has given him a new perspective.

"I never thought money would be my life five years ago, but now that I'm at a bank I love it! And being that I work for a bank, I feel that much more obligated to stay on track financially."

While he and I disagree on buying cutting-edge technology, Martin actually watches my TV show, and he "almost always" is simpatico with my message.

"I'm pretty good at hearing out both sides of things. If ever the topic of 'spending too much on gadgets when you should be putting more money into your 401(k)' or 'saving for a down payment on a house' comes up, I'll have to agree with [you].

"But you have to start living at some point!"

What can you learn from what Martin does or doesn't do when it comes to new technology?

Consider Android.

- While Apple gets the lion's share of media coverage, Android smartphones outsell Apple by a 5:1 ratio.
- During a recent ninety-day reporting period, 75 percent of the smartphones sold were Androids and only 15 percent were Apple. Yet based on the media coverage you see, you'd think it was 99 percent Apple and 1 percent everybody else!
- The general public just wants a deal. They're not as wedded to Apple as the media types are.
- I was looking at Virgin Mobile, which is a noncontract carrier for smartphones. They offer both the iPhone 4S and various Androids.
- The iPhone 4S is $650 because it's unsubsidized as a noncontract purchase. Yet you can get a highly capable Android for $199 noncontract. The difference is that stark.
- And if Apple keeps the price of iPads so high, they'll continue to be outsold by Android tablets.
- While the number of apps available for iPhone and iPad was many times greater than for Androids a year ago, today it's the opposite. The app developers go where the eyeballs are.
- There's no denying Apple makes works of art. But Android has good ease of use and opens you to the orbit of all noncontract carriers to get a much lower price on your monthly service.

Try a protective case for your smartphone.

- You could insure your smartphone, but I have a different Clark Smart way to protect it.
- A lot of people get their phone through the big contract carriers. So when you go in to get your Galaxy III from Samsung, or the latest HTC, or even the latest iPhone, you

get locked into that twenty-four-month contract. You also get a pitch for cell phone insurance from the salesperson.

- Cell phone insurance typically runs about $80 a year. You have a deductible to meet, usually around $50, and after paying that, you often get a refurbished replacement phone—not a new one.
- Not buying the insurance means that if you lose or break that phone before your contract is up, you could owe the unsubsidized price of $600 or $700 for a new replacement phone.
- But rather than paying for the insurance, why not get something like an OtterBox? It's a protective case for smartphones that can be clunky and ugly but really protects your smartphone in the event that you drop it.
- You can get a protective case like this on a discount site like eBay or Amazon. But even if you pay full retail price, it's still a lower-cost way to protect your phone. Visit OtterBox.com for more details.

Don't overlook cell phone repair shops.

- What do you do if you buy a smartphone and it breaks while you're in contract and you didn't buy the extended warranty plan?
- Try a local cell phone repair shop. They're spreading like wildfire across the country and typically specialize in Android and iPhone repair.
- If you go to one of these shops, the repairs tend to price out somewhere between $50 and $150. My executive producer Christa DiBiase recently went to a smartphone repair shop in metro Atlanta because she cracked her screen. She paid less than $100, though she concedes that's on the expensive end.
- Cracked screens are one of the most common repairs. I've also heard anecdotally that you can sometimes get a free replacement screen if you go to a retail outlet of your wireless carrier. Give that a try before going for the pay option.

Turn your e-trash into cash.

- When it comes time to upgrade your phone or tablet, do what Martin does: Sell your old gadgets.
- In addition to Craigslist and eBay, you can try these sites when you want to unload an old phone: Swappa.com (Android); Gazelle.com (Apple, Android, and BlackBerry); NewtonsHead.com (Apple products, even damaged iPhones); and NextWorth.com for phones, cameras, tablets, and games.

- But those aren't the only options. Coinstar is testing a kiosk called ecoATM.com that uses artificial intelligence and extreme digital photography to determine a value for any electronics gadgets you want to sell to the machine. You can get cash or cash equivalent on the spot. Visit the website to find a kiosk near you.
- Finally, as an alternative to selling your old gadgets, you might consider donating them to schools or senior centers. They're often looking for discarded devices for those who can't afford them.

RETILREMENT

A dime out of every dollar—it's a simple enough rule when it comes to saving for retirement. Yet life happens and many of us don't get around to saving. In the end, saving money is a choice; there's no requirement that you do it. No one wants to be a burden on family, and government is not riding to the rescue. So if saving is not something that's important to you, it simply means you'll probably have to work longer.

In this chapter, we meet four people who highlight the spectrum of possibilities when it comes to saving for retirement. And I'll show you how their choices play out so you can learn from their examples.

KEEP ON TRUCKIN'

Unable to retire, seventy-two-year-old
Grandpa John stays behind the wheel

Allen John Sokol climbs into his flatbed and prepares to haul another load of steel, pipe, and drywall from his home in Ben Wheeler, Texas, to Oklahoma, New Mexico, or somewhere else in the region.

His weathered face is highlighted by ageless blue eyes. But Sokol, who goes by John or Grandpa John, is far from ageless. He is seventy-two years old, and he is still working, unable to retire.

John has been a trucker for more than fifty years, since he graduated from high school back in 1959.

"I started on the big rigs in '62, and with a few interruptions, have done that since."

John tried to retire in 2002, and moved to a twenty-five-acre tract of land seventy miles east of Dallas. But it didn't work out. He didn't have enough money to cover his expenses.

His wife, Betty Veerkamp, had $100,000 in a 401(k) account and another $100,000 from an inheritance. John took early Social Security. But the bills for Betty's many medications—for high blood pressure, high cholesterol, and diabetes—proved too daunting. (Both Betty and John have insurance, but it doesn't help much. "The times we have to pay [are] in the gap, when the big discounts aren't there," John says.)

Betty retired in 2005 from Haynes and Boone, a large Dallas law firm where she worked as a word processor, preparing documents for the attorneys.

"I made the big mistake of retiring at sixty-two. I advise anyone not to do this. My wife had a 401(k), but I did not at the last job. Hers has been exhausted. I went back to work mostly to pay for her meds that insurance didn't cover."

Then there were also unexpected bills.

"The mobile home that was on the property [in Ben Wheeler] when we bought it began to fall apart, and rather than let it nickel-and-dime us to death, we replaced it. That was another $500 a month."

And because John started taking Social Security benefits at age sixty-two, he got less than he would have if he had waited.

So John went back to work two years after "retiring."

"I have had several jobs, beginning in 2004. One in 2008 was good money, and local, but died when the economy tanked."

The 2004 job was like what he does now, long-haul trucking in which he gets paid by the mile. The 2008 job was a temporary job for Averitt Express. John did pickups and deliveries in his local area and was paid by the hour. But then the recession hit.

John went back to work for a third time in 2011, at age seventy. And he had some trouble getting hired.

"I had put out résumés online to the headhunters and got replies from several companies, until they found out I had been working local for four years," John said. "For some reason nobody can explain, most don't count local work, even though it's driving."

John grew up in upstate New York. His parents divorced when he was four, and he moved in with his grandparents.

"This was during World War II," John said. "Everything was rationed, and Pop was supervisor of a town road crew, so he had access to things we needed. We even got our driveway plowed, which saved me from having to shovel it as I got older."

The family had a large garden and raised chickens, and John says he was nearly ten years old before he knew there was anything but a brown egg.

"We were very active in the church, and that laid a good foundation for the rest of my life. While I don't attend any now, I still get devotionals online."

When his mother remarried, John's stepdad worked for General Electric, and the family got transferred to Louisville, Kentucky.

"I finished high school there, and began driving delivery trucks and cabs. An ad I put in the paper got an answer from a gypsy trucker, and he taught me a great deal, even though he was only a year older. He passed away in '76 from emphysema."

John moved to Florida in 1967 and lived in the Fort Lauderdale area until 1977, then in Fort Myers until 1982, when he went to Texas.

Now he lives in Ben Wheeler, in northeast Texas, which sounds like a crazy, colorful place. The town bills itself as the "Wild Hog Capital of Texas," and holds events such as the Fall Feral Hog Fest and the World Championship Wild Hog Cook Off. The tiny town, named for the first man to carry mail into Van Zandt County, thrived during the late 1800s and early 1900s and is currently enjoying an economic and artistic renaissance.

When John is home in Ben Wheeler, you might find him tending his horses. He and Betty have four, all but one born in his care.

"I got interested in them while going to high school in Kentucky. Several of my classmates were into showing. I saved my money and took lessons from an elderly couple, who ran a riding school, a short bike ride from home. I attended camps with horses, and bought my first while in Florida."

His group includes Buddy, Bobbie, and two of their offspring, Sneaky and Finale.

Though he'd rather be home spending time with his grandson and his horses, John likes being a trucker.

"I like the travel. I guess it's wanderlust. When I was single, I'd leave the truck and ride a motorcycle."

But trekking to Minnesota or to the East Coast is rigorous, even for a younger man.

"You have to enjoy it or it's a hard job. I'm away from home for a week at a time, sometimes two. It used to be longer, but most companies are regional now."

John wishes Americans had more respect for truckers, who deliver food and other products across the country and are sometimes criticized for it.

"That's one of our pet peeves," said John. "The general population just can't relate the trucks on the highways with the merchandise on the shelves. Those so-called safety advocates, which are nothing more than truck haters, form lobbies to pile more and more restrictions on us, and make it nearly impossible to do a good job anymore.

"In the early days of my career, we pretty much just did it and were left alone," John added, "but of course the government just can't leave well enough alone, and now it's a mess."

How long will seventy-two-year-old John continue to work?

"I always like to say, as long as I can pass the physical, but I figure, realistically, about another year."

Know how much to save when starting later in life.

- I've always said that you should save a dime out of every dollar you make as a general rule of thumb. But if you're getting started saving for retirement later in life, the dime out of every dollar rule won't cut it for you. So for you, the *Baltimore Sun* has crunched the following numbers:
  - If you start saving at thirty-five, you need to save 20 cents out of every dollar to have a comfortable retirement at a reasonably young age.
  - If you start saving at forty-five, you need to save 30 cents out of every dollar.
  - If you start saving at fifty-five, you need to save 43 cents out of every dollar.

Seventy is the new sixty-five.

- Recent media reports scared people into thinking they will never be able to retire. Sure, a lot of people have trouble saving today for tomorrow. Don't believe the scare tactics. The overwhelming majority of Americans will be able to retire. The question is, at what age?
- We went through two generational cycles where people were able to retire at a younger age, relative to their life span, than at any time in history. Some people were calling it quits in their fifties because they had a pension and then Social Security later in life. So they never had to work another day in their lives. That meant people were having twenty or more years of retirement.
- Today, though, pensions are mostly gone and people are not saving enough. For most people, the new magic number is age seventy. Know your retirement horizon and work to meet your goals.

Find a job the old-school way.

- If you're entering the workforce again after being out for some time like John was, you've got to treat finding a job like a flashback to fifty years ago.
- Back in 1963, people found jobs through word of mouth and by relying on friends, relatives, and work colleagues to help them network. And that's right where we are today.
- Most jobs are filled by hirers who are likely to bring in someone they know or know of for an interview. A friend of a friend, a colleague of a colleague. People think that net-

working is passé. No way. Nobody likes to be asked for a job, but everybody loves to give advice. So identify some key people in your industry whom you can have a face-to-face meeting with and interview them for their career advice to make a successful re-entry.

Costco sells individual health insurance.

- With more people losing health coverage at work, Costco wants to fill the gap for its members with individual health insurance policies.
- The warehouse club is partnering with Aetna for what's called Costco Personal Health Insurance. Aetna has publicly stated that it will sell five varieties of plans to Costco members cheaper than what the individual plans are sold for elsewhere.
- The Costco Personal Health Insurance policies are so far only available to customers in Texas, California, Virginia, Connecticut, Illinois, Michigan, Arizona, Pennsylvania, Nevada, and Georgia.
- For Costco, the risk is selling something as a branded product that it won't have control of in an industry that hasn't exactly won a lot of love from customers over the years. Will it harm their otherwise solid reputation? It will be interesting to see how it plays out.

SILENT ENDURANCE

At thirty-two, Mandy has amassed almost $200,000 for her future

MANDY SPLAWN LIKES TO TAKE a fast and passionate approach to life. This is the kind of thing you learn early on about the Greenville, South Carolina, native.

Her recent exploits include skydiving in Elberta, Alabama, with the air force's Blue Angels skydiving team; taking her mother up for a hot air balloon ride over Asheville, North Carolina, on Mother's Day; and even burning rubber on her own during the Mario Andretti Indy Car Experience at Charlotte Motor Speedway.

"I got in an actual Indy car and raced it around the track for eight minutes all by myself! My top speed was 156.16 miles per hour," the thirty-two-year-old graphic designer says. "LOVED IT!"

Mandy's preparations for retirement are similarly high-octane. Since starting her career in 1996 at the age of sixteen, she's built up a nest egg of $160,000. Plus, she has another $13,000 in liquid cash savings.

But perhaps the most amazing thing about Mandy's story is that she's done all that—both the saving and the playing—while being a full-time caretaker for her father and mother in the wake of some devastating health developments.

Mandy's late father was diagnosed with Lou Gehrig's disease (amyotrophic lateral sclerosis) and lived for more than five years before succumbing to it. And her mother, coping with the stress of her husband's illness, suffered a stroke that left her legally blind in 2005 when she was forty-nine.

To deal with something like that, you have to be strong and resilient, and possess what

Mandy calls "silent endurance." Why do I tell you about her? To show you how somebody can overcome obstacles in life and still save for retirement like nobody's business.

Mandy got started saving early in her life on her dad's advice.

"My father told me early on . . . to get plugged into 401(k)s, Roths, IRAs, stocks, etcetera, [which was] something he had never done because of the era he was born in. He also taught me that if I don't see the money, I won't spend the money," Mandy says.

"So, since the age of nineteen, I've invested anywhere between 15 to 27 percent of my paycheck into these retirement options. I'm trying to do the very best for my own retirement while I have taken care of my beloved parents."

As you can imagine, Mandy has her personal finance ledger in tip-top shape with a less than 1 percent debt-to-income (DTI) ratio and excellent credit.

"I [got] preapproved through my credit union when purchasing a car. They said, 'Wow! You are extremely rare. You have less than 1 percent DTI. You can get a loan for any amount,'" she recalls. "Of course, being a saver, I didn't go crazy and buy a luxury car. Instead, I purchased a 2011 Jetta SEL for an outrageous price of $20,000. I will get my money's worth out of it, though."

When she was just sixteen, Mandy enrolled in a two-year drafting/design course at a local career center in 1996 that was being offered through J. L. Mann High School. The program allowed her to work in her chosen field for a few hours every morning earning $12 an hour and earn academic credit while completing her course work in the second half of the school day.

That training put her in good stead for her future and she found work doing geospatial mapping for AECOM in 1999. She's been there for almost fourteen years now. Over the years, she also put herself through Greenville Technical College as she continued working full-time—all while pulling double duty as a caregiver to her father (1998–2001) and her mother (2007–2010).

Ever the high achiever, she graduated in May 2010 with a 4.0 GPA!

Today Mandy earns about $70,000 annually, which includes income she gets from seasonal part-time work as a whitewater raft guide and a disc jockey on some weekends. In addition, she volunteers her time working with animal rescues and in senior homes, and helping those who are struggling in today's economy to get back on track.

"I call these side jobs my 'escape' jobs. They provide fun and entertainment, I get to interact with the public (which I love), and it's 'me' time."

Mandy's ultimate goal is to open an independent-living care home for seniors.

"I see a great need and desire to give personal attention to our dearly beloved elders who've experienced life and have all but been forgotten about. We have *so much* to learn from our elders and I don't want to lose sight of that. I want to love on them, care for them, and provide for them for the rest of their days," she says.

"That's important to me—it's in my heart. In fact, I've created my business plan and have met with a SCORE counselor to get this goal moving forward . . . the seniors need me and my heart needs them."

For those who don't know, SCORE is the Service Corps of Retired Executives, a group of retirees from corporate backgrounds who so love capitalism that they dedicate their time to help fledgling entrepreneurs realize their dreams.

Mandy's story points at the importance of having good guidance in your life, whether it's to help you reach retirement savings goals or craft a business plan.

"I find it extremely important to have mentors in your life—financial mentors, spiritual mentors, career mentors, and personal mentors. I pick my mentors wisely, as I desire much for my life.

"I have tendencies, at times, of not being a very patient person, as I'm a go-getter. I'm active and go at everything full force. I give my all in all that I do. In order to stay the course, I have to remind myself, 'Silent endurance!'"

What can you learn from Mandy's story if you're saving for retirement?

Gain financial literacy before it's too late.
- A new study from PNC Bank shows twenty- and twenty-one-year-olds have an average debt of $12,000. But by the time they reach twenty-eight or twenty-nine, the average person's debt load balloons to $78,000.
- Half of the debt load is student loans. Another quarter is credit cards. That's followed by car loans and mortgages. At the core of the problem is the level of financial literacy of our young people. Even whiz kids who work on Wall Street are clueless when it comes to everyday money decisions.

- If that sounds like you, you need to educate yourself. Try a free site like YoBucko.com that offers financial advice specifically geared to twentysomethings.

Never miss your money.
- Want to have more money in retirement? Switch to autopilot when contributing money to a retirement, investment, or savings account each pay period.
- It's easy to do this through a 401(k) at work; your employer simply diverts funds that you save in pretax dollars. But if you have an IRA, a Roth IRA, a SEP (simplified employee pension), or something similar, you might have to mark a date on your calendar every month or every pay period when you initiate an electronic deposit of funds to your account.
- If you can manage to pay yourself or your retirement first before you do anything else with your money, it's much easier to reach your financial goals.

Find a money mentor.
- I can't stress the importance of having the right money mentor in your life. It can be Dave Ramsey, Suze Orman, me, or any of a host of other financial gurus. Having the right guidance can make all the difference.
- Mandy says she picks her mentors carefully and I'm proud to have her call me one. "I don't often share my goals with those who are not my mentors, as I don't want to be discouraged in my desires," she tells me. "Everything is within reach and it's up to me to get there . . . and that I will."
- And remember, there really are no magic bullets that anyone can offer you that are going to make you insta-rich. While it isn't sexy to talk about compound interest and plain vanilla index funds, they do get the job done over time!

Get control of your money—no matter what it takes.
- Saving for retirement might seem hard, but it doesn't have to be. The first thing to address is how to get a real tactile sense of your money in a world of ATMs, auto-drafts, and debit cards, where money management has become so abstract that we've lost control.
- The brainiacs at MIT have developed a series of wallets that buzz when you spend money, become progressively harder to open as your money dwindles, and actually shrink in size as your account balance lowers!
- Working prototypes of what are called the "Proverbial Wallet" by product designer John

Kestner "communicate with a cell phone through Bluetooth, using its data connection to get financial information from the user's bank accounts." JohnKestner.com has a video of these devices with the promise that "a commercial version is in early development." You can also sign up for updates. Hey, whatever it takes to get the job of saving done, right?

THE EARLY RETIREE

Hilly hangs it up ten years early. You can too!

HILLIARD BARKER HAS BEEN DRIVING from his small farm in Goldsboro, North Carolina, to his job in Raleigh, North Carolina, a round-trip of 150 miles, for eighteen years.

And he's had enough. Hilliard, who is just fifty-four years old, is ready to retire.

"I've worn out three cars driving the distance to the moon and back twice, or to the West Coast and back thirteen hundred times," said Hilliard, who's never had so much as a flat tire on his long commute. "I feel lucky to have survived that trip unscathed so far. You know what they say, quit while you're ahead."

Hilliard makes about $54,000 a year as a distribution clerk at the U.S. Postal Service processing and distribution center in Raleigh. That would qualify him for a pension of $12,300, or about $1,000 a month.

Normally, he'd be penalized 5 percent a year for every year before age sixty-two that he retired. But the Postal Service is hemorrhaging money, and it's trying to encourage more people to retire.

So it's offering Hilliard, a twenty-two-year employee, a deal he can't turn down. He'll receive a onetime taxable $15,000 incentive, plus no reduction of his pension.

"The buyout is part of the reason I want to retire, not for the fifteen grand but for the fact I can retire early without the 5 percent per year penalty," Hilliard said. "Mostly it is because I am just tired of working."

His wife, Rhonda, also works for the U.S. Postal Service. She's a window clerk at the Mount Olive, North Carolina, post office, and she will continue to work.

"She loves her job and everybody in town loves her and she loves her customers."

Rhonda started with the post office about three years after Hilliard did, when she saw she could make twice the money she was making as a receptionist. She earns the same amount as Hilliard, about $54,000 per year.

The Barkers don't have any debt. Their house is paid for, as are three new cars, and they have about $400,000 in their Thrift Savings Plan. Plus, when Hilliard turns fifty-six, the Postal Service will pay him a special supplement that is about half of what his Social Security would be at age sixty-two. This comes to about $600 per month and he will receive it until he turns sixty-two.

Hilliard doesn't plan to get another job, even a part-time one, to occupy his time.

"The only way I would ever work again for money is if I had to financially," he said. "Getting a part-time job defeats the whole purpose, don't it? I do have a few friends with businesses that might need a hand every once in a while, and I plan to cut my wife's friends' lawns in the summertime. That's it!"

Some people dream of retiring so they can travel the world. But that's not Hilliard's plan.

"I've never been too big on traveling," he said. "I live on a ten-acre mini-farm in the country. I love being home and taking care of the place. If I did go anywhere, it would be Alaska. I'd like to drive that road they got going up there."

And the Barkers love North Carolina. Hilliard says Goldsboro is "perfectly situated between the mountains and the coast."

Hilliard does have a lot of hobbies, and plans to spend a good bit of time in retirement on those. His list includes hunting, fishing, gardening, caring for animals (dogs, cats, and chickens), quilting, winemaking, carpentry, swimming in the pool in the summer, and cutting firewood in the winter.

"And by the way, I've been playing bluegrass guitar for thirty-five years. Been thinking about trying to learn the fiddle."

Hilliard has had a hard working life. He and Rhonda were high school sweethearts in Falmouth, Kentucky. They got married in Falmouth thirty-eight years ago, and Hilliard dropped out of high school in the eleventh grade to support his wife and their baby daughter, Jessica.

He joined the U.S. Air Force at age seventeen, and that got them to Goldsboro, North Carolina—Seymour Johnson Air Force Base—in 1975.

After leaving the air force, Hilliard worked as a boiler operator at a Georgia-Pacific plywood plant in Dudley, North Carolina.

"We burned the sawdust we created to make steam to run the dryers to dry the veneer. Working indoors it was one hundred twenty degrees and outdoors you were breathing pine bark dust. Plus it was very hard work."

Fortunately, the cost of living was low.

"When we first moved to Goldsboro in 1975, we rented a place for $75 per month and were fortunate enough to not have the rent go up for fifteen years. We saved enough to buy our ten acres, then built our house on it. With my own two hands, I might add."

Hilliard's frugality helped him stay out of debt and accumulate enough money to re-tire early.

"Being debt-free is pretty easy if you earn decent money and don't live beyond your means," he said. "But you can't fly by the seat of your pants. You have to have a plan and be willing to sacrifice sometimes."

Hilliard is still nervous about making the decision to quit working.

"I know it's a big step, and I am apprehensive, but the way I look at it, you only go around once. I've heard too many horror stories of people working on up into their years, scared to retire, and when they finally do, are too old to enjoy themselves or, even worse, die soon after retiring.

"I think I've earned an early retirement. I'm not greedy or trying to rub it in on anybody, and I know I'll have to be frugal, but if it don't work out, I'll cross that bridge when I get to it," he says.

"Now I must learn to cook so I can have my wife's supper on the table when she gets home from work."

What can you learn from Hilliard's story?

Strive to reduce debt in your life.

- Being debt-free buys you so much freedom, as you can see in Hilly's story. And today it's easier to become debt-free than at any other time in our lifetimes because of dirt-cheap interest rates. If you're still paying high interest rates, like on a credit card, get a lower interest card if you can qualify and transfer the balance. Look at that box on your monthly statement and see what you'd have to pay to be debt-free in three years. Then resolve to pay that each and every month. You need to budget money to pay down your debt just as you would budget for rent or a mortgage or a car payment.

Save, save, save!

- Unlike Hilliard, many Americans no longer have access to a pension, are not saving enough money, and will get smaller Social Security benefits relative to living costs as the years go by. It's a perfect storm of circumstances that requires extra planning.

- Too many people tell me they can't afford to save. But I say start by saving just 1 percent of your salary in a retirement plan at work or on your own through a Roth IRA. Set up an automatic withdrawal every pay period so you don't even see the money. That's one penny out of every dollar you earn.

- Six months down the line after you've been saving 1 percent in a retirement account, I want you to bump your contribution up by just another 1 percent. Now you're at just two pennies out of every dollar you earn, or 2 percent. By doing it gradually like this, you won't feel restricted, squeezed, or pinched in the wallet. After five years, you're saving 10 percent of your pay and that's before any possible company match!

Know how much you need to retire.

- By age thirty-five, you should have one times your annual salary saved up for retirement, according to the latest numbers from Fidelity Investments. Five years later, you should have two times your annual salary. And on and on, until you reach sixty-seven, when you should have eight times your annual salary saved.

- Laid out visually, the Fidelity guidelines for individuals look like this:
  - By thirty-five, save 1 x gross annual salary
  - By forty, save 2 x gross annual salary
  - By forty-five, save 3 x gross annual salary
  - By fifty, save 4 x gross annual salary
  - By fifty-five, save 5 x gross annual salary
  - By sixty, save 6 x gross annual salary
  - By sixty-seven, save 8 x gross annual salary

Work longer than you expected if you're able.

- In the past, it was very common to retire and take Social Security at sixty-two. But for every year you wait after sixty-two, you'll have roughly 8 percent return per year on your

Social Security lifetime benefit. So if you wait until seventy, the amount that Social Security will pay you climbs dramatically.

- If you are physically able and plan to stop working in your sixties, but you don't have a lot saved, consider working as long you're healthy—especially if you're a woman, because women live longer, or if you know you're genetically blessed with longevity in your family. You don't want to outlive your money!

WELCOME TO THE
ELEVENTH HOUR

Mike is playing catch-up on his savings at fifty

MIKE POLLARD JUST TURNED FIFTY, and he says he's not above taking a job as a Walmart greeter if he can't afford to retire.

Mike is back on his feet again after a pair of layoffs in 2004 and 2008 upended any plans he might have had to build a retirement nest egg.

He's now gainfully employed as a communications manager at a medical center. His wife, Bonnie, makes a good living there as well.

But Mike, with just fifteen years until the traditional retirement age, has just $30,000 saved for retirement. He's in the eleventh hour and trying to play catch-up.

"Right now our retirement picture looks like they'll be wheeling me out of work on a gurney straight to the funeral home because I'll be working right up to my last breath," Mike said.

Mike is saving about 14 percent of his income now, 6 percent in a 403(b) and 8 percent in a Roth IRA. His wife is saving 6 percent of her pay in a 403(b). Both of their 403(b) contributions are matched dollar for dollar by the hospital on the first 4 percent they contribute.

His goal is to get close to two-thirds of his current income and retire at age sixty-seven. But he estimates he'll be about $4,000 a year short at the current pace.

"I need to work on making that up . . . somehow."

A friend is serving as the couple's financial adviser. He's gone over their expenditures and debts, and advised them to reduce their debt to nothing but the mortgage and max out their employer matches on their 403(b) plans.

Mike says he has a different attitude now about saving for retirement than he did at age thirty.

"Decidedly so. I wasn't worried about it as much then, but I was a newspaper reporter and used every penny for paying rent and bills, so I felt like I couldn't afford to save much. I didn't know much about planning for retirement, and didn't have any resources for learning what vehicles were available."

He characterizes his spending habits as "undisciplined." He didn't track his expenditures at all and didn't worry much about balancing his checkbook.

He didn't really splurge on big things, but he also didn't hesitate, in his premarried-with-children days, to go snowboarding a few times a year or on a road trip to the beach.

"So I've essentially prespent my retirement savings, probably one hundred bucks at a time."

Mike managed to save about $10,000 by 2004, when he was an associate vice president for a large bank, working on the team that ran the bank's management development program. But he was laid off after a merger.

In 2008, after hearing layoffs were coming following the mortgage crisis, he took a buyout from a large business credit corporation's small business division.

Mike went back to school in 2009—nursing school, in fact.

"I did not finish because I had to pause to work and get some more money in the bank to finish."

Then he found out that his current job was available. And his schooling has helped.

"Although it appears a shame to not have finished nursing school, the position I have now calls upon that clinical study and patient-care experience, as well as both my five years as a corporate trainer and my ten-plus years of marketing/advertising/journalism experience."

And he's making a lot more money than he would have earned in an entry-level nursing position.

Through it all, he's kept his sense of humor.

"A sense of humor is just a hallmark of my personality, but it's also a coping mechanism—it reminds me to keep perspective," Mike says.

He says he accepts the results of some poor financial decisions he made as a young adult but believes he did the best he could to feed his family when times were tough.

Mike lives in Winston-Salem, North Carolina, which he says proudly is the home of Wake Forest University, the former gateway to tobacco, and the birthplace of Krispy Kreme doughnuts ("There IS a God, and he coats manna in a delightful liquid sugar.").

He's spent most of his life in North Carolina in the northeastern coastal region where his mother was born and raised.

"We lived in St. Louis when I was age ten to almost sixteen, and that was a hugely valuable life experience. Great exposure to all sorts of things, including the Cardinals. I'm a die-hard Cards fan to this day. My dad took us to games a lot, even though he preferred a tennis court. But he thought it was a pretty cool thing to take his sons to a pro ball game, and he was right."

He has a twin brother who lives about a hundred miles away, and an older brother who lives in Manhattan and is very successful in global corporate marketing.

"Our mother was more of the primary force in raising us, as Dad was a workaholic textile executive on the rise. He provided very well for us and raised us all as fine young gentlemen. However, having been raised by his mother after his father's early death (he was eleven), he had no male role model, good or bad, for raising sons. He did his level best (we challenged him plenty) and the household was ruled maternally, with Dad as guidepost of principles and good hard work."

Mike likes to play guitar with friends, and once or twice a year, he builds custom electric guitars in a small wood shop in the back of his garage.

"My shop is pathetic, but my guitars are pretty damn cool. I'm an aging inland-trapped surfer, and I ride skateboards around the neighborhood with my daughters."

He and Bonnie love to go to the movies and watch sitcoms. Outside of all that, he says he spends the remaining nonwork hours of his life keeping their three dogs from devouring their new pet bunny.

"They don't get it. I don't force them to. They're dogs—I can't expect them not to . . . be dogs. I just ask them to cooperate. So far, so good."

It turns out, he says, that the tools in a guitar workshop are handy for building a bunny hutch that doubles as a dog-proof armoire. It also looks a heck of a lot better in his family room than a rabbit cage from PetSmart, he says.

Meanwhile, Mike will keep plugging away at saving for retirement.

"All I can do is resolve to do the best I can and move forward. I know I probably won't retire wealthy and I'm OK with that, although it doesn't quite dissuade me from buying the occasional lottery ticket."

Play catch-up with retirement savings.

- If you're fifty or older, you can make an additional $5,500 catch-up contribution to your 401(k) or 403(b) plans, or the federal government's Thrift Savings Plan. So instead of the $17,500 cap that applies to younger workers, you can sock away $23,000 if you have the means to do so.

- For the Roth IRA, the catch-up contribution for those over fifty is $1,000. Instead of being limited to the $5,500 cap, you can pile it up to $6,500. Take advantage of it if you're an older worker.

- One thing to keep in mind: Your Roth IRA eligibility gets phased out as your modified adjusted gross income hits $112,000 for individuals or $178,000 for couples. But there is a back-door way to do a Roth regardless of income, what I call "the two-step." It's where you put money into a nondeductible IRA one year and move it to a Roth the next year. It's complicated, but it works!

Be sure to only work with fee-only financial planners.

- Mike and Bonnie have decided to work with a friend who is a financial planner to meet their retirement goals. If you decide to enlist the services of an adviser, be sure he or she is working as what's called fee-only. That means they earn their income on an hourly or ongoing basis, not on commissions from the investments they steer you toward.

- Visit NAPFA.org (National Association of Personal Financial Advisors) for ongoing fee-only help planning for retirement or GarrettPlanningNetwork.com for one-time advice on an hourly basis.

Look to your employer for retirement planning advice.

- Still can't get your head around the thought of planning for retirement? The good news is now there's a lot more advice available to you. Most people don't need a great deal of advice to build a portfolio.

- First, all the discount stockbrokers, such as Fidelity and Charles Schwab, to name just two, now offer some level of counseling or expertise that ranges in price from free to really cheap. They'll sit down with you and help you draw up a simple strategy.

- Second, more and more employers as part of their 401(k) plans offer advice to you for free. This could be very useful, but note that if your employer's 401(k) is handled by a full-commission stock brokerage or an insurance company, you do not want the free advice.

Get an automatic pay raise at work without asking.

- Almost one in three people are eligible for an employer match in their 401(k) but don't take advantage of it, according to benefits administrator Hewitt Associates. If you're leaving an employer match to your 401(k) at work on the table, you're denying yourself an automatic pay raise.

- Think of an employer match like a bribe to get you to save money. I want you to take the bribe. You'll also be happy down the road that you put that money aside because it will be there to grow for you over the years.

- But note this as well: Only contribute as much as possible to pick up the maximum company match. After that, I want you to direct every additional retirement dollar to a Roth IRA. Earnings on a Roth are tax-free, and tax-free withdrawals can be made after age fifty-nine and a half. By contrast, every dollar in a 401(k) or 403(b) will be taxed when you use it in retirement.

INVESTING

So you've finally managed to save some money for the long term . . . now what? Investing is one of those things in life that can be complicated. Yet it doesn't have to be.

In this chapter, we meet five different types of investors who illustrate the right ways and the wrong ways to approach investing. I'll tell you about the hazards and opportunities facing the average Joe investor as you try to build wealth for the long term.

GOLD DIGGER

Rick puts all his eggs into one shiny basket

Rick Morris grew up in the California high desert and has worked there his entire life.

A contractor on large jobs for NASA and area school districts, as well as on small jobs for neighbors, friends, and family, Rick is careful to protect himself from the punishing sun. He often wears long-sleeved T-shirts and a straw hat that partially covers his silver hair.

Rick, sixty, typically drives old clunkers around town while running errands, leaving his rarely driven Porsches in their temperature-controlled garage at home.

The rugged Californian, six feet tall with a back that's straight as a board, is actually quite refined. He enjoys a great bottle of wine at fabulous restaurants. And he loves art. His collection includes pieces by the unique sculptor Bill Mack, paintings from Tom Everhart, and dishes by Izwin.

Rick also likes gold—a lot. He has 70 percent of his life savings invested in gold. The other 30 percent is in silver and he has a collection of $500 and $1,000 bills "in crisp, uncirculated condition."

I believe strongly in diversifying your investments, and while the value of gold has soared in recent years as I write this, I think it's unwise to have more than 5 percent to 10 percent of your investment portfolio in gold or other precious metals.

But one of the things I've enjoyed most about writing this book is meeting people who so fervently disagree with me.

Rick has almost all his money in gold and silver. The value of his gold alone is approximately $1.8 million.

Rick started investing in gold and silver in 1980, and he's done very well with it. He estimates he's invested a total of $400,000 and seen his holdings appreciate 600 percent.

"Gold and silver have been used as currency for thousands of years while paper currency is run through a printing press with ink slapped on it," Rick said. "In addition, nothing has the same feel in your hand as a gold coin."

Rick's primary interest in gold is his concern about the stability of the U.S. dollar, which he feels will plunge in value.

"I don't think the dollar will collapse completely, but I think it's going to get close to it," he said. "Just look at the exchange rate of the U.S. dollar to the Canadian dollar and the yen. I suspect the U.S. dollar will be devalued substantially to the point of even a new national currency. The one thing I know is that if there is a devaluation of the dollar and I need to buy a loaf of bread, I'm going to feel a lot better about paying for it with a one-ounce silver round than a U.S. dollar bill."

I asked Rick if he's concerned that the soaring price of gold has created an investment bubble, similar to the bubbles that saw technology stocks in the 1990s and housing prices in the early to mid-2000s soar and then crash.

He answered that gold and silver "are not in the same category" as tech stocks or housing.

"Those buying tech stocks are buying paper, while the housing market boom and crash was caused by the federal government lending money to basically anyone that could put breath on a mirror with little or no money to put down on a home. The federal government/lenders waved a carrot in the face of many people and they bought something beyond their ability to repay."

While some investors buy gold funds to avoid the fees and security issues that come with owning gold, Rick has physical possession of his gold, which he keeps "in a secure location."

Rick said he doesn't get butterflies in his stomach worrying about potential volatility in gold and silver prices.

"No, I enjoy the movement in commodity prices. It keeps it very interesting," he said. "Imagine if it just stayed at one price with no movement either way. How boring it would be. Besides, I bought a majority of my silver at $3.50 an ounce [it was more than $33 near the end of 2012] and most of my gold at $250 to $400 an ounce."

Has he sold any of his gold or silver to take profits?

"Not at all," he said. "Guess I'm really dumb or extremely brilliant."

Rick, who was born in McPherson, Kansas, and raised in California since he was a year old, specializes in federal and state construction projects, as well as solar projects. He recently installed a full solar array on his home in Palm Desert, California, and added air-conditioning to the garage to keep those Porsches cool.

While he expects the dollar to plunge in value, he doesn't have any fear of putting money in banks.

"It's certainly the way we conduct our personal and business transactions. Not a big concern about my money in banks. I don't keep too much in any one account, and if the banks closed tonight, I will surely be well prepared in many other ways."

One thing Rick and I do agree on is that if you don't already own gold, now is not a good time to start.

"Regardless of whose financial strategy you follow," he said, "buying high is never a good idea."

What lessons should you take away from hearing Rick's story?

Question the hype surrounding investing manias.

- Humans are pack animals. We tend to go with the herd more often than not—even if we think we're marching to the beat of our own drummer. Gold is just the latest example.

- For those who took economics in college, you might recall the Dutch Tulip Mania from almost four hundred years ago, when people speculatively bid up the price of tulip bulbs in the Netherlands, which they thought would appreciate sky-high. Unfortunately, generations of wealth got wiped out when the bubble burst.

- Manias happen in so many ways. In the late 1990s, it was the tech stocks. The "this time it's different" mentality drove people who had resisted other manias to sink their hard-earned cash into the overvalued tech sector. Then the market collapsed and today the NASDAQ (an index of mostly tech stocks) has only a little more than half the value it did twelve years ago.

- Could it be the same with gold? It's anybody's guess.

Own gold the Clark Smart way.

- With worries about the weakening value of the dollar, people are continually asking me if they should take everything they've got and buy gold. In general, I only recommend putting 5 or 10 percent of your overall portfolio into gold or other precious metals.
- While Rick favors physical gold, my preferred way for you to own gold is through a gold exchange-traded fund (ETF). You buy ETFs exactly like you would a stock—preferably through a zero-commission broker—and you can sell your holdings at any time.
- See "Limit your investments in gold or precious metals" on page 196 of my last book, *Clark Howard's Living Large in Lean Times*, for a rundown of my favorite gold ETFs.

Consider online pawning.

- Not everyone is sitting on nearly $2 million in gold like Rick. But a lot of people have some gold jewelry that they could bear to part with—if they desperately needed money and couldn't get access to funds any other way.
- Enter online pawning. With pawning, you take something of value like, say, a ring that might be worth $500 and you hawk it at a pawnshop or online. The pawnshop lends you a fraction of the value, maybe $100, against that $500 ring, and they charge you an interest rate on the money.
- Meanwhile, while you're paying back that loan, the pawnshop is holding your ring as collateral. Most people never quite get around to paying off the pawnshop loan, so it becomes the lender's property to liquidate.
- Once confined to struggling blue-collar workers, pawning is now finding a new middle-class audience online. Sites like Pawntique.com and PawnGo.com are attracting customers who would never normally think about setting foot in a brick-and-mortar pawnshop.

Get the best value for your gold without getting ripped off.

- There's an easy way to figure out the real intrinsic value of gold in your jewelry. Start by looking for the karat, stamped directly on the gold. Then use a kitchen scale to weigh the jewelry and an online calculator like Dendritics.com to convert the weight (based on karat) to determine the value at today's market price.
- No one will pay you full retail market price because they've got to make a profit. But jewelry stores and pawnshops are typically the best places to sell a few loose pieces. Avoid those who won't tell you how much they're paying for gold over the phone. Chances are they want to lure you in to lowball you.

Determine the value of your gold coins and other collectibles.

- If you receive a collection of coins, stamps, or even autographs after a relative passes away, there's a new game in town for getting a fair valuation.

- According to the *Los Angeles Times*, Collectors.com will give you an objective valuation of your gold coins and other collectibles based on third-party authentication and grading. Using Collectors.com is *not* cheap, but they only specialize in valuation, so they will not try to buy anything from you. You send in whatever you've got, they evaluate it, and then they give you a report and send your stuff back to you.

- In the past, I've talked about going to a coin show when it's in town and going booth to booth to get quotes for individual coins, never for the whole collection. But that's a very shoe-leather-intensive approach. Collectors.com makes it easy.

BRIGHT FUTURE

....

Mike is under twenty-five and sitting on a $50,000 retirement nest egg

MIKE ZACCARDI WAS AN EIGHTEEN-YEAR-OLD high school senior when he heard me speak about one of my favorite financial tools, the Roth IRA, and he really liked what he heard.

He heard me describe how a Roth allows you to save money for retirement with the money growing tax-free, not tax-deferred like a regular IRA or 401(k). And you can withdraw the money in retirement without paying state and federal income taxes on the amount you take out.

The Roth doesn't give contributors an income tax deduction like the other plans do, but teenagers typically don't earn enough to need deductions.

Mike worked after school and on the weekends at a golf course driving a golf ball picker. It was a minimum-wage job, but he was earning an income. He took home about $120 a week from the golf course and another $80 a week at his other job at Publix, a popular Southeastern grocery chain.

Scraping up the $3,000 he would need to open a Roth at a particular low-cost mutual fund company would be tough, but Mike was able to meet his self-imposed challenge by the end of the year after tithing, paying for gas for his car, and other odds and ends. (He didn't realize at the time that he had until April 15 to make a deposit for the previous tax year.)

That was in 2005. After making the maximum Roth deposits of $4,000 in 2006 and in 2007, and $5,000 a year after the limit on contributions was raised, Mike Zaccardi, now all of twenty-four years old, has a retirement account worth $50,000!

"My goal is definitely to retire young," said Mike, who graduated in 2011 from the University of North Florida in Jacksonville. "The Roth is just one piece of the puzzle, but an important piece."

Mike doesn't really have a particular sum in mind for his retirement nest egg, because inflation can change the amount he might need. "But certainly at least $2 million discounted to today's dollars."

He's definitely on track. Even if he never contributed another dollar to his Roth IRA, the twenty-four-year-old, like most investors, could expect to see his money roughly double every eight years, to $100,000 at age thirty-two, $200,000 at age forty, $400,000 at age forty-eight, $800,000 at age fifty-six, and $1.6 million at age sixty-four.

But Mike, of course, isn't finished saving. With his double major in investment finance and financial services and planning, and a minor in economics, he got a job with a major brokerage/mutual fund company.

He was planning to put the maximum into his Roth 401(k) when I spoke to him, and plans to save a large percentage of his income going forward. Wow!

I asked Mike if it's ever been challenging for him to be such a good saver.

"I have found I am a bit strange in that I find joy in saving money," he said. "I think I get the same thrill about saving as others get about buying a new car, iPod, or surfboard. It has not been very difficult, but it has required working my butt off at times."

Mike also made some smart, frugal choices about his college education. He chose to attend college near his home in Jacksonville and to live at home, only a few miles from campus. That allowed him to save more and to work more, as there are more opportunities in Jacksonville than he would have expected to find in a college town.

Being in Florida, he also benefited from the Florida Bright Futures scholarship program. He had some tuition to pay that wasn't covered by the program, but Publix supermarkets had a tuition reimbursement program that took care of that. So he graduated from college with no student loans.

"Speaking of college, I *never* paid full price for a rip-off college textbook!" Mike said. "I would typically buy a used book that was an older edition for literally pennies on the dollar of the new current edition book. In fact, I probably profited from selling my textbooks in my final couple of years."

Mike has also been very careful with credit cards, another source of financial trouble for many young people.

Following my advice when he was in college, he opened a credit card account just to establish a credit history and to begin building it. It had a $250 credit limit and he used it only to pay for an occasional small purchase, and then he immediately paid it off. He now has eight credit cards and never uses more than 20 percent of his available credit limit to keep his credit score high. (Your credit rating suffers if you use too much of your available credit.)

Mike uses the cards mainly to take advantage of cash-back rewards, and he pays each off every month so he doesn't incur interest charges or accumulate debt.

He has this advice for kids and students in particular who want to save for their future: Get a job.

"I started making minimum wage and made it a point to save money where I could."

A Roth IRA is a great way to do it, he said, because you can withdraw your contributions—not the earnings on the money, just your contributions—at any time, tax- and penalty-free.

"I understand not all students may have the drive to save as much as me, but if they were to simply look at what $1 today can grow to over the decades, I believe they would be amazed at the power of compound growth! At a minimum, students need to save for college—do not depend entirely on student loans."

He also thinks parents who can afford it should help their working children contribute to a Roth. If a teen works and earns $5,000, then the parents can contribute up to $5,000 to the child's Roth IRA account for them. Or the parents can contribute $2,500 and the child $2,500. The student probably can't put every cent he earns into a Roth, but the parents can help, as long as the student has earned income. I often encourage parents to match their child's contribution to a Roth, which doubles the child's saving power.

What other tips can you draw from Mike's remarkable savings efforts?

Start saving early.

- A fifteen-year-old who saves $2,000 each summer for seven years and lets the money grow in a retirement account until sixty-five can easily amass $1 million or more. That's without ever contributing another penny after twenty-one!
- I know that's a big claim, but it was recently corroborated by *Chicago Tribune* financial columnist Gail MarksJarvis. (Her exact figures require a sixteen-year-old to save $2,000 annually for six years and retire at sixty-nine, not sixty-five.)

- Gail's numbers assume a 9.4 percent average gain annually, the average return on the stock market since 1926—in spite of all the ups and downs of the 1930s Great Depression and all the bear markets of the modern era.
- Of course, inflation will greatly eat away at the purchasing power of $1 million when your fifteen-year-old retires, but I want to suggest that it can be easy to build some level of comfort and security into your later life if you just start saving early! Most people don't start thinking about saving until they hit forty. Begin early and it can make a big difference down the road.

Invest equal amounts of money on a set schedule.

- My goal is to have you automatically put in a set amount of money regularly to build the habit of saving and reduce your overall risk to market ups and downs.
- By making regular contributions each month or each pay period in equal amounts, you are doing what's called "dollar cost averaging." That's just a fancy way of saying that you're pacing your investing against the market. With the same dollars each month, you're buying more shares when prices are low and fewer when they're high.
- Over time, saving money in this way—rather than all at once in big lump sums—reduces the possibility of panic and keeps you steady as you go. And staying in the game makes you more money over the long haul.

Diversify your portfolio.

- Spreading your money out among both domestic and international investments is one of the safest ways I know to invest.
- I recommend mutual and index funds over individual stocks. Pick four or five mutual funds for your portfolio with at least one being an international fund. When you're younger, you want more stocks and fewer bonds in your portfolio so your money has the optimal time to grow. As you age, you can do the reverse with more bonds and fewer stocks.

Do discount investing.

- A couple of years ago, *Los Angeles Times* financial columnist Kathy Kristof reported on findings that the typical investor who makes an annual $4,000 contribution into an IRA can lose 54 percent in fees alone each year.
- There are three fees most commonly associated with commissioned investments: the "load," which is the commission itself; 12b-1 fees, a dubious marketing charge that pays

for advertising to attract more money to the fund; and an annual management fee, which should always be lower than .5 percent.

- The takeaway here is simple: Don't buy your investments through full-commission brokerage houses or an insurance agent. Instead, buy your investments commission-free (aka "no load") through discount brokers that hold down the other expenses too. Vanguard, Fidelity, and T. Rowe Price all do a great job of this.

BIG SKY, BIG SAVINGS

*Cathy and Ned realize it's the little things that make
the biggest difference in your financial picture*

CATHY AND NED COONEY were both born and raised in Southern California—back when Orange County meant open spaces and orange groves.

But in 2004, the husband and wife team traded in the heat, smog, and congested freeways of the Inland Empire for snow, suicidal deer awaiting roadkill status, and threatening skies over the Flathead Valley, just adjacent to Glacier National Park.

"Our idea of a traffic jam is having four cars waiting for a light at an intersection," Cathy quips.

Making the move from the Golden State certainly took a leap of faith for the couple.

"Many of our colleagues probably thought we were crazy. The economy of the Inland Empire was booming and we both had good-paying jobs. We moved to Montana with no jobs though we knew that my husband wanted to start his own [philanthropic] consulting business," Cathy told me.

Today she's at the epicenter of the nonprofit world in Montana in her role as program director for the Montana Community Foundation.

"Everyone who wants to know about community foundations gets referred to me," she says. "I have become the 'go-to' person for our sector for the whole state. I'm a fairly big fish in the tiny pond of the nonprofit/philanthropic sector in Montana."

Cathy lives in Bigfork and is proud to have visited all of Montana's fifty-six counties many times over as she's helped launch nearly a dozen community foundations. These include the Greater Polson Community Foundation, the Ruby Valley Foundation, and the Wibaux Endowment Foundation.

Nonprofit work isn't known for its high pay, but the fifty-three-year-old program director has found a niche that allows her a comfortable income. She makes a little more than $50,000 annually.

Ned, forty-five, runs a nonprofit consulting firm called Ascent Strategic Development, and has income that mirrors her own, although it changes from year to year.

"That's a very good joint income for Montana, especially working in the nonprofit sector. We are very lucky," she says. "When we moved here eight years ago, we had a joint income of $120,000 working for two nonprofits in Riverside, California. We may never get back up to that salary, but that's OK!"

As for a lot of people, Cathy's early efforts to get a solid investment plan in place were upset by a previous divorce.

"I do feel like a slacker when I hear about twenty-year-olds buying homes or people my age who already can retire. Overachievers!" She laughs. "I have to admit that I got a slow start because my ex-husband was terrible with money, and I paid off his old debts and had to build up his retirement savings, which he promptly emptied and spent once I divorced him."

But Cathy has made some simple yet smart tweaks to her investment portfolio that will make all the difference for her down the road. I want to tell you what she's done because these are the same kinds of things you can do today, no matter what kind of income you earn.

When it came to making her money work for her, the first thing Cathy did was pay attention to who was managing it.

From her days at California nonprofits, Cathy had amassed a sizable nest egg in her 403(b)—the retirement plan common in the teaching and nonprofit fields—but it wasn't with the right administrator. So she moved it.

Many 403(b) plans are administered by life insurance companies that load them with massive commissions and huge ongoing fees, especially when your money is in a variable annuity. Good providers are generally few and far between.

"I definitely think that people in the nonprofit [and] academic fields are not aware of the high fees. . . . I had an account with Mutual of America for years. I had all my funds invested in a Fidelity mutual fund," Cathy says. "I thought I was paying low fees because my money was invested in Fidelity Investments, but then I realized that Mutual of America must be adding more fees so I moved the money into a Vanguard IRA."

A simple difference of 1 percentage point in fees can mean tens of thousands of dollars in the long run.

For example, the average variable annuity might charge fees of 2.25 percent annually; the average mutual fund might charge 1.4 percent annually; and the average no-load index fund, 0.18 percent annually, according to Meridian Wealth Management.

That means a $250 monthly contribution with 8 percent growth over thirty-five years will amount to either $336,320, $409,585, or $548,750 at retirement, depending on whether you paid fees of 2.25 percent, 1.4 percent, or 0.18 percent. Which one would you want?

In the same vein, Cathy insisted that her current employer put her retirement match into an account at Vanguard instead of at a full-fee company.

"My employer was very cooperative. They actually put 6 percent into an individual SEP [simplified employee pension] since we don't have a regular 403(b) plan [at the Montana Community Foundation]. It took a little extra work, but my employer was willing. We have a small foundation with seven full-time staff, and so we don't have to deal with lots of bureaucracy to get things done."

She and Ned also have Roth IRAs that they max out each year.

"I just pay the Roth contributions automatically like I pay our mortgage and utility bills. It's not optional. Luckily for us, we don't have kids, we don't have credit card debt, we aren't extravagant, and we have seen our income rise slowly but steadily in the eight years we have lived in Montana. Also, when we built our house four years ago, we built a 1,200-square-foot house, not a 2,500-square-foot house. Our contractor said it was the smallest house he had ever built, but we knew what we could afford."

Today Cathy has a total of $228,000 invested, putting her on track for a nice retirement. Clearly, she is no slouch when it comes to money.

But another cornerstone of her investing strategy is that she anticipates working beyond traditional retirement age. I can't overstress the importance of that choice, particularly for women.

Women tend to live five years live longer than men on average. Yet they save far less money for retirement than men, and most women tend to invest too conservatively. Working longer, if you're able, can really help right the ship of your retirement.

"As a woman and an ex-Jazzercise instructor who is health conscious, I assume that I will live a long time and outlive my husband. It would be stupid for me to not think about how I'm going to afford my old age," Cathy says. "I certainly plan to work part-time well into my seventies. I love working and having that professional identity."

Cathy attributes a lot of her money smarts to her parents, both poor German immigrants who left their country's struggling post–World War II economy for a better life in Canada and then the United States.

"They worked hard, saved, and now are the classic 'millionaires next door.' They actually could have done even better if they had invested some of their money in equities rather than just saved it in CDs, but they did invest in some real estate over the years in Orange County and Santa Barbara and did reasonably well with [it].

"My parents really believe in saving and living within your means. I inherited some of that outlook, although they don't believe in using any of their money to enjoy their lives, and I just think that is so wrong. There is a balance."

What lessons can you draw from Cathy's story?

Start with a Roth IRA first.

- For any nonprofit worker or teacher saving for retirement, your first step should be to do a Roth IRA on your own. You can contribute up to $5,000 annually ($6,000 for those fifty or older). A Roth is vastly superior to a 403(b) plan. Make your contributions automatic like Cathy did so the question of discipline in saving doesn't even come into the picture. Do this especially if there's no company match into a 403(b), which there often isn't.

Know what's in your 403(b) plan.

- If you get new plan info on your 403(b), find out what's in it. Don't be intimidated or confused by the verbiage. Look at the expense ratio. Most 403(b) plans are over 2 percent. You want that number to be below .5 percent. Vanguard in particular can be as little as .2 percent.
- That's why Cathy moved her 403(b) money to Vanguard. But there's also another company I like called TIAA-CREF. If you are offered a 403(b) with them, do it. They will charge you as little as one-twentieth in junk fees what you would pay to a typical insurance company offering a 403(b) plan. Visit TIAA-CREF.org for more details.

Invest like a man . . . or a woman.

- Are men or women better investors? In general, women end up with less money over time because they're hardwired to be conservative to a fault. They also live longer on average, so they have less money that has to stretch over a longer period of time.

- Generally, women tend to pick "safe" choices like CDs for their money. Men, on the other hand, trade stocks excessively and hurt themselves by buying and selling too much. Yet the average man ends up with a lot more money at the end of a working lifetime—even accounting for income differences. That's because if a woman puts money in CDs, she barely keeps up with inflation and loses in the long term.

- The *Sun Sentinel* found that women in the state of Florida have a 50 percent greater chance than men of being impoverished after age sixty-five. And if they've worked fewer years because of child rearing, women get less of a Social Security check too.

- That's a pretty bleak picture. But it doesn't have to be anyone's fate. Make it your personal goal to learn a bit of the opposite sex's investing style and let it temper your own.

Keep it simple.

- If the alphabet soup of 401(k)s, IRAs, and 403(b)s ever gets too much for you, keep it simple. Investing doesn't have to be complicated. Discount investment houses like Fidelity, T. Rowe Price, and Vanguard offer targeted retirement funds, where you just select the year that's closest to your expected date of retirement and pop your money in. Then the fund's manager allocates it for you. No muss, no fuss on your part. When you're young, they have you heavily in stocks. Then as you age, you get fewer stocks and more bonds.

ALL THE RIGHT MOVES

Matt realizes saving for his future is as easy as pie

MATT JOHNSON HAS JUST GOTTEN started in his life as an investor, but he enjoys telling people that he celebrated like a billionaire on his last birthday.

Matt, thirty-four, lives in Omaha, Nebraska, with his wife, Vivian, and their year-old daughter, Hannah Marie.

For his thirty-third birthday, Vivian decided to take Matt to the Bohemian Cafe, a local restaurant just south of downtown Omaha in the Little Bohemia neighborhood.

That's when he met legendary investor Warren Buffett.

"It's not a fancy restaurant by any means, but carries quite a bit of the ethnic flavor of the immigrants that settled in that part of town over one hundred years ago. I'd been wanting to try it for some time," Matt recalled.

"As the maître d' showed us to our table, I couldn't help but notice the 'Oracle of Omaha' sitting at a booth right around the corner from ours. It turns out his birthday and mine are one day apart, so he was there celebrating with a few members of his family."

A billionaire celebrating his birthday in Little Bohemia?

"Having lived in Omaha for a while, I've heard stories about Warren Buffett preferring to eat at smaller, locally owned restaurants rather than much fancier and much more expensive places that he could easily afford," Matt said.

"It was fascinating to see such stories confirmed in real life. I was also quite surprised to see that he didn't seem to have any security detail with him, either. There were no tough-looking bodyguards escorting him to an armored limo outside the restaurant when we were done eating—just a few family members I guessed were his wife and kids."

One of those family members took a picture of Matt and Vivian with Buffett, which Matt displays proudly on his website.

One thing Matt didn't do is ask Buffett for investing advice.

"I'd actually just finished watching a series of videos on YouTube where he explained his strategy of value investing. His advice for people like me, however—people who don't have time to invest as a full-time career—was just to put money away in index funds on a regular basis, which is what I've been doing."

When I spoke to him, Matt was earning about $50,000 a year as a graphic designer for MOSAIC, a nonprofit that helps people with intellectual disabilities, and doing freelance work on the side. He saves 10 percent of his income in a Roth IRA.

(Matt later e-mailed me to say he and MOSAIC parted ways one week before Christmas in December 2012. He was still freelancing while looking for new full-time work at last check.)

Vivian, thirty-three, worked at a local day program for seniors and people with disabilities before becoming a stay-at-home mom.

Together, they have accumulated $32,000 in four retirement accounts:

- Matt's 403(b), which he had at MOSAIC. He used to get a 3 percent match, but that ended in 2009, so he no longer contributes.
- Matt's Roth IRA with Charles Schwab. He opened it in 2008 and has contributed regularly, upping the amount when the match for his 403(b) went away. He now contributes 10 percent out of every paycheck automatically via direct deposit.
- Vivian's 457 (with ING, now owned by Capital One), which she got with her previous employer. She opened the account a few years before Matt met her and made automatic contributions, but she didn't know exactly what they were invested in. He took a look at the account and saw she was entirely in cash positions, so he gradually moved her into a few Vanguard index funds instead (large, small, and mid-cap funds).
- Vivian's Roth IRA. Matt opened this with Vanguard while she was working and contributed around 10 percent into the STAR Fund (VGSTX) and then a target retirement account once they dropped the minimum investment to $1,000.

Matt is also interested in a little-known federal tax credit, the Saver's Credit, that encourages people to save for retirement, subject to income limits. Savers get a 10 percent,

20 percent or 50 percent match if they save up to $2,000. Because he's on the higher end of the income scale, Matt would be eligible for the 10 percent match, or $200.

Is that enough incentive to spur people to save? Sure, Matt says.

"It actually keeps me motivated in the sense that I'd be silly not to save for retirement—it's like getting an employer match in a 401(k). I would be leaving money on the table if I didn't take advantage of it."

Matt's goal for retirement is to have enough so he can withdraw 4 percent of his money each year and match his current income without depleting his savings. At a salary of $50,000, that would require $1.25 million ($50,000 divided by .04).

He might not be on track for that yet.

"I feel I should be saving more, but I believe if I keep putting away money consistently over time, I'll be a lot better off than many of my peers, who haven't saved a dime."

Young couples with small children are often torn between saving for their child's education and their own retirement. I've long said that retirement should be the first priority, because there are many ways for a child to get through school and only one way for a couple to retire.

Only once you've fully funded your own retirement should you begin to put money away for a child in a 529 college savings plan. A 529 plan allows you to save money tax-free and spend it tax-free on qualifying college expenses down the road. (See pages 85–86 in my last book, *Living Large in Lean Times*, for more on 529 plans.)

"I believe retirement is my top priority as well, since I don't want my little girl to have to support my wife and me in our old age," Matt says. "I am still putting a little away in a 529 account now, however, because I still have seventeen years ahead of us to save, and if we're going to save anything at all [for Hannah Marie], I believe it's better to do it now rather than later."

One thing Matt wishes he'd known earlier is how easy it is to open a retirement account.

"The company I worked for didn't offer any kind of 401(k) or pension plan, and everyone I talked to about opening an IRA was a commissioned broker who made the process sound far too hard to do on my own."

One adviser suggested maxing out a Roth IRA for the current and previous year, which at that time would have meant a deposit of $6,000. That was too much for Matt to come up with. But after listening to my radio show for a few weeks, he realized opening a Roth was no harder than opening an online bank account.

"I've enjoyed learning about index funds and target retirement accounts, which make it very easy to have a well-balanced portfolio with extremely low expenses," he says.

Matt enjoys investing, but he has other passions too. He has been part of an Omaha-based online comic book community for years. That interest even took him to London to meet with other like-minded comic book fans. Over the years, a comic book collective that he was with had one of their titles selected for Free Comic Book Day. And one of his own comics was even translated into Russian!

He also loves swing dancing, doing vintage moves like the Charleston and the Lindy Hop. And he loves food. On his blog, the *Cornstalker's Journal*, he says Omaha is a great place to eat, that Vivian is a great cook, and that they have plenty of friends who know how to cook.

And if he ever becomes a billionaire himself, he can look back and realize that it was his love of a good meal that allowed him to meet the legendary Warren Buffett.

What can you learn from Matt's story?

File for the Saver's Credit if you qualify.

- People come up to me and say, "All that stuff you talk about saving is great . . . for people who make a lot of money. But what about the rest of us?"
- More than ten years ago, Congress passed the Saver's Credit with the goal of assisting savers who make a decent living but not a huge income. If you save $2,000 in a 401(k), IRA, 403(b), or 457 plan, the government will match your money with as much as 50 cents on the dollar, up to a maximum of $1,000. Income caps apply—$29,500 for single filers; $44,250 if head of household; and $59,000 if married filing jointly.
- You won't automatically get this tax credit if you qualify. You have to ask for it using IRS form 8880. Visit IRS.gov and search keyword "8880" for more details. Full-time students are not eligible for the credit.

Save for retirement before saving for a child's education.

- A few years ago, a Country Financial survey revealed that more men than women think saving for a child's education is of greater importance than funding their own retirement.

- As parents, we all know it would be great to do *everything* possible for our kids. But the most important thing you can do is provide good guidance and discipline, plus ensure the feeding and care of your children in a safe, healthy environment.
- There are no scholarships for retirement. But there are grants, work-study, regular jobs, scholarships, loans, and other ways to pay for college. So your hearts are in the right place, but your heads are not. You've got to do the practical thing and save for your future first.

Don't pay a "professional" to manage your money.

- If two years ago you put your money in an index fund instead of into individual stock picks, you would have done better 84 percent of the time versus if you had your money actively managed by an "investment guru," according to data from Standard & Poor's.
- The results of the S&P study were back-tested over ten years and guess what? Go back five years and 61 percent of the time you'd do better with an index fund versus actively managed money. Go back the full ten years and again there is a similar finding.
- I like index funds because they give you wide exposure to capitalism. You can buy little slices and dices of many companies in one index fund. Some of my favorites include the Fidelity Four-in-One Index Fund, the Schwab Total Stock Market Index Fund, and the Vanguard Total Stock Market Index Fund.

Look at exchange-traded funds.

- Matt is doing great by diversifying in index funds. But he might want to consider adding some exchange-traded funds (ETFs) to his portfolio. ETFs are becoming fantastic for individual investors since Charles Schwab, Fidelity, Scottrade, TD Ameritrade, and Vanguard started offering them without any buy/sell commissions.
- ETFs are bought and sold just like stocks. They typically have a better tax treatment than a mutual fund, plus lower management fees. So while the typical mutual fund might have annual management fees of 1.5 percent, you can buy ETFs with annual management fees of less than .10 percent.
- My favorite starting point is the Schwab Total Stock Market Index ETF, which charges only 0.04 percent per year.
- Let's say, unlike Matt, you're the kind of investor who hires a professional to handle your money, and maybe you pay 1 percent in management fees, plus the expense of the actual investments. Well, now it could actually be cheaper to hire a brainiac to manage ETFs for you than it would be to pay for mutual funds that you pick yourself!

SCARED STIFF

Burned by the stock market, immigrants Victoria and
Dan stash money under the mattress

(WHILE ALL THE PEOPLE *in this book are real, several did not want me to use their real names or locations. That's the case here. As you read Victoria's story, you'll understand why she requested a fictitious name and location.*)

It's just after ten o'clock on a weekday morning and Victoria Lim is sitting near the fireplace in her Savannah, Georgia, home. Fragrant plumes of smoke rise from small decorative candles in the mouth of the hearth.

Victoria is clad in blue jeans and a comfy plum-colored sweater, sipping coffee from a white ceramic Starbucks mug. The steam from hot arabica beans flushes her cheeks to a rosé color that offsets her obsidian black hair and olive skin. Several copies of *Architectural Digest* lie piled up on a nearby ottoman.

It's a rare moment when she's not at work, dropping her kids off at school, or running one of many errands. In short, it's her time.

"My time is usually quiet and relaxing," Victoria says. "I love reading, but with the hectic schedule, I mostly have time for browsing magazines."

Victoria, forty-two, works part-time at the front desk of a medical office two days a week. Her husband, Dan, also forty-two, is a self-employed contractor in the telecommunication and security industry. Together they have two kids, twelve-year-old John and seven-year-old Chloe.

"Because our business fluctuates, our annual income varies widely. In 2009, we made over $100,000," Victoria tells me. "In 2011 and 2012, we made just $60,000. Nothing much has changed, so we expect about the same this year."

But while she works hard and can allow herself to enjoy a precious spare moment to unwind, something else is not working quite as hard in Victoria and Dan's life: their money.

Victoria and Dan have saved up $100,000 and it's just about as liquid as can be.

"All in cash," she tells me. "Not in the bank, not in the market, not in any type of equity. It's somewhere in the universe where I can have quick access. Probably a very unsafe place, but I have no trust in the market, or banks, or anywhere, anyways.

"I came up with the figure of $100,000 because I thought that it would be enough to start over if a catastrophic event happened—natural disaster, stock market crash, 9/11, Y2K," she says.

Catching the paranoia in her voice, she adds with a laugh, "Too much TV?"

What Victoria has told me scares me. Not because I fear the standard media fare of potential disasters she's outlined. But because over the years, there's something ready to eat the couple's money alive.

It's called inflation.

If you're sitting with cash and you're afraid to invest it, you have to get over that fear. If you won't need the money for ten years or longer, I want you to step out on the risk equation to give your money the opportunity to grow beyond the rate of inflation.

Victoria and Dan have spent the last eleven years saving their six-figure nest egg in cash. A few bumps along the road delayed them: a 20 percent down payment for their house, a deposit for their two cars, and a job loss in the early 2000s that left Dan unemployed for a year and a half.

Both Dan and Victoria are native Koreans who spent their formative years in South America before immigrating to this country and attending college. Victoria came to the United States when she was nineteen and has been living here for twenty-two years.

Being an immigrant from the Third World greatly shaped her thinking about money.

"How many times [have I] heard of banks in South America going bankrupt, being corrupt, and not having cash anymore? Didn't I see in the news images of people standing in line to withdraw their money from bankrupt institutions?" she asks rhetorically.

"What ensures us that it won't happen here? I am also uneasy about the U.S. government . . . [and its] ability to access and freeze accounts. Besides, we also have to pay taxes on interest income."

Then she draws back a bit.

"My fear could be irrational, emotional, and a bit mythical. Add some misinformation and I could have full-blown paranoia!"

As with so many things in life, there's more here than meets the eye. There's another layer that's adding to the fear and it comes from direct experience. She and Dan lost some money earlier in their marriage in the stock market because they violated one of my key rules of investing: Minimize the amount of stock you own in the company where you work.

"I was just married and my husband was working at MCI WorldCom. For the first time, we opened a retirement account, our first dip into the stock market, all in company stocks. We never thought that such a large telecom business would ever go bankrupt. Hard lesson learned and we lost all our 401(k) there—about $20,000 at that time. It just reassured me that cash was king."

Interestingly, though, life isn't black and white and Victoria and Dan haven't turned their backs on the stock market entirely, even though they were badly burned once.

On the insistence of her friends, her boss, and even my advice, Victoria opened two Vanguard Roth IRAs—one for herself and one for Dan—about seven years ago. She has money deposited to the accounts by automatic draft, twice a month.

Victoria originally told me it was "play money." But upon digging deeper, I learned that the couple's combined balance was a little over $60,000.

"Not play money anymore, but I'm OK that it's just a number now that can go drastically down or up any day," she says. "Lately my boss is urging me to sell ''cause it won't go up anymore,' but I'm keeping it there since I have another twenty years to recover if anything happens. My emergency cash savings keeps me a bit at ease."

I think it's great that Victoria has the wisdom to know that her retirement horizon is way off. So she keeps some money in the game, contributes steadily as she goes, and rests assured knowing that's the key to building real long-term wealth.

I just wish she'd do something with that $100,000!

As I mentioned earlier, the problem with Victoria and Dan's strategy is that their $100,000 won't keep up with inflation. Just to give you an idea, BankRate.com reported that a $100,000 salary in 1990 would have had to grow to $172,103 in 2011 in order to keep up with inflation.

Victoria tells me she's very concerned about inflation too—but her desire to stockpile the bulk of her retirement portfolio in cold, hard cash trumps all!

"I've been playing with the online financial calculators to see how much I'm losing [by sitting on the $100,000]. I'm more concerned about inflation than the money being lost or stolen," she says. "But the peace of mind it gives me, to know that whatever happens, I'll have quick and easy access to cash anytime—no trading, selling, buying . . . or waiting to access it—is the price that I can deal [with] for now."

And while $100,000 might sound like a big amount to keep on hand, Victoria doesn't see herself or Dan as extreme savers.

"We take vacations abroad once a year, dine out twice a week, send the kids to summer camps, and contribute weekly to our church.

"We are not spendthrifts, either: Our cars—paid off in two years—have been driven for over ten years; my husband does all auto oil changes and repairs—learned on YouTube; we bank at a credit union; the kid's clothes are from Target; we shop at Walmart and Costco, buy generic, never had cable TV; if we go to the movies, it's always a matinee; we use Groupon for restaurants and discount coupons for grocery and department stores."

In the end, Victoria and Dan will probably keep doing what works for them. After all, they've built up six figures by sticking to their guns. "I am constantly looking for savings without affecting our standard of living. We try to live within a certain budget and save the rest. My goal is another $100,000 in cash by my fiftieth birthday."

That's less than ten years away, but I have every confidence that Victoria and Dan can do it!

Victoria is like a lot of people who are afraid of the stock market, though her fear of banks is a bit unusual. What can you learn from her story?

Get protection beyond FDIC limits through CDARS.
- While my bias is for you to invest money you won't need for ten years or more, I understand some people won't heed my advice. If that sounds like you, I want you to know your money is safe up to $250,000 on deposit through FDIC protection (for banks) and NCUA protection (for credit unions) at any participating institution.
- Yet many business owners, people with inheritances, and local governments have deposits that exceed that limit. What can they do to avoid getting burned in the event of a bank collapse? The Certificate of Deposit Account Registry Service extends FDIC protection up to $50 million by spreading your money among a number of participating

banks. You receive one rate, one statement, and the rest is handled for you. That way you never have more than $250,000 at any one financial institution. Visit CDARS.com for more info.

Find the highest yield for your money.

- If you prefer to find a parking spot for your money rather than investing it, I want you to at least get the highest rate of return possible.
- Some smaller banks and credit unions offer a new oddball checking account that pays higher-than-average interest. Usually called a "maximum earnings" account, this type of checking account offers interest rates that can be 30 to 60 percent higher than the national average on deposits generally $25,000 and under.
- To qualify for the higher rates, you typically have to do direct deposit and at least ten or twelve signature-based debit transactions each month. The reality is merchants pay exorbitant fees whenever you run a debit transaction as a credit card and sign for it. So the bank, in essence, rips off the merchant and then passes along a part of the bounty to you.
- Visit DepositAccounts.com or CheckingFinder.com to find max earning accounts. As I write this, I'm seeing several offers for 3 percent APY interest on balances up to $15,000.

Go light on buying the stock of a company where you work.

- Most investors have a bias for the familiar. They work at a company, they believe in that company, and so they feel safe having their retirement tied up in employer stock. But when market conditions change, that could wipe you out entirely, like it did Victoria and Dan.
- That's why I've long recommended that you diversify your 401(k) and have as little as possible in your employer's own stock. You never want to tie up your paycheck and all your retirement eggs in the same basket.
- If you feel *not* having employer stock in your portfolio is being disloyal to your employer, then it's OK to have up to 10 percent of your retirement money in employer stock. Especially if you're getting a discount on the purchase of the stock. But anything more than 10 percent in company stock is too risky.

Diversification is key.

- As I noted earlier in this chapter, diversification is one of the main keys to long-term growth of your money. You have to spread your money out to lower your risk. A lot of people make the mistake of taking all their money and putting it into a stable value fund because they're afraid of the stock market. That might sound like a sure thing, but it basically treads water, just like Victoria and Dan are doing with their $100,000.

- I prefer that you have money in a total stock market index fund, where you own pieces of thousands of companies. Sure, it's not as "sexy" as putting it all into a single company and letting it ride. And it's not as "safe" as stashing it under the mattress. But investments should be about long-term security, not the dazzle factor or a safety valve.

ENERGY

Advocating everything from alternative-fuel vehicles on the road to LED bulbs in the home, I have always been a pioneer in the field of energy savings. I believe it's critical to reduce our dependence on foreign oil, and that going green can actually put more green in your wallet.

In this chapter, I'll introduce you to other pioneers paving the way for lower energy costs for the rest of us. I'll show you what you can do right now to reduce your energy overhead no matter where you live or what you drive—and regardless of whether you rent or own a home.

BBQ MY RIDE

Raye and Jay use kitchen grease to fuel over
$2,000 in auto savings a year

EVERY MONDAY, JAY DILLON DRIVES over to Three Li'l Pigs Barbeque in Troutville, Virginia. But it's not for the pork tenderloin medallions smoked to perfection with apple wood and marinated in Jamaican jerk sauce.

It's not even for any of the signature hickory-smoked North Carolina–style barbeque dishes on the menu, each one slow-cooked at a place where the motto is "We sell no swine before it's time."

He's actually there to pick up a giant vat of used fryer grease for his wife Raye's Mercedes.

The Dillons were introduced to the idea of "greasecars" by an independent film called *Greasy Rider*. The 2006 documentary really intrigued fifty-seven-year-old Raye and fifty-six-year-old Jay as it followed a journalist and his friend driving across America powered by used vegetable oil.

"Jay did some research on diesel engines and identified the [Mercedes] early '80s models as ideal for grease fuel. We went to eBay and found a 1983 200D for $2,000," Raye told me. "We then contacted a company [called] GreaseCar.com and ordered a conversion kit for $1,000. Jay was able to do the conversion in a weekend. He is a pretty fair mechanic, and the company was available for questions."

That same conversion kit starts at $1,295 these days and it's for diesel vehicles only. It includes a controller, valves, a fuel tank, a tank heat exchanger, fuel lines, and a feed line.

The kit basically equips a car with a dual-tank system—one for traditional diesel and another for vegetable oil. Raye starts her car using diesel fuel and, when the engine is heated up, flips a switch to change the fuel line to vegetable oil. A minute or two before she's reached her destination, she has to switch back to diesel to prime the lines again.

While many Americans struggle with $4 per gallon of gas becoming the new normal, Raye uses about $20 worth of diesel fuel each month. She has a round-trip commute of more than fifty miles three times a week to work her twelve-hour shifts as a registered nurse for the Carilion Clinic health system in Roanoke.

Jay, meanwhile, is a longtime truck driver on routes to Washington, D.C., North Carolina, West Virginia, and many places in Virginia. He's home every night and is considered local.

The couple also has two grown sons ages twenty-four and twenty-eight who work as certified pharmacy technicians.

"My husband works [out of a terminal] five miles from where we live, so he uses very little fuel. Our other Mercedes, our 'good car' is a '95, and we usually only drive it to church on Sundays," Raye confesses. "Ha, ha, ha, the truth! Or if we go somewhere together."

The used fryer grease Raye runs her '83 Mercedes on requires surprisingly little TLC before it's ready to be poured into the fuel tank.

"Jay has a filter station set up in an outbuilding where he heats the oil in a turkey fryer and then pours it through a one-micron sock filter into a clean receptacle," Raye says. "We also have a 250-gallon clean storage tank that is at least half full."

Three Li'l Pigs Barbeque doesn't charge the Dillons for hauling away the twenty or twenty-five gallons each week. "At Christmas, I always show [them] my appreciation with a large basket of home-baked goodies," Raye says. "They love my biscotti."

When I first talked to Raye, before I actually saw her car, I told her that I loved the idea of running a high-end car on discarded fryer grease. Well, she just about fell over laughing when I said that.

"It is anything but! Jay for the most part refuses to [drive] it," Raye told me. "The car is an absolute rattletrap and has so many idiosyncrasies that most people, or their husbands, would not feel it's worth it. But I'm such a skinflint—not including extortion—I will do it."

Among those idiosyncrasies are a broken air conditioner, a starter that's still temperamental despite two replacements, and a broken window crank on the driver's side. That last one requires Raye to store the crank in the door pocket for when she wants to roll her window up or down.

As you might imagine, she has a bit of a reputation in her neighborhood and at work because of her preferred ride.

"I get a little ribbing about making the road workers hungry when I go by [because of the grease smell]. But most of the head shaking is more because of the condition of my car. An '83 really has no pickup so I don't dare 'shoot the gap' or try to pass anyone unless it's a tractor and we're going downhill. I have had several people at work tell me they are interested in alternative fuel just because of what I drive."

But bystanders aren't the only ones who have to do a double take when they see Raye's car. Think of the confusion for the occasional passenger who glances at the speedometer in Raye's European ride and doesn't expect to see the speed in kilometers per hour instead of miles per hour.

"I remember transporting my friend's little girl and she was astonished that we were going one hundred twenty," Raye recalls. "I got a laugh out of that. Of course we were actually going seventy-two!" (Raye has simply learned to do the math in her head, multiplying the speed shown by 0.6. But not all her passengers are so proficient in math!)

So why does Raye do it? Why does she put up with the hassle of a beat-up old grease car?

You could say that it's all about the money. Raye estimates that using mostly fryer grease versus filling up exclusively with diesel fuel saves close to $200 a month during the summer and at least $150 a month in winter. (It takes longer for the engine to heat up in winter.)

Those extra savings help her and Jay pay their phone and electric bills, or it's more than enough to buy hay for the four horses named Cody, Trooper, Callie, and Little Gray that the couple keeps on sixteen acres of pasture at their property.

Still, there's a deeper reason.

"I grew up poor, although I didn't know it at the time. Everyone in my family is thrifty. I shop at Goodwill for clothes, I buy from eBay, I grow a garden and can a good portion of our food. I [even] buy my canning jars used wherever I can find them. I [also] make my own laundry detergent and hang my clothes out on the line [to dry]," Raye told me.

"Every year our neighbors give us what deer [meat] they don't want. I almost never buy beef. We have our own chickens, and I have a few egg customers that offset my feed cost. We raise rabbits for meat. We eat out less than once a month—I'm not exaggerating."

Fortunately, Raye's thrifty lifestyle has paid off with an unexpected dividend: It allows her to be more charitable.

"Even though I'm cheap with my own house, I tithe faithfully with a cheerful heart, and if I see something I know a friend or family member will like, I buy it for them. I truly believe in 'casting my bread on the water.'"

Consider retrofitting your ride.

- There's an old expression, "Pioneers get slaughtered and settlers get rich." I've been a serial pioneer when it comes to energy independence and I keep getting financially slaughtered, especially in the arena of alternative-fuel vehicles.
- A few years back, I had my hybrid, a Toyota Prius, converted into a plug-in hybrid so I could charge it at night in my garage. The cost for the conversion kit and labor was $9,000. I'll practically never make my money back at that price!
- But don't let that steer you away from investigating aftermarket kits if the price is right. After all, Raye's diesel engine conversion kit cost $1,000 when she bought it. Be Clark Smart in researching aftermarket alternatives like the Dillons, not like me!

Find your fuel connection.

- The cost of energy independence doesn't have to be an arm and a leg. The Dillons found a restaurant in their area that gives them used grease for free. Approach a few restaurants in your town to see if you can work out a similar arrangement. Be prepared to give the restaurant a fifty-gallon drum with a lid, and arrange a regular pickup schedule that works for everybody.
- You'll probably want to avoid restaurants that do too much batter frying. "Fast-food oil doesn't work very well because there is usually a lot of breading. If they deep fry a lot of chicken or other meat, too much breading and animal fat gets in the oil," Raye says. "The best restaurants are ones that only fry french fries."
- If you can't find a free hookup in your area, visit Biodiesel.org to find a retailer who can sell you biofuel.

Don't fall for the lure of gas additives.

- I always get a lot of questions about fuel economy boosters when the price of gas gets high. During the energy crises of the 1970s, we first started seeing people selling pills and additives for your gas tank to supposedly increase fuel economy. That's only continued unabated in recent years as $4 per gallon has become more and more the norm.
- Yet you shouldn't fall for these ploys. Out of nearly one hundred gas-saving devices

tested by the government, only six gave a tiny improvement in fuel economy—and even those were nothing to write home about. Visit EPA.gov and search "Aftermarket Retrofit Device Evaluation Program" to see the full study.

Replace a gas-guzzler when it's time.

- For the most part, the price of gas is out of our control. What you can do, when it's time, is replace your current vehicle with the most fuel-efficient choice you can afford. But don't dump your old gas-guzzler before its day has come. Wait until it reaches the natural end of its life.

- You can visit Edmunds.com and search keywords "gas mileage savings calculator" for a helpful tool. Their calculator can help decide whether it makes sense to keep a gas-guzzler or dump it and get a brand-new gas sipper.

- Before you play around with this tool, know that the cost of a car is more than just the price of a gallon of gas. You have depreciation, maintenance, insurance, repairs, and interest on the loan. But this tool gives you a starting point to make that decision.

Don't overlook what's already on the market.

- With so many fuel-efficient auto options on the market today, it's hard for a consumer to know what to do. The *Los Angeles Times* crunched numbers on hybrids versus the closest gas engine version to help you out.

- Owning the Toyota Camry hybrid will save you more than $1,000 over a five-year cycle versus owning the gas engine version. The Lincoln MKZ hybrid offers payback almost from the get-go. The Toyota Prius V, meanwhile, saves more than $3,000 versus the VW Jetta SportWagen. And you don't have to buy all that oil from OPEC. (I should point out that Volkswagen makes a full line of diesels that get fantastic fuel economy and are very affordable to operate even though diesel fuel is more expensive than gas.)

- If electric cars appeal to you, a word of warning is in order. A TrueCar.com analysis shows that my newest car, the Nissan Leaf, takes more than eight years to make back its cost versus the Nissan Versa. But if you think that's bad, the Chevy Volt takes twenty-seven years for payback versus the gas engine equivalent of the Chevy Cruze!

- Of course, I didn't buy the Leaf (or the first hybrid ever sold in America, the original Honda Insight, back in 2000) for return on investment. Instead, I buy these cars as a symbol to get us to think about ways to become independent of foreign oil.

- So some fuel-efficient cars already make financial sense, while others don't. But over time, they'll get cheaper for all of us. As I said before, pioneers get slaughtered and settlers get rich. . . .

Do what you can right now.

- Many people won't want to go whole hog into the world of "greasecars" like Raye did. So for you, shift the focus from energy independence to doing the no-brainers that can improve fuel economy on your existing vehicle.
- The reality is that you have to do the simple things to get better fuel economy. We've all heard them a hundred times. But almost nobody remembers to do them—unload your trunk, keep your tires properly inflated, and slow down on the road. Make a resolution and do these things! Finally, the twofer here is to walk short distances because it saves money and improves your health.

SOLAR SAVER

For Steve, being green is all about the money

STEVE BUZALKO ISN'T EXACTLY what you'd call a "green" kind of guy. He works with wood for a living, meaning his job involves a nasty little thing called "deforestation" that's bemoaned by environmentalists the world over.

"I am a cabinetmaker by trade, so we must cut a few trees to make things. They grow back," Steve deadpans to me. "[But] I do believe in doing the right thing and helping people."

He is, however, interested in another kind of green—the kind that pads your wallet. That's why the fifty-four-year-old craftsman decided to install a solar system at his Pottsville, Pennsylvania, home back in April 2010.

Steve built his two-thousand-square-foot raised ranch himself, and he shares it with his wife, who is a high school guidance counselor in Schuylkill County. The upper floor of the home is residential, while the bottom floor houses the workshop of Buzalko Woodworking. When I spoke to him, he was working on a library made of cherry wood for a nearby Hindu temple.

Having a workshop onsite means two electric meters on the property, one residential and one commercial.

As a cabinetmaker with twenty-seven years of experience, Steve wasn't used to researching the best prices for solar photovoltaic (PV) systems in his normal line of work. But he got some guidance from a weekly newspaper that had an article on alternative energy for farmers—published, ironically enough, deep in the heart of neighboring Amish country—and soon found three companies that could install the system he was interested in.

"While [I was] on the phone with each company, they looked at my house on Bing maps and determined [it] would be a good candidate for solar because of its southern exposure," Steve recalled. "The lowest price was [from] the only commercial electrical contractor. The others were newly formed solar [installation] companies. This particular company sent an electrical engineer, the others sent salesmen. That also helped me to choose them."

Based on his energy needs and his electric bill, Steve decided on a 10-kilowatt (kW) solar system consisting of fifty roof-mounted 200-watt panels at a cost of $55,000.

He paid for it up front using a home equity loan, and then received a $19,500 grant through Pennsylvania's Sunshine Program, plus a $16,500 federal tax credit on his 2010 taxes. His final out-of-pocket cost for the system was $19,000, and he paid off the home equity loan in two years.

The 10-kW solar system now provides for all of the Buzalkos' residential energy needs, while Steve's commercial work space is still powered by the local utility company.

Before the solar system, Steve's residential electric bill was around $120 a month. (Recent rate increases would have bumped that up to $180–$220 a month.)

Today, though, he generates enough of his own energy to pay zero, zip, *nada* each month to the utility company for his residential electric needs—except a customer service fee of around $8 a month. The junk fee allows him to have his system hooked up to the grid so he can sell the power he generates down the line.

"What I produce when the sun shines I use," Steve says. "Any excess electric will feed back into the grid for others. During those times of excess, my electric meter spins backwards. During times of no sun, I take from the grid and the meter spins forwards."

Each 1,000 kilowatt hours of energy his system produces above and beyond what he uses is equal to one credit, and Steve produces about twelve credits a year. Those credits are reported to an aggregator (he chose his installer) who charges a flat fee of $10 per credit to accumulate and sell them to large electric generative companies.

When Steve first installed the solar system in early 2010, each credit sold for between $300 and $350. Add that to the minimum $120 he saves each month on electric, and he was trending toward a return on his $19,000 investment in 4.7 years. (The magic number for a payback period at today's low interest rates is ten years.)

But now, with more people installing solar and selling excess energy on the open market, the increased supply of credits means each one only commands about $20 to $30 in Steve's area. The way things are going now, Steve figures he won't make his money back until 2016 or 2017. But you have to remember that he has no residential power bill.

Still, return on investment wasn't exactly the foremost thing on his mind when he decided to go solar.

"[My wife and I] are looking at retirement and are motivated by one less bill to pay and being more self-sufficient," Steve tells me. "We have our own well and septic. No bills for water or sewer. As hobbies, [we] grow vegetables and jar them. We keep chickens, and I make my own wine and beer. It all sounds like a Mother Earth [thing], but it's not. We enjoy the modern world. I do not consider myself a 'greenie.' I just believe in doing no harm and being responsible. Nothing more.

"I am happy I bought the system and would recommend anyone with the means to do it. Just do your homework, and get all the grants and credit available to you."

Steve adds that you should get at least three quotes for your system and ask a lot of questions of potential contractors. The questions he asked included the following:

- How long has the company been in business?
- How many systems have they installed?
- How long will the installation take?
- Who pays for the permits?
- Is it a roof-mount system or ground-mount system?
- Who applies for the grants and submits all the paperwork?

As for me, I believe solar energy is a huge part of what we need to be about as a nation. My wife and I have a vacation place at the beach in Florida that is a near net zero energy home. We've put in the compact fluorescent lightbulbs, the efficient HVAC, and even a solar system.

Over the course of a year, we sell more power than we buy from the power company in Florida, just like Steve. So we have no utility bills. And that's saying something because even though we're not there all the time, we have to run the air conditioner all year round—otherwise we'll have mold growing in the high-humidity climate.

To give you an example, a few months ago our power bill at the beach was $4.15. The bill after that was negative $26—the power company owed me instead of the other way around because of what I generated and sold down the line.

Get ready for your quote.

- The process starts by going online to a solar company's website and putting in your street address. This will allow the company to use a satellite map to pinpoint your home and assess your solar potential. Have your past year's electric bills handy, because you'll be asked about your energy usage.
- Your property will also need a fairly clear shot of the southern sky. Don't worry if your roof is too shaded. You can still have ground-mount panels installed in a sunny spot on your property.
- Some of the more popular solar companies include SolarCity.com, Sungevity.com, SunRunHome.com, and Us.SunPowerCorp.com. Know that it is an unstable field, so there will be casualties as some companies go out of business and others start up.

Consider a lease.

- While Steve bought his system outright, most people put solar on their home through a lease agreement. With a lease, there are no up-front installation costs for you. You just pay a flat monthly fee or rate for the equipment and the energy you generate. The solar company typically handles necessary permits and takes any tax breaks or renewable energy credits—not the homeowner. They're also the ones who handle ongoing maintenance and repair.

Explore your alternatives.

- You might want to consider solar shingles if you live in a restrictive covenant community that prohibits traditional panels. The solar shingles are small and they look just like the traditional asphalt ones you're used to. They even get nailed to your roof in the same way! You just need an electrician to hook them up to your home's electrical system.
- Solar shingles are not as efficient as traditional solar panels, but *The New York Times* reports they can offset your bill by 40 to 80 percent, and they're typically 15 percent cheaper than a solar panel system. Visit DowPowerHouse.com for more details. So far they're only being sold in California, Colorado, and Texas.

Go green to get more green at resale.

- The long-standing assumption in the real estate market is that buyers don't really value energy-saving stuff like putting in solar panels. But that turns out to be wrong.

- In 2011, the Lawrence Berkeley National Laboratory released the results of a nearly dec-adelong study of home resale values in California. The study found the typical home with whole house solar sold for $17,000 more than a home that didn't have it in the state. That difference can recoup virtually all of the installation costs.

- In a similar vein, green-certified homes can command 9 percent more in offers when it's time to resell. That's according to a 2012 study out of UCLA that looked at sales of more than 1 million California homes between 2007 and early 2012.

OFF THE GRID

Laura and Rutherford's EcoManor shows you can
save big bucks with small changes in your home

A LOT OF US HAVE FATHERS who patrolled the house when we were young, turning off the lights in unoccupied rooms and imploring us not to waste energy and money.

But for Laura Turner Seydel, that fatherly lesson was taught by Ted Turner, the billionaire philanthropist, environmentalist, and founder of CNN.

"He didn't believe in wasting money," said Laura, still blond, blue-eyed, and youthful at fifty-one.

She's now a mother of three and an environmental advocate and speaker who lives in one of the nation's most environmentally friendly and healthy houses. But more on that later.

First, I want to share with you a few of Laura's stories about growing up as the daughter of Ted Turner, and how that has guided her life and career.

Laura said growing up after the Great Depression strongly influenced her father's attitudes.

"Dad always said he didn't get rich by wasting money. He got rich by spending it very wisely and saving it as well. So anything that was considered wasteful, like leaving lights or televisions on when not in use—or turning up the thermostat instead of donning a sweater when you were cold—was just not acceptable."

Laura remembers regularly picking up bottles and cans with her dad and taking them to the store to be recycled. And once, while they were visiting Machu Picchu in Peru, Laura said Turner surprised an eco-guide by reaching down to pick up a piece of trash.

The guide told Laura, "In all my years of taking these celebrities through, I've never seen somebody of his status bend down and pick up somebody else's trash."

In the 1990s, Turner created the cartoon series *Captain Planet and the Planeteers*, in which the world's first and only eco-superhero, Captain Planet, taught children about crucial environmental challenges and other issues of global importance, including war, AIDS, and the threat of land mines.

Captain Planet ran for six years as a new series, a total of 113 episodes, and was rerun for years afterward. It was seen in more than one hundred countries and translated into twenty-three different languages.

After the merger of Time Warner with AOL, Ted and many things that he cared about were jettisoned, including the green-lit full-feature *Captain Planet* movie, the cartoon series, and the associated Captain Planet Foundation. The Foundation was offered to Turner, who didn't have the time to take it on. But Laura did, and two decades later, she continues to chair the organization.

The foundation, which has given grants for more than twenty years to schools and youth groups in all fifty states and in twenty countries worldwide, provides hands-on environmental-service learning projects such as recycling programs, testing and monitoring water quality, gardens of every type, renewable energy projects, wetland restorations, and tree plantings, to mention a few.

"You name it, we've done it, and there are some very impactful projects we've supported," Laura said.

In the early 2000s, an act of God spurred Laura and her husband, attorney and Atlanta Hawks co-owner Rutherford Seydel, to create one of the nation's most environmentally friendly houses. The house, known as EcoManor, is so innovative that it has its own website, EcoManor.com. It was the first house in the Southeast and the second in the country to be certified under the U.S. Green Building Council's LEED program (Leadership in Energy and Environmental Design). Rutherford and the other Hawks owners also gained LEED certification for Philips Arena, the first NBA and NHL LEED EB (for existing buildings) arena in the world.

But EcoManor might not have been built had it not been for a fallen tree.

Laura and Rutherford had lived for sixteen years in a house that was built in the 1920s. They had made some energy-wise improvements, such as replacing the heating and air-conditioning system with one that was more efficient, adding insulation, and wrapping the pipes. But there was only so much they could do with the house, and there weren't really any nationally recognized environmental standards to follow. (The best standard at the time, a local program called EarthCraft, was primarily for building new houses in a way that was moderately energy- and water-efficient.)

The couple bought a house adjacent to their 1920s house and was planning to renovate it and resell it.

"But days after we bought the house, a terrible storm came through—one of the new developments of our heated climate—and a tree was blown down from our neighbor's property and destroyed half of the house."

After a long fight with their insurance company, the house was declared a teardown, and Laura and Rutherford, who had heard about a new environmental certification for houses, set out to build the first house to secure the new designation.

"We would have been first if not for a broken pipe and resulting flood in our basement that set us back several weeks, which was just enough to let somebody else in California get ahead of us," Laura said. "But we did make it first in the Southeast, and I can't even begin to tell you the amount of interest in our project on behalf of the media because it was so new."

Everything about the house was designed to conserve energy and water, from the cistern that collects rainwater from the roof and pipes it to the toilets; to the system that allows gray water from the showers, sinks, and laundry to percolate back into the ground; to high-efficiency appliances and LED and compact fluorescent lighting.

"I really like all the natural daylight," Laura says as she walks through her front door, cell phone to her ear, and describes what she sees. "I love that I can come home to my house, like I just did, and there's not a light on in the house. Even when it's overcast outside, there's plenty of light, and it always feels good."

The house has a series of solar tubes—basically mini-skylights—that redirect natural light to windowless places such as closets and bathrooms.

And the house was designed to take maximum advantage of the sun.

"We had built the frame of our house," Rutherford said, "and I went over there many nights at sunset and many days, mornings and in the middle of the day, to see if I was right about how the sun was going to come up and how it was going to come through a room and light it up. And we changed some things around so that in the morning the sun would come in one way and in the afternoon it would come in another way."

They widened openings and changed door and window locations to allow in more natural daylight.

EcoManor consumes less than half the energy, per square foot, of the average U.S. home built from 2000 to 2005, according to Southface, a nonprofit dedicated to sustainable construction.

EcoManor, which includes approximately eight thousand square feet of space, has a 6.5-kilowatt rooftop solar array that reduces its conventional electricity and gas use. The Seydels are planning to add more solar capacity for 2013.

Laura says she loves the aesthetics of the house, including the rugs that were made from natural fibers and the plank flooring that was milled from downed trees. Because her concerns extend beyond energy and water efficiency to indoor air quality and toxicity, she loves that the paints used to decorate the house do not emit volatile organic compounds. She also uses natural cleaning products rather than harsh chemicals that could harm her family's health and find their way into the local water system.

Outside the house, Laura and Rutherford planted drought-tolerant indigenous plants so little water is wasted watering them, and they use no chemicals in their yard or veggie garden. These practices earned EcoManor another coveted certification given by the National Wildlife Federation for managing their yard in such a responsible way.

They also used a type of vine called Virginia creeper to help shade the brick on the southwest side of the house.

"During the summer, this wonderful, leafy, beautiful plant goes up the brick wall. But most of what it's doing is acting like a big shade tree. It's shading the brick from getting heated by the sun. In the winter, when it's gone, the brick warms up. So it's a great natural way to provide shade for that side of the house."

The couple also grows food for the family in their garden, and has four chickens to provide a regular supply of fresh eggs.

"I give them away to neighbors because we produce more eggs than we eat. It's fantastic," Rutherford said. "Then the chickens walk around the yard and help fertilize so we don't need chemical additives."

He says besides the red wiggler worms that turn their food scraps into nutrient-rich compost, they're the best pets he's ever had. And they all help with positive net cash flow! In addition, the hens thankfully coexist well with the Seydels' beloved cocker spaniel, Boo.

Laura also set up a beehive on the property, hoping to help the increasingly threatened pollinators. But that ended up in disaster. The cause was the overuse of weed killers and pesticides in Laura's affluent Atlanta neighborhood, which found their way into the hive.

"The beekeeper who was helping me said she'd never seen anything like it before in her life, and she manages thirty different beehives around the city. She said the honey and the pollen were so toxic that the bees actually encapsulated it because they couldn't remove it from the hive. So they formed this shield around it."

But it didn't work. "It was a sad day for me when I learned all the bees had died."

The beekeeper said the most successful and best honey-producing hives are in low-income communities because they don't have the discretionary income to spend on lawn and garden applications.

"And the worst case she'd ever seen was in my neighborhood, which has all these big homes and these perfectly manicured lawns and not a weed in sight."

Laura's growing awareness of toxic chemicals poses some unique challenges to Rutherford. She has cautioned him about buying jewelry because of the toxic chemicals and heavy metals used in the mining process. Diamonds that could be related to armed conflict zones are out as well, as are cut roses, which Rutherford said are often grown with the heavy use of pesticides.

So what's a guy to do for a Valentine's Day or anniversary gift?

"I can go out in the backyard and cut something and make a nice bouquet and give it to her," he said. "And chocolates are still on the list."

But for their most recent Valentine's Day, they gave each other an enhanced purification system that helps oxygenate and alkalize tap water and turns it into "live water" for our 65-to-70-percent H_2O-based bodies.

Of course, being a stringent environmental advocate can sometimes get discouraging. Rutherford recounts the story of the great Jacques Cousteau, the French scientist and explorer who studied the sea, telling Ted Turner that he was becoming increasingly negative about the future of the world's reefs, whose ecosystems were breaking down.

"Ted looked at him and said, 'Wait a minute. You're a scientist, and every scientist has a degree of probability that you could be wrong.'"

So even if that chance was only 1 percent, it was enough to work to try to change things, Rutherford said.

Laura sees a big source of encouragement in the Planeteers, nearly six hundred thousand Millennials who grew up watching *Captain Planet* on TV and who are now, as young adults, communicating with one another on Facebook.

"Now they're young career professionals and college students, but they are saying what an impact the cartoon made on them," Laura said. "They're organizing in their communities. They've also made career choices based on the ethic that was developed watching the cartoon. We are starting, at the [Captain Planet] Foundation, to get grant requests from these formalized groups of Planeteers, including groups from Bangladesh, Ethiopia, and Ghana. It really was the gift that kept on giving, that cartoon, and it really matters what kids grow up watching."

Both Laura and Rutherford work hard to get people to change their energy-wasting and polluting ways. Rutherford knows that he is privileged and is humbled to live in a house like EcoManor. But he thinks there is huge potential for more meaningful, healthy improvement in any apartment or dwelling.

That improvement, he says, will come from more and more people making millions of incremental but efficient changes.

An environmental group they started installs rain barrels on even the most basic houses. And Rutherford says it's relatively easy now, and inexpensive, to buy such things as high-efficiency dimmable compact fluorescent lights and low-flush toilets and to use paints and cleaners that do not emit volatile organic compounds.

"There's lots of options," he said. "When we built our house, there weren't lots of options, and that was seven or eight years ago. We didn't even have smartphones back then. The world has evolved and people will always want to save money and live a more healthy, better quality of life . . . so there is hope."

What can you do in your home right now to make it more energy efficient?

Find your entry point into savings.

- Rutherford describes monthly utility bills as a "utility mortgage," because they must be paid and they drain cash from a house's owners. "I don't know of anyone that sits around and says, 'I can't wait to pay my utility bills,'" he said.

- But where do you begin reducing what you pay? For most of us, a good basic starting point is changing your lightbulbs to CFLs (compact fluorescent lightbulbs) or the even more energy-stingy (light-emitting diode) LED bulbs. They might cost more up front, but they'll save you a lot over time.

- Another basic entry point to savings is your windows. Don't change them thinking that you'll get a payback; caulk them instead. Weather stripping will also make a big difference.

Get a smart programmable thermostat.

- Programmable thermostats can reduce heating and cooling costs in your home by 25 to 30 percent. But it's hard to get excited by this device that your dad probably loves.
- Enter the Nest Learning Thermostat, which was designed by a former Apple executive and borrows the clean, minimalist design of the classic iPod click wheel. The Nest uses algorithms and artificial intelligence to learn your living patterns and figure out when to bump the temperature down a few degrees to save you money.
- It can be self-installed if you have technical ability or you can hire a local installer who will also sell you the unit. Retailers carrying the Nest, which sells for around $250, include Amazon, Best Buy, and Lowe's, among others.
- I've now tried the Nest at my home and am very happy with its performance. I've found it reduces my energy bill by about 20 percent. Visit Nest.com for more info.

Reduce your water consumption.

- I had a low-flow toilet put into my house that took us from 3.5 gallons a flush to 1.1 gallons a flush. The toilet actually has two buttons—one that delivers 1.1 gallons and another for 1.6 gallons. This is a G-rated book, so use your imagination to understand when to use which button!
- *Consumer Reports* gave its vaunted "best buy" check mark to two toilets that both sell for about $100—the single-flush Aquasource AT1203-00 (available at Lowe's) and the Glacier Bay Dual Flush N2316 (available at Home Depot).
- In addition, try installing a low-flow showerhead that uses a blast of air to simulate a strong stream of water. You might qualify for a rebate if you outfit your home with water-efficient devices. Check with your municipality to see if they participate.

Insulate your attic.

- If you have an attic, be sure to insulate it. You can either pay a professional to do blown-in insulation, or if you do it yourself, be sure to wear proper gloves and a mask.
- Joel Larsgaard, my associate producer, whom you read about in the Homes and Real Estate chapter, recently did it himself at his new house. He got free rental of an insula-

tion blower with the purchase of twenty bags of insulation ($11 a bag) at a local big-box home improvement store. Then he grabbed a friend to help him.

- "It took us roughly an hour and fifteen minutes to blow twenty-three bags of cellulose insulation into my attic, and it was actually kind of fun doing it," Joel told me. "Bonus, I looked like the Snuggle bear afterwards with a thick coat of lint all over me."

- The real bonus is that Joel got a reimbursement from his local power company. They covered half of his $274 total bill for the job! Visit DSIREUSA.org (Database of State Incentives for Renewables & Efficiency) to see similar incentives that might be available where you live.

- Meanwhile, you can follow Joel's adventures in money saving at his blog, SaveOutside theBox.com.

LIVING BELOW YOUR MEANS

Too many people who lived above their means before the recession found they couldn't weather the storm when it hit. In the wake of the damage, it became very chic to talk about living within our means. Yet what we should have been talking about all along was living below *our means.*

In this chapter, we meet several people who have found unique ways to take a scalpel to their expenditures and cut, cut, cut every which way possible.

MAKING LEMONADE
OUT OF LEMONS

Darcy exemplifies resilience by finding freebies and silver linings

THERE'S A LITTLE PACKAGE of cocoa butter that's long since dried out inside a $1 plastic container in Darcy Miller's apartment. It's frayed around the edges and the brand name has rubbed off even though it was never opened.

Little wonder about the sample size's condition—it came Darcy's way eleven years ago when she first started perfecting the art of getting freebie products online.

"The first year of doing freebie searches panned out to be nothing. The only thing I got that whole year of filling out freebies was that small pack of cocoa butter and a bunch of spam in my e-mail inbox," Darcy recalls. "[But] I didn't let it bother me and that's why I continued. To this day, I still have that small pack of cocoa butter as a reminder of where I started."

Darcy is a self-confessed "freebie-aholic." Getting free samples online is a way of life for her. The forty-seven-year-old divorcée really knew she was on to something when she was able to supplement part of her shopping list with freebies.

"I have not had to buy shampoo, conditioner, toothpaste, toothbrushes, or deodorant in ten years," she told me.

Clearly, this is one lady who knows how to pinch a penny. But you have to when you're living on $678 a month in disability and $158 in food stamps.

Darcy lives in northern Indiana's Amish country, in a town called Nappanee, which lies between South Bend and Fort Wayne. It's just over one hundred miles from Chicago across the Illinois-Indiana border, but it is worlds away from the hustle and bustle of metro areas.

Nappanee is the kind of place where you can still see a homemade stop sign that reads "Please Stop! Horses Have the Right of Way" on the outskirts of town. Darcy lives about half a mile off Main Street in a town where Main Street still signifies the place where people gather to talk about the news of the day over a cup of coffee.

Darcy has embraced the slower pace of life in Nappanee but not willingly. She's disabled and spends her time at home in a wheelchair. She started receiving disability in 2011, a dozen years after she first had back surgery to remedy debilitating childhood scoliosis.

Still, she makes it a point to get up and out of the chair once a day to move around with the assistance of a walker. Every morning, she vacuums and dusts, picking up after the three pets that she says keep her "sane."

With maybe too much time on her hands, Darcy is the kind of person who is always ready to share the latest from the hours she spends on the Internet researching freebies and money-saving options.

She effuses over e-mail when talking about Dollar Tree's recent decision to start accepting coupons. ("So basically, you pay a dollar for something, and if you have a coupon, you can get it close to free—if not free!")

On the phone, Darcy is eager to pass along a tip about the giant loaves of herb and garlic bread on Walmart's bakery racks for $1.19. ("If you put them in the fridge, they will last a full month. But if you leave them out, they'll spoil in just a couple of days.")

She rents a one-bedroom in Nappanee for $290 a month—paying an extra $10 each month for her pets. There's Joe the dog, Baldy the cat, and another stray feline named Tangerine, who literally came flying into her apartment in 2011 when the screen door was open and has never left.

"I've always had pets since I was a baby. I've never been without them. My ex-husband wanted to keep Joe and Baldy . . . but that's not going to happen," Darcy says, "knowing how he took care of them, which was zero. I wasn't having it."

Darcy could pay less for Section 8 housing, but that would be in a high crime area and she wouldn't be able to move very well in the event of a home invasion.

Five years ago, things were going somewhat better for Darcy. She was working part-time as a salesperson at Olan Mills, a chain photography studio—six hours a day, three days a week, at $8 an hour. Back then she could afford to earn $7,488 annually because she had a husband who worked.

But that marriage ended in 2011, Darcy says, because of domestic abuse and infidelity on her ex-spouse's part. It was her second marriage.

Fortunately, she has developed a couple of coping strategies to survive the lean times.

Darcy has saved money on furnishings by outfitting her apartment on the cheap. She found a bed, a nine-drawer dresser, and a couch for under $250 through the Salvation Army. She got her recliner for free on FreeCycle.org, a website that connects people who are giving things away with people who are looking for select items.

She's also a big fan of dollar stores. Because she is handicapped, she has to pay a driver $15 once a month to go shopping for perishables and nonperishables.

"I found a Dollar Tree that has refrigerator and freezer stuff. I get a dozen eggs for a dollar, hot dogs for a dollar, and large sour creams for a dollar."

When it comes to the online freebie front, time has taught Darcy what not to fall for when looking at beguiling offers of supposedly free samples online. Requests for your Social Security number and being asked to pay shipping and handling charges for a "free offer" are among the most common red flags.

She religiously reads all the mice type on contracts. That places her among a small minority of Americans who are actually *not* contractually illiterate. But inevitably, Darcy has had several run-ins with errant companies trying to charge her for goods they advertised as free, including a leading publisher of romance novels and a Big Four wireless provider.

In both cases, she just had to get tough, reread the fine print, and show the companies why their own language substantiated her point.

With the romance publisher, she thought she was signing up to be a member of a free book club that required her to respond to an e-mail with feedback on the three or four titles they would send her. But then the bills started coming.

"I e-mailed them and told them that I would not be paying for the books that they sent me through the free club when I followed all the instructions by answering the questions and sending them back."

Minor mice-type scuffles aside, Darcy has perfected the art of getting freebies to supplement her small income. And if things ever get too grim, she has Joe, Baldy, and Tangerine to see her through.

Decorate your home with free or gently used furniture.

- Furnishing a home or an apartment can cost thousands of dollars. But it doesn't have to. Darcy furnished her apartment on the cheap by paying for gently used furnishings at the Salvation Army and getting a free recliner on FreeCycle.org.

- If you're not familiar with FreeCycle, it's a free site that matches up people who are giving stuff away with people who are looking for select items. One time the sister of a close friend of mine saw a funny post on FreeCycle where someone was looking for my books! I love that the individual was really getting my message about being extra thrifty.

- Twitter.com/Yoink offers a hyper-local version of this idea catering to New York City. When Hurricane Sandy hit in October 2012, Yoink went into overdrive as a crowd-sourcing response tool to help connect desperate New Yorkers with food, clothing, and more—all of it free for the asking.

- Make sure you thoroughly inspect any items before bringing them home because of the possibility of bedbugs. Be sure to cover every mattress and box spring, new or used, with the highest quality cover you can buy. It's cheaper to deal with a potential problem proactively rather than after the fact.

Stay out of the store to save money.

- One of the challenges we face in our nation is that everything is available all the time. It's hard to overcome "affluenza" and "want-itis" when stores are open twenty-four hours a day.

- Darcy's limited income and the difficulty she has moving around means she's locked into shopping only once a month for both perishables and nonperishables. That's a pretty unusual situation. But there's a certain wisdom in voluntarily adopting what she's forced to do.

- You can buy groceries on a weekly basis, of course, as your situation allows, but why not try to shop for nonperishables and other necessities only eight or twelve times a year? The more you stay out of the store, the more you limit your opportunities to overspend.

Know the deals at dollar stores.

- In *Living Large in Lean Times*, I include a list of the best deals at dollar stores. More recently, I saw a cute item on Yahoo! News with their tally of screaming deals.
- Unfortunately, the list was as dull as dishwater, with mostly products for household chores making the cut. It included dish soap, bleach, fabric softener sheets, dishwasher detergent, toilet cleaning bleach tablets, bleach spray cleaner, and sandwich bags.
- My favorite dollar store buy? "Belly Flops" at Dollar Tree and 99¢ Only stores. They're bags of irregular jelly beans for a buck!

Beware of free trial offers.

- Free trial offers are a dime a dozen all over the Internet and on bad late-night TV. Most require you to divulge a checking account, debit card, or credit card number so they can bill you for a nominal shipping and handling charge.
- But that small fee is just a ruse to get your account information. Once they have that, the marketer typically says you missed your chance to cancel the trial, and they begin posting huge charges to your account without your permission.
- There is a way under the law for you to stop the funny business. See "Suspend automatic drafts from your account" on pages 175–177 of my last book, *Clark Howard's Living Large in Lean Times*, for an explanation.
- If you're already going through this ordeal, it's up to you to watch your account like a hawk going forward. Let's say you think you've gotten the mischief stopped. Don't be surprised if the same marketer re-emerges anywhere from six months to two years later and tries to pull from your account again!
- Perhaps the simplest rule of all is this: It's much easier to get into trouble than to get out of it. When you see the free trial offer, *don't do it.*

Read the mice type.

- When you're presented with a contract, do you know what you're reading? Most of us don't. In fact, *Business Week* reports that only one in eight Americans can read a long, dense passage of text and comprehend it.
- If we expect consumers to sign agreements, we should also expect that contracts be written in simple English. The nation's newspapers usually write at a sixth-grade level. If

they can tackle world issues at that level, why is it that we don't require our contracts to be written in plain English?

- My guess is that if you knew what you were agreeing to in a contract, you would never sign one! But capitalism functions best when there's complete transparency. Until that time, you have to do your best to read all the mice type like Darcy.

Don't give up.

- Darcy's story offers a great example of how to handle being thrown curveballs in life. As I've noted elsewhere in this book, everything I write for you in these pages—all the advice, all the guidance—none of it will work if you just give up on life. You've got to steel yourself when you face challenges like Darcy has done, and you've got to do it in the kind and gracious way she has. Darcy, you truly know how to make lemonade out of life's lemons. This glass is for you!

THE THRIFTY DENTIST

*On the edge of "affluenza," Steph and Steven pull
back and decide to live more modestly*

LIVING BELOW YOUR MEANS can mean different things to different people. For Dr. Stephanie Aldrich of Copley, Ohio, it meant backing out of a deal to purchase a dream home when the price wasn't right—even though she has a nearly million-dollar practice.

Steph, as she likes to be called, opened Akron Dental Concepts in March 2000. Her business started growing by about 10 to 15 percent annually after she began accepting insurance, and it's been about even for the last two years in the aftermath of the recession. Most other private dental practices in her area don't accept any PPO plans.

At thirty-nine, she lives on less than half her net income—not a difficult feat for a dentist, but a noteworthy one when so many of her colleagues seem bent on living a lavish lifestyle.

"The general public thinks that dentists are rich and drive fancy cars and live in expensive houses. And some of them do . . . [but] I have decided to break the stereotype," Steph told me.

Why might she want to do that? Consider the extreme price tag for dental school and the burdensome loans necessary to establish a successful practice.

In Steph's case, that amounted to $176,000 for her studies, $250,000 to buy and renovate her first practice in 2000 from a dentist who was selling, and $252,000 to buy and renovate an adjoining practice in the same building in 2005. That's a total price tag of $678,000 before you factor in the interest.

"I know how [it] feels to be in debt up to your eyeballs and to know that it all lies on your shoulders," she says. "A couple of years ago when I was pregnant with my son, I told myself that I didn't want to ever borrow money from a bank again if I could help it. I want to pay everything in cash, and if I don't have enough cash for the purchase, then I have to wait for it."

To be exact, Steph lives on 44 percent of her income and is the primary breadwinner in her family of three, while her second husband, Steven, studies to be a dental hygienist.

She gives herself a weekly stipend for spending and avoids credit cards at all costs. Whatever doesn't get spent at the end of the week makes it back into a spare money jar.

"I feel that just because you have a high-paying career, business, or job that you can still clip coupons and not have the latest iPhone that's out there—I still use a regular cell phone with no data plan, just text and talking," she says. "I don't need it. If you want to get ahold of me, I'm either at home or I'm at the office.

"It's funny, I've sacrificed [by doing everything from] staying after work to paint my office so I didn't have to pay a painter to do it to doing my own website—I learned how to do it and all about search engine optimization."

Frugality was practically coded into Steph's DNA from birth. Her father often held two jobs to feed his family of four and her mother pinched the pennies that came into the house.

"Early on, I watched my mom stretch the dollars that my dad gave her. She always had a stash of cash somewhere. Either for birthday presents for us, or for school clothes, or for Christmas. It wasn't until I was an adult that I realized how much money my dad really made. Some people would think that it wasn't a lot, but I never felt like I didn't have anything.

"We always had toys. We always had clothes. We always went on vacations. I guess there were things that we didn't have, but to this day I still couldn't tell you any of them. Somehow my mom stretched those dollars and made us feel rich."

When it came to her days of higher education, Steph paid the bill through a combination of federal student loans, scholarships, and grants, plus some parental contributions during the undergraduate years. She also followed her dad's lead and held two jobs on campus.

"I saved my money working my summer jobs so that I could party with all the other kids. In dental school, I definitely didn't have any extra money, so I worked at a pizza shop for three years, twenty hours or more, and used that money to help pay my utilities and living expenses."

Yet for all the messages about living below your means that she had internalized during her middle-class upbringing, she was a hairsbreadth away from living a financially high-voltage lifestyle when she had a brush with trying to play the role of the affluent dentist. Such a misstep would have meant extending her student loans and the loans for her practice way beyond 2013, when they'd otherwise be paid off.

It all started when Steph and Steven were tempted to play keeping up with the Joneses with another couple in their neighborhood. Let's call their "friends" the Johnsons.

The Johnsons convinced Steph and Steven to join a local country club with a nearly $4,500 initiation fee so they could all hang out and play golf. But Steph and Steven never once hit the links or socialized with the Johnsons when they did join.

"After two years of feeling inadequate with the country club patrons, we quit. We spent thousands of dollars a month trying to fit in at a place that just wasn't us," Steph says.

And back when the Johnsons were getting ready to build their dream house, Steph and Steven also got caught up in the excitement.

So they bought some land in 2009—a deal that was contingent on getting a loan for the dream home—and told the Johnsons' award-winning builder that they wanted a 3,200-square-foot ranch for $400,000. But when the architectural plans came back, they were way over-budget.

"We got the quote back from the builder and it wasn't even close to $400,000. It was $699,000 and it didn't even include a finished basement!" Steph recalls. "When I saw that quote, my heart sank. I didn't want to spend that kind of money on a house. Could I have done it? Absolutely. I could have taken out a jumbo loan for thirty years and put every last dime I had saved into the down payment. But I knew in my heart I couldn't do it. I didn't want to put my husband or me in that predicament."

The Johnsons went on to build their dream home for even more money than Steph was quoted. Steph, meanwhile, declined the builder's quote and got out of the land deal without losing a penny.

"The architecture plans were around $2,600," Steph says. "I still have those plans and once in a while look at my expensive pieces of paper . . . Ouch! But that money was worth it to me [instead of] making a [big] mistake that would put us in the hole!"

Instead, she and Steven found a twenty-year-old existing home in a rural part of the Akron metro area for less than half the price tag of their "dream home," put 10 percent down, and got a fifteen-year mortgage at 3.25 percent.

"My property taxes are less for two acres than they were for the .25 acre lot I had in the 'burbs. My house payment is $500 more a month than my other house, but I only have fourteen years left on it instead of twenty-two years and I'm only paying a grand total of $29,000 on the debt over the entire loan compared to over $100,000 I would have paid for my other house at 6.25 percent for thirty years," Steph says.

"It may be considered a 'rich dentist house,' but with house prices the way they are around the country, I got a great deal on it. It needs some work and we will be doing that over the next few years—doing a lot of it ourselves."

And how are the Johnsons doing in their dream home?

"Well, they're in the middle of a divorce right now, and their house is up for sale at their rock-bottom price. They just want to get out from underneath it. It's sad," Steph says. "But I didn't want the pressure that a house payment like that would put me under . . . and with the economy taking a dive in 2008, it was one of the best gut decisions I ever made."

So what's next for Steph after she pays off her education and practice loans in 2013? A splurge on something big? Not for this dentist!

"Now that I'm at the end of my [student and business loan] debt road, you would think that I would want to buy something extravagant and frivolous. But instead, the last couple of months, I've been learning different ways to invest," she says.

"I will be forty next year and will finally start to save for retirement. I want my investment and bank accounts to grow and hopefully someday help put my son, and his children, through school, as well as act as 'family banks,' where they can borrow money to buy houses or emergency purchases so they don't have to go to traditional banks and pay all the unnecessary interest payments that most people get trapped with—me being one of them."

Steph does allow herself some smaller splurges along the road to financial independence, like the Mercedes she leases. It's Steph's "rich dentist" car, and I just hope she got it on a factory-subsidized lease deal because that's one of the only ways a lease for a luxury car can make sense in somebody's life! (Steven, meanwhile, drives a Toyota RAV4 for the fuel economy.)

"I'm hoping the country club and the dream house fiascos will be my last lessons in keeping true to myself and my personality without trying to keep up with the Joneses, or should I say, 'the Johnsons,'" Steph says. "I can shop at Target and get a good deal on a good pair of socks and feel good about it, you know?"

Go cash only.

- There's something wired in many of us that if we are given permission to borrow and spend, we will. The immediate gratification of having access to the ability to buy what we want instantly is so seductive that a lot of us get ourselves in over our heads. If you know that you will spend if given the plastic, *you must live on a cash basis and turn away from credit.* Period. Doing so will create a lot more security and sanity in your life.

Know the difference between wants and needs.

- A cell phone might be a necessity these days, but must you have the latest and greatest smartphone? Steph has a feature phone that just allows her to talk and text, not surf the Web or do e-mail. She knows what she needs and she sticks to it.

- In a similar way, do you really need the most expensive pay-TV package? Try dialing back on your programming or cutting the cord. You can get network TV with an over-the-air antenna and supplement some Internet programming on the cheap from sites like Netflix.com or Hulu.com.

- Ask yourself this question: What's a need and what's really just a want in your life? I want you to sit down and make a detailed list of both. Put the list aside for a day or so and then come back to it. Having that time away from it will allow you to really reflect on what you need and what you just want. You'll be able to see both clearly and then budget accordingly.

Don't shy away from sweat equity.

- Steph wasn't afraid to learn how to build her own website or put in the time to paint the walls at her dental practice. If there is something you know you can do with just a little extra effort, why not give it a try to save money? Stepping a little bit outside your comfort zone can keep more money in your life. As Steph told me, "I'm not too proud to scrub my own floors or try to fix something that's broken. Why pay someone else if you can do it yourself?"

Have the right role models.

- Like many of us, Steph gives credit to her parents for modeling thrifty behavior during her upbringing. But not everybody has the best role models at home. What about a close friend or distant relative? Is there someone in your life who is handling money well? Study what they're doing. Talk to them about the way they manage their finances. If you want to live below your means, you probably don't want to hang around with somebody who spends like there's no tomorrow. Find a better role model. The right people can help you along your way to financial freedom.

EL CHEAPO MAN
AND WIFE

*Living below their means gives Matt and Jamie the
freedom to enjoy small splurges*

WHEN I SPEAK ABOUT why it's important to save money and spend less than you earn, I try to explain the benefits of that choice. Some people, unfortunately, equate saving with sacrifice—not getting what they want or the lifestyle they want.

So I present to you Matt and Jamie Cowan, a New Mexico couple who live beneath their means and enjoy a wonderful life with lots of freedom and very little stress.

Matt, forty-one, is a lieutenant colonel and the director of the pharmacy at Kirtland Air Force Base in Albuquerque, New Mexico. His wife, Jamie, has a marketing degree and has worked for several companies, mostly in retail, but is currently a stay-at-home mom to the couple's two young children.

Matt says socking away money gives him and Jamie the freedom to make choices that are right for them. For example, during a break in his service from the air force back in 2004, Matt was working for a pharmacy automation company.

"I was in the process of returning to active duty service in six months but received a surprise when I was one of twenty-five people laid off," Matt recalled.

Instead of worrying about how to feed his family or pay his bills, Matt took a part-time job with a retail pharmacy and used the time off to take his family on a seven-day trip to London and Paris. His low expenses and money in the bank gave him the freedom to make that choice.

"We believe this freedom allows us to take advantage of opportunities as they arise and will eventually put us in a position to work because we want to and not because we have to," Matt said.

Another outstanding benefit of living beneath their means is the lack of financial stress in their marriage.

"We simply do not argue about money," Matt said. "Overall, I cannot put a value on the amount of psychological income this generates. My disclaimer is that my wife did question me a little when I bought a six-month supply of cereal during one trip to the commissary when it was available to buy with a coupon for $1.05 a box."

Fortunately for Matt, his wife shares his financial values.

"She is motivated and understands the principles, but thankfully to a lesser degree than I do. Her strength is derived from working at retail clothing stores. She is great at price adjustments and finding the deals on clothing."

Jamie has also done a great job with yard sales and selling the stuff that the kids have outgrown, Matt said. One of her latest moves was to purchase a trampoline, in great shape, for $80.

"I credit premarriage counseling and her father for us being on the same page. Her wonderful dad gave her the book *Smart Couples Finish Rich* by David Bach and recommended that she read it. This generated some good discussions and got us off to a good start."

Their kids are learning to be like Mom and Dad. The oldest loves finding money on the ground, Matt said, and after she lost her first tooth, she looked forward to a future visit from the Tooth Fairy. Her comment: "I hope my pillow bleeds money."

As for his youngest child, Matt said, "the financial fire does not burn as bright yet," but he is hopeful.

Matt earns a very good living, about $132,000 a year, including base pay of $7,763 a month, an annual retention bonus of $15,000, and monthly base allowances for food ($240) and housing ($1,764).

But he wasn't always doing so well. He joined the air force in 1995 as a second lieutenant, making about $28,000 while his classmates graduated and took jobs for $55,000 a year.

"My long-term financial view at that time, desire to serve, and the fact that I did not have any student loan debt allowed me to take a job that was not just about the money," he said.

Matt still has no debt. He and Jamie spend about $3,500 a month, with their top five expense categories being housing (17 percent), vehicle/gas (13 percent), travel (11 percent), food/restaurants (10 percent), and merchandise supplies (44 percent). They run most of their expenses through their Costco American Express credit card, to earn cash back, and pay the bill in full each month.

"We have been receiving about $65 a month back out of $134 allotted for utilities because of low energy use—I guess those CFLs I bought at Costco for 84 cents have helped decrease our electric bill."

That leaves plenty of room to save. Matt and Jamie save 35 percent to 40 percent of their gross income, contributing the maximum amounts to their Roth IRAs and Thrift Savings Plan (TSP) federal retirement account. They have savings and investments valued at $630,000.

"I started maxing out my IRA in 1995," Matt said. "A deployment in 2010 allowed for a $49,000 contribution and the conversion of my IRAs to a Roth with minimal taxes because of very, very low net income that year. I am quite proud of those moves."

Everyone knows how frugal I am. I once bought a Jacksonville Jaguars sweatshirt just because it was only $3! Think about it: I got a logo sweatshirt for less than I could buy a non-logo sweatshirt. And I still wear that sweatshirt proudly to this day!

Matt shows his frugality by telling people he'd rather have two dollars, the cost of a greeting card, instead of the card.

"Before we were married, Jamie and her mother made me a card out of two one-dollar bills with a note inside. It was a great moment."

Matt drives a 2001 Subaru Forester that he purchased used for cash, and he tells people he has transportation rather than a car. A splurge for him might be a nice restaurant when coupons are not used or the purchase of tickets to a play.

"A future splurge will likely have to be a smartphone," he said. "The lobbying has begun."

Matt and Jamie would like to have saved $1.6 million by age sixty, which would allow him to work part-time "for the sake of my mental and social well-being. Plus, I figure the extra money will allow for the splurges."

For now, he said, "I feel good that my family is provided for while enjoying a comfortable lifestyle and a good quality of life. My wife and I are very thankful."

Thanks for your service, Matt! You're outstanding in so many ways.

Reduce the small expenses one step at a time.

- Market research firm Accounting Principles found Americans spend nearly $1,100 annually drinking coffee away from home and another $1,900 eating lunch out. That's $3,000 a year!
- Say you're used to going to a fancy coffee place every day. What if you skip it one day a week and brew a cup at home? That's a few hundred bucks back in your pocket every year. Same thing with lunch. Brown-bag it one day a week and you'll have close to an extra $500.
- Between the two, that could be $700 or $800 back in your pocket annually. Once you get used to brewing at home and brown-bagging lunch one day a week, maybe you'll do it twice a week, and then you're up to over $1,000 saved.

Control your spending in stores.

- I have a no-cart rule when I'm shopping at retail. I just use my arms; whatever I can carry in them limits what I buy. When something catches my eye as I'm walking to the checkout, I have to assess what I'm bear-hugging and decide what I want to put back. I use that as a way to control my wants. Plus, I like to shop in stores with concrete floors. If I'm in a fancy store, I know I'm paying for the rarefied environment with higher prices. So I avoid them.

Adopt a lifestyle of voluntary simplicity.

- There's a book called *Money Secrets of the Amish* by Lorilee Craker, and one thing the author heard again and again from her Amish interview subjects was "Use it up, wear it out, make do or do without."
- How do you put that into practice in your own life? Go back to basics: Never borrow money for lifestyle. Never make purchases through those "*no* payment, *no* down payment, and *no* interest until . . ." plans that are so popular at furniture stores, electronics stores, and elsewhere. You want to buy with real money—not with borrowing.
- I don't want you to have the "I owe, I owe, so off to work I go" mentality in today's economy. Jobs can be shaky these days. What happens if you're suddenly without one?

Teach your kids about money.

- If you have a family, like Matt and Jamie, you've got to teach your kids about money or they'll learn their lesson at the school of hard knocks. Unfortunately, one talk won't get the job done with your kids. You have to do it every time a teaching moment arises.
- One of my favorite things to do is sit down with a dollar in coins and ask, "How much of this goes for housing? For our car? For our food?" Pretty quickly kids realize the dollar is gone and we haven't even talked about a present for them yet! You use finite resources that a kid can get their hands on to teach them.
- There's no one formula, no one way to teach your kids. You have to keep trying to meet them at their level to increase their knowledge and responsibility. For more tips on how to have a financially healthy family, see the Family chapter.

ENTREPRENEURSHIP

Everybody wants to be their own boss, right? While getting there is possible, it isn't easy. In this chapter, we meet entrepreneurs who are billionaires and those who are just starting out. Each shows us how to travel that hard road of generating an idea, product, or service; finding the funding to make it a reality; and then nurturing it over time.

SELF-MADE MAN

*Fired at thirty-five, Arthur Blank goes on to co-found
one of the world's most successful companies*

IT WAS 1978, AND ARTHUR BLANK had just received some bad news. He picked up the phone to call his wife, Diana, to tell her that he and his mentor and friend, Bernie Marcus, had just been fired. Blank, thirty-five, had been vice president of finance, and Marcus was president, of Handy Dan Home Improvement Centers, which at the time was the largest and most successful chain of home improvement stores in the country.

"She started laughing, thinking I was joking with her," Blank recalled. "Eventually, after she started getting phone calls at the house from business media reporters, she realized it was true."

And that is the beginning of one of the most remarkable stories in the annals of American business. Blank and Marcus rebounded from their Handy Dan firings to found The Home Depot Inc., the world's largest home improvement retailer, the sixth largest retailer in the United States, and the eighth largest retailer in the world. As I write this, the company is valued at more than $89 billion.

Blank also went on to purchase the NFL's Atlanta Falcons, and he and Marcus, both billionaires, have become noted philanthropists.

Yet back in 1978, he was shocked about being fired because he didn't see it coming.

"Bernie got caught in the middle of a political situation and power struggle with the chairman of Daylin Corporation, which was the parent company of Handy Dan," Blank said. "His name was Sandy Sigoloff, and internally he was known as Ming the Merciless, a title that actually made him proud."

Instead of looking for another executive position, Blank decided to tap into his inner entrepreneur.

"I was young and confident enough to know there would be other opportunities for me. A friend asked me to open a CPA practice with him, but I didn't want to go in that direction. And I had offers to run other retailers. . . . But Bernie and I decided to stick together and build something on our own."

The two started out by sketching their ideas on a clean sheet of paper in a local coffee shop, and eventually came up with a business plan.

"Bernie and I always knew the kind of home improvement retailer that Handy Dan would not be able to compete with: a large-format, deep-discount, high-service home improvement retailer. So we already had a Home Depot–type formula in our heads."

For Blank, the seeds of his Home Depot success were planted early. Blank's dad, Max, a neighborhood pharmacist, died of a heart attack when Arthur was just fifteen. Max was only forty-four.

It was a formative moment for the young entrepreneur-in-the-making. Max Blank had little life insurance, and his death forced Arthur's mother, Molly, to take over Sherry Pharmaceutical, the mail-order pharmacy business that Max had created.

As Blank recounts in *Built from Scratch*, the story of the founding of Home Depot, his mother, despite having no business experience, did a very good job. She grew the tiny enterprise into a business with several million dollars in volume.

"She showed us by example that with hard work and resilience, you can be successful," Blank said.

Blank's parents, and his mother in particular, instilled values in him and his brother, Michael, as youths that shaped their adult lives.

"She also taught us the value of giving back. We had very little financially when I was growing up, but my mother always found a way to give back to the community, to help others. 'You are your brother's keeper,' she would say. Everything we do in life is a gift. It's our responsibility to share that gift, and to give back what we can to the world." Today, at ninety-seven years old, she would say the same thing.

"So I think it was probably a combination of confidence, values, and some good DNA passed on from both my parents that molded me."

In college, Blank started a couple of small ventures. He paid for his education in part by starting a landscaping business. He also ran a dry cleaning– and laundry-delivery business.

He earned a degree in accounting in 1963 and postponed joining the family business to take a job with the Big Eight accounting firm Arthur Young & Company. A few years later, he decided to join the family business to help his mother and brother. But working with family was hard. His mother eventually sold the business to Daylin Corporation, and a couple of years later, Arthur became chief financial officer of Elliott's Drug Stores/Stripe Discount Stores.

Blank soon became president of the division. Then, in 1974, Daylin went through some tough times and sold several divisions, including Blank's. That's when Bernie Marcus, who had met Blank at Daylin corporate events, called with an invitation.

"I joined Handy Dan in 1974, at Bernie's request, as corporate controller, and had worked my way up to vice president of finance—effectively their CFO—at the time we were fired, which was in 1978."

Together, Blank and Marcus came up with their idea for Home Depot, a big-box store that would have a huge variety of home improvement items, great service, and very low prices.

"Bernie and I were an interesting duo because, while we both had a high degree of confidence in ourselves, we also had enough humility to realize we didn't have all the answers. I think one of the key reasons Home Depot became so successful is because we hired the best people we could find and listened to them. More importantly, we listened to our customers and then *responded* to them. It's a pretty simple formula, but you'd be surprised at how many mistakes are made in business by giving customers what we *think* they want as opposed to what they *say* they want."

(Somebody like Apple innovator Steve Jobs is obviously the ultimate exception to this rule. He came up with products that people didn't even know they wanted but then went on to crave.)

Getting funding for their new venture wasn't easy, because, Blank said, they were selling a dream rather than a financial model.

"We didn't make it about hammers, nails, lumber, etcetera; it was about fixing people's problems and making their dreams come true."

After a number of failed attempts to attract investors, co-founder Ken Langone was able to put together a group of investors who provided the seed money for the business to get started.

The challenges were many for Blank and Marcus in the early entrepreneurial days of Home Depot. For one, most of the inventory in the first store was fake.

"We didn't have enough capital to fully stock the stores—to create the wow factor we needed—so we borrowed empty boxes from one of our vendors to put on the top racks, and we stacked empty paint cans ten feet high."

Even with some money, convincing vendors to supply the new company with merchandise wasn't easy.

"For some vendors, it took years to convince them to sell their products to us. Kohler, the kitchen and bath products supplier, is a good example. We knew we needed products like Kohler's to satisfy our customers. I don't know how many meetings, dinners, and attempts at wooing Herb Kohler it took, but I know it took us years to convince him."

Believe it or not, Home Depot's founders had a hard time in those early days getting customers to come into their stores.

"On the day we opened our first two stores in Atlanta, we kept our kids out of school and put them in the parking lot of our stores handing out seven hundred one-dollar bills to entice customers in. I remember thinking we'd be able to get the kids back to school by lunchtime, but by the end of the day they were still in the parking lot—with the money. Bernie, Pat Farrah—a co-founder and our senior merchant—and I met for lunch that day and just looked at each other. Our big day had not gone as we had planned."

The company's first two stores got off the ground much more slowly than they had anticipated, and the company went through half of its seed money in the first nine months of operation, Blank said.

Home Depot's advertising also wasn't paying off—customers just weren't showing up. Then, one of their ideas clicked.

"Pat Farrah had an opportunity to buy a truckload of fireplace screens at a greatly reduced price. Rather than applying a normal markup, Pat marked them up just two dollars and placed an ad in the newspaper. A fireplace screen that normally sold for $139 was advertised for $35, and people came in droves to buy them. We sold out in four days."

After that, word of mouth started to take hold.

"People drove to our stores from faraway cities because someone had told them about our big stores, great prices, and great service. That also led us to change our advertising focus from products to more of the Home Depot "concept," meaning the size of the store, the scale of inventory, and the levels of service.

"All of these things put us on the right path," Blank said.

So what advice does one of America's greatest entrepreneurs have for people who want to start their own business?

"Find something you believe in and have a passion for," said Blank. "Be resilient during setbacks, and develop the ability to handle adversity. Surround yourself with people who share your vision and can work together to make it happen.

"Finally, don't buy into the notion that it's too difficult to start a new business in today's environment. The things that made Home Depot successful—wide assortment, low prices, great service—are not restricted by the government, bankers, or SEC regulations. Let the attorneys, board members, and bankers worry about those constraints. Our country needs people with the creativity, unencumbered minds, and risk-taking personalities to carry on the American Dream."

What lessons can you draw from Blank's story?

Be prepared to rebound from setbacks.

- Blank's road to the top wasn't always paved smoothly and yours probably won't be, either. The Home Depot co-founder got axed from Handy Dan before he and Bernie Marcus could regroup and flesh out the concept for what would be a mainstay of American capitalism. So often in life we need to face adversity to rise above it. Every setback in business is a learning experience. When you're an entrepreneur and something doesn't go as you planned, you need to ask yourself, "What did I do wrong and how can I improve it next time?"

Gain industry experience.

- After the Handy Dan firing, Blank didn't choose to launch a new business in some field that he hadn't the first clue about. He went back to basics in home improvement retailing, the very market that he had been unceremoniously booted from. And therein lies the lesson: Know your market intimately.
- If you're an entrepreneur eyeing a field that's ripe for your idea, product, or service, I want you to consider first working in that field for somebody else. This is particularly true in franchising, but also when you're talking about a built-from-scratch operation like Home Depot. Don't let your employer know your plans. You want to learn on their dime and make mistakes on their dime, not on yours, until you perfect your vision.

Use loss leaders to build a customer base.

- In the company's early days, Home Depot struggled until they hit on the idea of deeply discounted fireplace screens to get potential customers excited. In business, that's what's called a "loss leader."

- It's the idea that you offer a low price on a product or service to introduce your business to new clients. The goal is to build repeat customers who get wowed by what you have to offer at regular price.

- Daily-deal websites like Groupon tried to make the idea of loss leaders viral. But the shortcomings of that approach are now apparent; too many people tend to buy the face value of the coupon being offered and not a penny more, and they don't often make the conversion from one-time customers to long-term clients.

- You probably don't want to advertise your loss leader in a newspaper like Home Depot did. But you could use Facebook. Consumers are increasingly looking to the social media world, particularly Facebook, to deliver the deals from businesses they like.

Romance your employees.

- Most successful capitalists get that way because they use enlightened self-interest. They romance their employees so the employees will romance their customers—in a non–sexual harassment sort of way, of course!

- My late dad always used to say about business, "It's never the horse, it's the jockey." The idea is that it isn't the product or service you're selling, but how you execute your business and treat people who work for you.

- After Blank's tenure at the company, Home Depot started lagging in the customer service department. Bob Nardelli had come in and fired the full-time employees. They hired cheaper part-timers who didn't have nearly the level of experience or knowledge to offer customers. As a result, sales suffered mightily, and Home Depot has spent the last few years trying to undo the damage now that Nardelli is gone.

- In business, you've got to execute. And that always starts and ends with how you treat your employees.

DRESS FOR SUCCESS

Raymond turns T-shirts into treasure with $2,000

RAYMOND LEI MIGHT not be a millionaire just yet. Like many people, he prefers not to discuss such details of his personal finances.

But he's been successful enough as a small business owner to have "unenrolled" from the University of California at Berkeley during his second year to focus on his innovative T-shirt business, ooShirts.com.

What's innovative about a T-shirt company? Well, Raymond doesn't actually design the shirts, nor does he print them himself. Raymond, who started the business while in his junior year of high school, uses a network of screen-printing shops to make the shirts. Customers design them on his website using software developed by a programmer from India that Raymond hired with his $2,200 start-up investment.

Raymond, who was still just twenty-one when I interviewed him, is the California-born child of two computer engineers. His mother works at Broadcom Corp. and his father works at a small Web company.

He came up with the idea for ooShirts.com while ordering T-shirts for his high school's tennis club.

"I searched endlessly for a company to order from but was never able to find one that had both solid quality and reasonable prices," he said. "It was very frustrating to be unable to find good prices on such a commonly bought item, so I decided to do some research on my own."

Raymond's digging confirmed what he suspected: The T-shirts themselves weren't that expensive to print; it was the inefficient practices of printing companies that drove their prices up.

So just months later, he decided to start his own company.

His goal was modest—to sell affordable printed T-shirts to other student clubs at his school.

He did that and more. The company has grown to include six employees and now has annual revenue of more than $3 million.

One of Raymond's biggest challenges early on was getting the word out to potential customers, a challenge that faces many new companies.

"Part of the way I managed to make our prices low was by making our margins lower," he said. "Though this meant lower prices for customers, it also meant I had less money to spend on advertising."

However, over a couple of years, the company's website became more and more accessible to customers through search engines, he said, and it started getting a lot of repeat and word-of-mouth customers.

Raymond used his computer savvy to improve his rankings on search engines when people entered search terms such as "custom T-shirts."

He doesn't claim to fully understand the complexities of search algorithms. He said search engines basically rank a site by seeing how many other sites link to it.

"In the very beginning, we had very few customers and very little potential to attract links, so we were ranked poorly. Many new websites face this problem. But over time, as people started using our service and being very happy with it, we started seeing more and more links build up."

Raymond doesn't profess to have a magic formula for building high rankings.

"I think that if you focus on building a great website and on satisfying your existing customers, then, over time, you'll see search engines pick up on these natural signals and reflect it in their rankings."

Raymond loves everything about owning a business. He loves that he's built something from nothing and loves the creativity he can express, the control he has over where the company goes, and the excitement that comes with growth.

"The company's success, in the end, is measured by how much value it provides to others," he told me.

Raymond has no interest in going to work for an employer. Whether tomorrow or ten years from now, he expects to spend his energies building a company, whether it's ooShirts or something new.

"This applies until I'm sixty, give or take twenty years."

Despite Raymond's success, he lives modestly. He has a studio apartment in Berkeley that includes a sofa from Costco, a desk from IKEA, a mattress from a discount store, and a computer he built himself. He says his total expenses are roughly $2,000 a month.

His parents have supported and encouraged him along the way. "Despite being academically focused when I was younger, my parents were actually the ones that gave me the idea to drop out of school," he said.

I asked Raymond if he has any entrepreneurial role models. He named Amazon's Jeff Bezos, Zappos's CEO Tony Hsieh, Elon Musk of the Silicon Valley–style space transport company SpaceX, the fictional billionaire Tony Stark (aka Iron Man), and "whoever is in charge of Costco." (Costco co-founder James Sinegal retired at the end of 2011 and was succeeded by Craig Jelinek.)

One of the big lessons to take away from Raymond's success is that you don't need a lot of capital to start a business. ooShirts.com is what's known as an "ultra-light start-up," the kind of company that lets entrepreneurs use the power of the Internet to get started on the cheap. Ultra-light start-ups leverage every creative technique and the use of the Internet to do everything for free or for very low cost.

Everything Raymond is doing is based on holding down the use of capital and at the same time generating revenue. It's not the easiest thing to do, but it is possible.

"Having so few resources at the very start forced me to value efficiency more than entrepreneurs with more funding," Raymond said. "I think that frugality has stuck with the company. It's this constant drive to produce more for less that's causing the company to grow today."

Here are some tips to keep in mind if you would like to launch an ultra-light start-up:

Get a business plan in place.
- If you need help writing a business plan, the Service Corps of Retired Executives (SCORE) is a group of volunteers who provide free advice and counseling to people who

want to start a business, grow an existing business, or are in trouble with a business they already have.

- Depending on the chapter near you, a SCORE mentor will either meet with you or you can attend a class on how to write a business plan. Visit SCORE.org to get started.

Find the talent you need to realize your idea

- When Raymond launched ooShirts.com, he didn't design the website himself—he hired somebody else to do it. Thanks to technology, you too can hire the best tech, design, marketing, accounting, and back office freelance contractors to help you realize your business idea.
- Sites like crowdSPRING.com, Elance.com, Guru.com, and oDesk.com let you post a job and field bids from qualified vendors around the world. These sites are in a category called "virtual hiring halls" because they're a modern adaptation of the union hall idea where workers would go to await job orders.

Get a free website for your small business.

- If you don't have a website these days, it's like you don't exist to your potential customers. Thankfully, it's easier than you might have heard to establish a Web presence if you don't want to hire someone like I suggested above. Google has teamed up with Intuit for a joint venture called "Get Your Business Online." Simply log on to gybo.com. You'll get free twelve-month access to an easy-to-build Intuit website, a customized domain name, a year's worth of free Web hosting, and more.
- After the first year, you'll have to pay $2 per month for your domain name and $5 per month for hosting. Additional e-mail support is available for $8 a month after the first thirty days.

Get financing from someone who knows your business.

- If you're an ultra-light start-up visionary, the last place you probably want to get capital is at a big bank. You need somebody who thinks and works like you do. That's where a site like Kabbage.com—an online lender exclusively dedicated to online businesses— comes in.
- The Kabbage application process is streamlined and simple. Among other factors, they'll look at your transaction history as an Amazon or eBay merchant, user feedback ratings, and even your social media participation to make a decision on your loan application.
- Upon approval, the money is issued through PayPal in just minutes. One caveat, though: The interest rate is only marginally good, sitting at somewhere between 10 and 18 percent.

Go mobile for your credit card payments.

- Let's say you're a vendor at an arts and crafts fair, or you have a hot dog pushcart in a busy downtown area, or you're some other kind of merchant who doesn't do business at a fixed location. You can accept credit card payments from customers using a little mobile credit card processor that plugs into a smartphone. Below are some no-contract services where the plug-in device itself that you use to run the card is completely free; you just pay per transaction with no contract.

- SquareUp.com for Apple and Android phones charges a simple flat merchant fee of 2.75 percent on every swiped transaction. PayPal Here (PayPal.com/Here) for Apple and Android phones charges 2.7 percent, though if you do more debit card transactions than credit card transactions, you can lower your transaction cost to about 1.7 percent. And Intuit's GoPayment.com for Android, iPhone, and BlackBerry charges 2.7 percent per swipe.

DYING—EVERYBODY'S DOING IT

Mike turns a personal tragedy into a thriving business to help grieving families

WHEN I WROTE MY FIRST BOOK back in 1993, I included a section on funerals. Some might consider that a strange topic for a consumer book. But I've always been troubled by how, at a very vulnerable time in a person's life—after the death of a loved one—they are required to make a very large purchase with almost no information to help them.

So I was very interested to hear about a new business, eFuneral.com, that gives consumers price quotes and service reviews to help them make these tough but important decisions.

Co-founder Mike Belsito came up with the idea for eFuneral in October 2010, after the unexpected death of his cousin Ed.

Amid the shock of Ed's death, Mike and his family had to figure out how to plan a funeral. Which of the twelve funeral homes near where they lived in Cleveland, Ohio, should they choose? How willing would each funeral home be to work within their budget?

"We ultimately selected a funeral home to work with and moved forward—but the lack of information we had going into making that decision bothered me," Mike said.

Later, Mike recalled how he and his wife had tried a new restaurant, making their decision based on positive reviews they had read online.

"It bothered me that we actually had more information to use to make a decision about which restaurant to choose for dinner than we did for Ed's funeral service—something that was certainly more important and two hundred times more in cost."

So Mike and his business partner, Bryan Chaikin, started eFuneral. They expanded from Cleveland to Columbus and Dayton, and have launched in other cities around the country.

Some have described eFuneral as the "Angie's List of funeral homes."

"We've heard that several times, and we're pretty flattered," said Mike. "Angie's List has built its reputation as a company that brings more consumer transparency to the industries it is involved in, and that's certainly our goal with eFuneral."

Unlike another entrepreneur we profile in this book, T-shirt company founder Raymond Lei, Mike and Bryan started eFuneral with a fair amount of capital. As of June 2012, they had raised $600,000 in funding from various sources—including grants, low-interest loans, and investments from angel investors and a venture capital group.

That funding was enough for them to quickly build a team of five full-time employees, develop their initial release of eFuneral, launch it into a handful of markets, and give them a runway to continue to develop their idea.

To alleviate their quite natural fear of inviting investors into their company, Mike and Bryan attended a local accelerator program called 10xelerator, which helped them prepare for the process of raising this kind of start-up or "seed" money.

"Even still, fund-raising was perhaps one of the areas that we greatly underestimated in terms of how much time and energy would be required."

As innovators trying to make a go of it in a very traditional business, the eFuneral founders confirmed some theories but found some surprises.

After getting to know dozens of funeral directors in Ohio and other states, they confirmed their assumption that most funeral directors rely on personal relationships they have built in their communities. They still spend money on marketing to families—but the methods are mostly traditional (including television advertising and Yellow Pages advertising).

"One of the things that surprised us has been how willing individuals are to use an online service like ours to compare funeral options," Mike said. "At this point, we've seen all types of individuals and organizations that are not only intrigued by eFuneral, but are actively using it to help ease the process of funeral planning."

The reaction from funeral homes has been mixed. Mike says some love eFuneral because it helps set them apart from their competitors.

"Of course, since some funeral homes don't even have websites or e-mail addresses, they have been more hesitant, mostly because of their fears of utilizing such technologies."

I've always been a fan of funeral and memorial societies, which allow consumers to preplan—but not prepay—funerals so they don't have to make decisions, or have family make decisions, when they are beset by grief. (See Funerals.org for more info.)

"We think funeral and memorial societies are great but serve a bit of a different purpose," Mike said. "Most burial and memorial societies are very much focused on providing pricing information, which is one part of the equation."

The other part, of course, is service: eFuneral provides verified reviews to evaluate service quality, and gives people price quotes for the specific services they want.

"By going through our process, individuals can learn more about the various options and request a quote for the specific services they need," he said.

Mike runs eFuneral with his partner, Bryan. So I was curious to see how they divide their responsibilities, and whether Mike has any advice for people who are thinking about starting a business with a partner.

Mike said Bryan oversees all technical aspects of the business while he oversees business functions.

"But we stay very close together to ensure that we're on the same page. Our desks are literally a few feet away from each other—and we have both daily and weekly meetings to stay focused."

And the advice part? Mike said having a partner can be great.

"When you go through the inevitable ups and downs of creating a start-up company, having somebody with you in the trenches can provide a great benefit. More than that, having a partner allows you to go farther, faster. There would be no way that eFuneral could have achieved some of the technological innovations we have if it weren't for my partner. He's a 'tech guy,' and innovating through technology is what he does."

And the downside?

"I will say that, in many ways, having a business partner is very similar to being involved in a marriage. In fact, Bryan and I end up spending more time together than we do with our respective wives. Because the business partner relationship is so important, it's essential that one doesn't make the decision of partnering with somebody without a lot of thought."

Mike said there are actually "founder matching" events where people looking for business partners can hook up with somebody, and on that very night link up to become partners. That would be like going to a speed dating session and deciding to marry your speed date that night.

"Regardless of how you find a partner," he said, "just be sure to have complete trust in that person, and they in you, before you decide to take that leap together."

What should you know if you want to start a business with a partner?

Find a partner at your own speed.

- If you're going to have a partner, it's key that you have the right one. When you sign up at free sites like StartUpWithMe.com and FounderDating.com, they'll screen potential co-founders to make sure they're not looking to poach your talent and suggest matches based on complementary experience, skills, and expectations.

Consider working with a start-up accelerator.

- Mike and Bryan used 10xelerator—a start-up accelerator program out of Ohio State's Fisher School of Business in Columbus, Ohio—to get up and running. There are organizations like this around the country providing professional development, networking, training, consulting, and other opportunities for entrepreneurs. Visit GlobalAccelerator Network.com to find one near you.

Get start-up capital online.

- Peer-to-peer lending sites like Prosper.com and LendingClub.com can help when you're looking for start-up capital. With sites like these, you're borrowing money directly from individuals, not banks, at an interest rate determined by your creditworthiness.
- A new evolution called "crowdfunding" is the latest wrinkle in bankless borrowing. With crowdfunding, you let others know about your business idea online with an appeal for funds. Kickstarter.com is the most popular crowdfunding portal, but if you don't get 100 percent funding for a potential project, you get no money at all. IndieGoGo.com, on the other hand, allows you to get whatever money is pledged even if you don't reach 100 percent funding.

Consider the freemium model.

- "Freemium" is a very hot word right now. Under a freemium business model, especially when you're talking about a technology-based business model, you give away something for free and then require customers to pay for an upgrade if they want more of what you've got.
- For example, *The New York Times* reported that the iPhone game Temple Run wasn't getting a lot of downloads at 99 cents a pop. So the makers started offering it for free.

Suddenly, it had more than 40 million downloads. As the game makers discovered, when the game was initially given away for free, people ended up spending money to upgrade to a premium pay version over time.

Don't ignore your retirement.

- Nearly one-third of all entrepreneurs aren't saving anything at all for their retirement, according to a new survey from nonprofit The American College. They're too busy pouring every penny back into their business, thinking that will be their big score. Maybe, but maybe not.

- Here's my alternative: As a self-employed person, you have access to a simplified employee pension (SEP). The paperwork to set up a SEP is simple, and you can even open one at a low-cost investment house like Vanguard.com, Fidelity.com, or TRowePrice.com at no cost.

- SEPs work like a traditional IRA or 401(k), with a current year tax deduction. Withdrawals are taxed at retirement. SEPs also offer flexibility because you can put in from zero a year to as much as $51,000. That's helpful during the feast or famine start-up years. Don't miss this opportunity to save for your future! For more info on retirement planning, see the chapters on Retirement and Investing.

TRAVEL

Back in 1981, I launched a travel agency that grew into a chain with locations across metro Atlanta. In 1987, I sold the company at thirty-one and retired. Travel has remained a lifelong passion ever since.

In this chapter, we meet four people who I think have the idea of cheap travel down pat. In addition, I'll show you the latest and greatest ways to save money in an era of high airfares and fuel expenses.

AROUND THE WORLD
ON A DIME

*From Dumpster diving to couch surfing, Michael made a
once-in-a-lifetime journey to Antarctica*

MICHAEL WIGGE WAS SITTING on the couch at *The Tonight Show*. On his left was *Tonight Show* host Jay Leno. On his right was the beautiful singer Katy Perry. And Wigge was telling these highly paid celebrities about how he had completed the ultimate low-budget trip around the world—not just for very little money but for nothing at all.

Michael, thirty-six, a television travel reporter who grew up in Berlin, Germany, had wanted to visit Antarctica since childhood.

"It's one of the very few untouched places in the world and I really wanted to see it," he told Leno in his German-accented English.

I have been addicted to travel for most of my adult life. During that time, I've been to every continent *except* Antarctica. (Truth be told, I'm just waiting for the first McDonald's to go in at McMurdo Station before I make the trek!)

As Michael found out himself, you can't just fly from Berlin to Antarctica. You have to fly to Argentina, then take a luxury cruise ship there.

That got Michael to thinking. Maybe he could come up with a way to get there for free. And while he was at it, why not see the rest of the world as well?

Michael spent a year planning his adventure. With the help of more than one hundred people, he managed to get free food, free lodging, and free transportation for his 150 days across four continents and eleven countries.

He found free places to stay on CouchSurfing.com, a website that allows people to search for others who will let them sleep at their houses and apartments at no cost. And he found other ways. In the tiny Ohio village of Berlin, Amish farmers let him sleep in their barn.

For food, Michael would ask people to feed him, or go "Dumpster diving," looking for sealed packages of food that had been thrown away by supermarkets.

He crossed the Atlantic Ocean for free by working on a container ship. To get to other places, he hitchhiked. That's how he got from the Grand Canyon to Las Vegas.

If all else failed, he would offer his services in exchange for a meal or for cash. In San Francisco, Michael got two pillows and offered to have a pillow fight with people for one dollar. Fifty people took him up on it.

He ran into some trouble at the outset in his home country. While hitchhiking on a German highway, Michael had to go to the bathroom.

"So I went into the gas station," Michael told Leno in his *Tonight Show* appearance, "and it costs 50 cents." The attendant wouldn't let him use the toilet for free, so Michael found a nearby bush instead.

"The little things could be very difficult on that trip," he said.

Michael also had trouble at the Peruvian Inca attraction Machu Picchu, located high in the Andes. Michael wasn't in good physical condition, and the climbing, he said, was a nightmare.

His scariest moments were in Cusco, Peru, where he stayed in the house of a German expat.

"Unfortunately his apartment was on fire because of a problem with his self-built oven," Michael said. "We could leave the burning place early enough to rescue ourselves. But it was very scary and I had to stay outside all night long."

On the plus side, there was Colombia, which was "amazing," and where people welcomed him into their homes. And Hawaii. "I just love those islands," he said.

Michael learned some things about himself on the 25,000-mile journey.

"I learned to be on my own for a long time. I also learned to live without money by using the barter system. It was a great experience."

He also learned that most people in the world "tend to be nice and helpful."

Michael is back to using money, but he said he values small things much more than he did before the trip.

Michael grew up in the German countryside. His father was a truck driver.

"I often traveled with him throughout Europe. I think that made me start to like traveling a lot."

So what did he learn that could help people save money on travel, even if they don't want to hitchhike or rely on people to feed them for free?

You can go by the barter system, he says.

"If you want food, just offer to clean the store or at least tell a funny story. People will appreciate that."

He shares some of his tips on his website, HowToTraveltheWorldforFree.com.

He really likes CouchSurfing. "It's wonderful and people are trustworthy. I am going to use it again next week," he said.

One thing he learned not to do was get too dependent on one person.

"Always keep plan B and C in your pocket," he said.

What can you learn from Michael's unique perspective on travel?

Keep flexible on dates and destinations to save on travel.

- A great way to save money when you're going on vacation actually involves *not* planning.
- When I see a travel deal, my longtime philosophy has been to buy the deal first and then figure out why I want to go there. By doing that, I've gotten to visit every continent except Antarctica and every state except North Dakota. And I've done it on the cheap.
- Allow the deal to drive the vacation, because if you let the destination or the calendar drive the trip, you'll pay more.

The best time to book airfare is . . .

- There's some debate about whether you'll get a better deal booking forty-two days (six weeks) or twenty-one days (three weeks) out before your date of travel. My experience? Generally, both can be true. Those two times are points in the calendar with significant dips in fares. Particularly if you're flying to Europe, six weeks out is going to be a time to find a real deal.
- You can also define your departure and arrival points at websites like Kayak.com and Bing.com/Travel (formerly Farecast.com) and set up a fare alert. With a fare alert, you're automatically e-mailed when a good price pops up online wherever you want to go in the world. By the way, the Bing travel site also offers a price predictor that tells you if

fares are on their way up or down. That way you can know the optimal money-saving time to book.

Know the best money-saving travel sites.

- There's a new ranking of the best travel sites for bargains as decided by you, the traveler!
- Booking.com claims first place on the J.D. Power and Associates 2012 Independent Travel Website Satisfaction Report—though it's for accommodations only, not airfare. In second and third place, we have Hotwire.com and Priceline.com, respectively. Both of those sites are blind booking sites where you pay nonrefundable money before you find out where you're staying. I book more travel on Priceline than anywhere else, principally for hotels and cars.
- The traditional players like Orbitz.com, Expedia.com, and Travelocity.com were all in the middle of the heap. And two bargain sites for air travel didn't get great scores: cheapOair.com and CheapTickets.com.
- No one site will offer the best deals all the time. So you've got to shop around.

Go with easy blind booking for hotels.

- I detailed my complicated procedure for researching and bidding through Priceline and Hotwire for hotel rooms on pages 217–219 of my last book, *Living Large in Lean Times*. Fortunately, there's a site that basically automates my process and makes it much simpler.
- With TheBiddingTraveler.com, you pick the town where you want to stay and your dates of travel. Then you set the minimum you're willing to bid and the maximum you're willing to bid, plus you identify any neighborhoods in the area you're *not* willing to occupy.
- Many people don't like the idea of having no idea where they're going to stay (aka blind booking) until *after* they've paid nonrefundable money. Yet this is among the best ways to really save money on travel.
- TheBiddingTraveler.com can do in three minutes or less what takes me fifteen or twenty minutes (for select cities) to do. It is far superior to the way I have always booked my own rooms. Give it a try!

THE SAVVY BUSINESS TRAVELER

Professional road warrior Chris reveals his secrets for
scoring great deals on the go

WHEN CHRIS MCGINNIS was a child in the 1960s, he and his family would fly to Ottawa, Canada, for summer vacations at his mother's family lake house on Big Rideau Lake. They often took Eastern Airlines, which Chris knew as "the turquoise airline," while Delta Air Lines was "the blue airline."

He loved flying from the start.

"While my brother and sisters were frightened, pale, motion sick, and frequently putting 'barf bags' to good use, I was up and out of my seat, talking to passengers, checking out the different views from other windows, chatting up flight attendants, and scoring wings and decks of cards and occasional visits to the cockpit, something that is no longer allowed."

Decades later, Chris, now fifty-two, has a different view of travel as a well-known correspondent and consultant. He's been the business travel columnist for BBC and a travel correspondent on HLN, and now that he lives in San Francisco, he's the editor of the *Frequent Travel Advisor* blog on the *San Francisco Chronicle*'s website.

He's also the author of two books about business travel and appears frequently on TV, online, and in print offering tips and advice to those seeking the wisdom of the road warrior.

Chris started his career as a management consultant in the 1980s, at about the time when frequent flyer programs were ramping up. He designed a traveler training program for new employees at his company to help them deal with the rigors of the road.

"For most new employees, the extent of their frequent travel up to that point had been spring break to Florida or Mexico."

Eventually he took that idea and formed Travel Skills Group and offered a similar program to *Fortune* 500 companies. That resulted in a lot of media attention, and led to a newspaper column about business travel.

"That's how my writing career began. Eventually, due to my location in Atlanta [at that time], CNN began to call, and I parlayed that into gigs there as 'CNN's business travel expert' and travel correspondent for HLN."

Few people know more about business travel, so I asked Chris to share his expertise with me, and you, about the state of business travel today.

I wondered whether business travelers and their companies are more focused on saving money today, in the wake of the Great Recession, than they were years ago. But Chris believes they have always tried to find a happy medium between cost savings and traveler comfort.

"The focus is more about cost savings during lean times and traveler comfort in good times—and I've watched the tide turn three or four times since I've been covering the business travel beat since 1990.

"For example, the traveler who is worried that he or she might not have a job next year is likely to accept traveling in coach to Europe for an annual sales meeting. But a high-performing salesperson at a company reporting record profits who is flying to Europe to seal a multimillion-dollar deal or enter into a tough business negotiation is going to fly up front where he or she can get a good night's rest and be ready to hit the ground running."

Interestingly, Chris does not believe business travel is more difficult today than it was a generation or two ago.

"I know I'll get a lot of disagreement on this one, but having watched business travel closely over the last twenty years, I'm confident to say that business travel has improved enormously, and this has a lot to do with the transparency brought on by the Internet."

Chris says we have far more control over our trips than we used to—and control is all-important to the business traveler.

"Think of all the other advances we have now . . . Wi-Fi on planes; no smoking on planes; safer, newer hotels; big, bright airport terminals; seats that fold into flat beds for sleeping on overnight flights; modern trains from airport to city; a fast and easy rental car process. All of these were dreams of business travelers back in what many like to call 'the golden age of travel,' when everyone dressed up to fly. Hogwash!"

Chris has several key strategies he uses to save money on his travels. For one, when he's visiting big cities that have good transit systems, he'll avoid expensive downtown hotels by booking a hotel near a transit stop.

"These hotels usually have several reasonably priced restaurants in the vicinity, and most offer free Wi-Fi and a free breakfast. I also think that airline premium economy seats are a good value for your money—you typically have enough room to work on a laptop in premium economy, which makes it worth the extra cost."

One of his new favorite tools for savings is Hotel Tonight, an app that lets you book last-minute deals in a city you've just landed in—or if, as happens frequently in business travel, you end up having to stay over an extra night.

"For research, I like meta-search sites like Kayak.com that provide me with what the going rate is on airfare or a hotel in a given city. Once I know that, I'll go to the individual supplier site to make the booking."

To find a good place to eat in an unfamiliar city, he likes Eater.com. (My preference for user-generated reviews of local eateries wherever I go is Yelp.com.) And for travel trends and industry information, he's recently discovered Skift.com, which curates good business travel content.

"When I'm going to a new city for the first time, I like to buy (or download) the helpful (and gorgeously designed) DK Eyewitness Travel guides." Visit TravelDK.com to see what Chris is talking about.

Chris and I disagree a little bit on credit cards that offer travel miles as rewards. I'd rather you get a card that rewards you with cash, which you can then use for travel or any way you want. Chris thinks they're a nice way to build up points to redeem for free trips, "but since you typically only earn 'bonus points' they don't help achieve the holy grail of business travel, which is elite status."

On frequent flyer programs, Chris thinks it was a mistake for airlines to base the programs, and the perceived loyalty of their customers, on miles flown instead of dollars spent.

"Southwest, and more recently Delta, are the first major airlines to move in the direction of tying loyalty to dollars spent [so-called revenue-based programs], and I think other airlines will soon follow suit."

I believe using loyalty programs can end up costing you more than you might otherwise pay, but Chris says, "Once you reach elite levels with airline or hotel programs, I think the benefits, especially for business travelers, make it worth choosing a supplier based on program instead of price."

With hotels, Chris advises business travelers to always ask for a specific room when they check in.

"Get the person behind the desk involved in choosing a good room," he said. "If you don't, a computer will assign you a room that could be a dud. The person behind the desk knows which rooms are 'good' and which ones are not. Ask for something specific, like a room with a view, one away from elevators, or one away from the noise of the pool area—that way, they can't leave the choice up to the reservations system."

Chris doesn't do as much traveling today as he used to.

"My family is very proud of the fact that I've been able to create a company and a lifelong career doing what I love and being my own boss. But they don't like the fact that I'm away from home so much. And as I get older, I'm finding more joy on the home front, and only travel when I have to these days compared to before, when I was willing to jump on a plane anytime to anywhere for any reason."

Having heard Chris's story, what tips can you keep in mind to save money as a business traveler?

Get corporate-negotiated hotel rates as an individual.

- There's a particular site that I really like called QuikBook.com for business travel. Quik-Book began principally to offer small businesses and individuals access to corporate-type rates on hotel bookings. They're a big player in a handful of markets, including Boston, Chicago, Las Vegas, Los Angeles, Miami, New York, Orlando, San Diego, San Francisco, and Washington, D.C.
- They use a blind booking model with mystery rooms and you don't find out which hotel you're getting until after you pay nonrefundable money. But again, you can get a room at a price that's a fraction of what it would sell for otherwise to the average business traveler.

Know the best use of your rewards miles or points.

- I'm not a big fan of credit cards that offer frequent flyer miles or points toward a hotel stay, because the airlines and hotels are always raising the bar of what it takes to redeem a ticket. But I know people love them and many have a lot of miles to use up.

- If that sounds like you, there are several free websites that will take a scalpel to your rewards account to tell you the best use of your miles or points for a particular airline or hotel. These include MileWise.com, GoMiles.com (recently acquired by Traxo.com), and AwardWallet.com.

- You give these sites access to your loyalty accounts and they alert you to deals, warn you if any miles are expiring, and make suggestions about the optimal use of miles or points at any given moment. It's a great way to leverage the value in what you've got, though not every one of these sites works with every airline or hotel's loyalty program.

Re-shop your car rental before your trip.

- It's common that when somebody books an airline ticket, they also book their rental car. But rental car reservations are, as a general rule, fully changeable: You pay no money up front, just at the time you rent the car. So I routinely re-shop the rental car rate again a week before my trip—whether it's for business or pleasure.

- For example, my family and I recently went to Denver for a ski trip. I originally booked the car for a week at $273. But when I re-shopped just before the trip with another company, I found a rate of $99 including junk fees. Wow! That was a lot of money back in my pocket.

- Anecdotally, I'd say I save money at least 90 percent of the time by using this method. I can't say it works 100 percent of the time, because there are some times when it's actually more expensive. In that case, I just stay with my original booking.

- Finally, I want to tell you about a website called AutoSlash.com that will automatically track your car rental rate each day before a trip and rebook you at a cheaper rate when they find something better. AutoSlash only works with a limited number of rental companies, but it's still worth a look. (By the way, there's a similar service for hotels called Tingo.com that will book your room for you and then continually re-shop your rate. If a better deal pops up on your same room, they'll automatically rebook you at the new lower rate.)

Avoid add-on fees at the car rental counter.

- Be sure to investigate alternate ways you might be covered for temporary use of a rental car other than paying for add-on coverage.

- Car rental companies love to sell you what's called "collision damage waiver" (CDW). When you're at the rental counter, you will probably be warned about the consequences of not accepting the CDW, also known by the codes LDW (loss damage waiver) or

PDW (physical damage waiver). But certain credit cards or even your auto insurer will provide this coverage in lieu of the expensive add-on CDW coverage.

- Personal effects coverage might also be offered at the rental counter. This covers you in the event something is stolen from your vehicle. Again, you can forget about it; your credit card might cover you.

- Know before you go, and a call to your credit card company and your auto insurer is all it takes.

STAYCATION PARADISE

Tony and Peggy show that sometimes there really is no place like home

TONY BARTHEL AND HIS WIFE, Peggy, own the Featherbed Railroad Bed and Breakfast Resort in Nice, California. Nestled in Northern California's wine country, the Featherbed Railroad is a collection of nine restored cabooses for rent on a five-acre wooded property on the banks of the Clear Lake.

Each caboose that sits among the resort's centuries-old bay laurel trees has a unique theme.

La Loose Caboose is decked out in the lurid neon reds of a New Orleans bordello. The sign upon entering warns you to "Beware pickpockets and loose women."

Over in the Easy Rider caboose, the queen-size bed boasts a headboard made with motorcycle handlebars. Everywhere you look are the iconic orange, black, and chrome colors of Harley-Davidson.

Moving from Hog heads to Parrotheads, the TropiCaboose is decked out with a coconut color scheme, wicker furniture, and the music of Jimmy Buffett wafting in as if on a gentle breeze.

Many of the cabooses have in-room Jacuzzis and second-story cupola seating for two. The Featherbed takes its unique name from the genuine goose-down bedding that comes standard in all accommodations.

It's a great place for a staycation—if you happen to live in neighboring communities like Santa Rosa, Mendocino, Healdsburg, Calistoga, Ukiah, and Willits, or farther-flung cities like San Francisco and Sacramento.

But I decided to include Tony in this book because he had some solid tips for staycationers, based on his experience as a B&B owner, that he was willing to share.

The first thing Tony recommends is asking innkeepers if they have a "locals" mailing list that you can subscribe to for spur-of-the moment kinds of deals.

"Many lodging properties are more inclined to offer a discount last minute than they are for a reservation made months in advance. . . . At our place we have our mailing list divided up into several segments, including 'super locals.' These are people who can make a buying decision and be here within a very short period of time."

In addition, many properties make special deals available for their Facebook and Twitter fans. Tony recommends liking the page of your favorites to get in on the action.

"We also post specials [on social media sites] for last-minute getaways. . . . Obviously if you're planning a business trip months in advance, you can't get this, but if you're in the next neighborhood a deal happening this weekend is a good thing that one can, potentially, take advantage of."

Tony is even toying with the idea of taking the promotions one step further.

"I've also been considering setting up a text messaging system to send out messages for last-minute deals. A prospect or guest could ask the property if they've got a text messaging deal system in place. Apparently this is the wave of the future."

Another thing some staycationers forget to take advantage of is coupon books offered at properties. But that's a mistake. In fact, Tony says those kinds of coupons can work better for staycationers than for out-of-towners.

"Nobody can dine at ten restaurants while they're here for a couple of days, but they certainly can enjoy these coupons if they have stayed with us and live in the area. They can parlay these coupons into deals over time and, done right, completely work out the price of the room by savings on local products and services."

Even if the property you're staying at doesn't have a coupon book, many local businesses will offer discounts to guests of certain properties.

"So if someone goes out to eat or rents a boat or whatever, they should ask if there are discounts for guests of XYZ property," Tony says. "Oftentimes there will be, and they only have to show their key to take advantage of these."

Of course, one of the greatest things about staycations is the money you save on fuel when you're staying close to home!

Tony is a car enthusiast who once single-handedly self-syndicated his own newspaper column about automobiles to more than two hundred newspapers. Nowadays he does *Curb-*

side TV, an automotive blog and car show calendar that he lovingly refers to as "the pothole on the information superhighway."

He also wrote a book in 2007 called *Wedding Horror Stories (And How to Avoid Them)* that drew on his twenty-two years of firsthand experience as a mobile DJ in Southern California.

His wife, Peggy, meanwhile, has a master's degree in geology and once worked for a geotechnical construction services company while cleaning up Edwards Air Force Base. She did her master's thesis on the source of the groundwater in Zzyzx, California, at the Desert Studies Center in the Mojave Desert. (Rhyming with "Isaacs," this former spa settlement is the last word, literally, in the tally of names of places done by the United States Board on Geographic Names!)

Tony and Peggy became owners of the Featherbed five years ago. The Barthels had just sold their house in El Segundo, California, when they decided they wanted to build a B&B rather than wait to realize the retirement dream of owning one.

It was 2008 and they went under contract on a piece of property where they would construct their dream B&B. But fate intervened.

"We were in escrow on an avocado ranch and the whole thing burned down," Tony says.

Later at an innkeepers' conference, they learned it's better to buy than to build. So when Peggy saw the Featherbed for sale online, they visited—after convincing Tony to leave his beloved Southern California.

"We bought it in 2008 right at the worst time to buy a place," Tony concedes. "It had sat on the market for two years with no bids."

The rest is history. Today, their dogs Zora and Ginger roam the property barking at squirrels. And there's even Pippin, a resident desert tortoise named after one of the Hobbits in the J. R. R. Tolkien fantasy novel *The Lord of the Rings*, on the grounds!

Tony offered quite a few tips for staycationers. What else should you keep in mind if you're doing a staycation?

Take all the vacation you have coming.
- A new survey from Harris Interactive showed that the average American left nine days of vacation on the table in 2012. That's almost unbelievable. Compared to the Europe-

ans, we get almost no vacation at all. And here we have people forfeiting almost two full work weeks!

- We went through a phase where people were working themselves silly because they thought they'd be laid off if they took a vacation. While that might have been true in some cases, that trend has now mostly reversed, and people should be availing themselves of what's called "paid time off" (PTO) at many companies.

- I take a good amount of vacation. I believe it makes me a better employee. I'm just fresher for the next six weeks or so when I come back from vacation.

Don't overlook free attractions in metro areas.

- I know money still remains tight for many. Yet you can find a way to get away without having to break the bank or remain tethered to your home or apartment during a staycation. Popular options include going to state parks, renting a cabin, or even staying at an inexpensive motel.

- I recently spent a weekend in Boston with my seven-year-old son, Grant. He had the best time ever. At the monument at Bunker Hill, Grant ran all three hundred steps up to the top while all of us adults were huffing and puffing. The cost of Bunker Hill? Free.

- We also went to the USS *Constitution* for free. We walked the Freedom Trail and went to Boston Commons for free. The cost of the carousel at Boston Commons and souvenirs: $3 and $15, respectively. My point is there's something to do for either free or very cheap wherever you are.

Social media can help score a deal.

- As Tony points out, social media has become the "go to" way for travel providers to give out deals and for customers to get them. Particularly if you're flying U.S. full-fare airlines or discounters, you want to look at buying an airline ticket using social media. More and more specials are posted for those who friend or like an airline on Twitter or Facebook—not through the traditional outlets. That same holds true for vacation properties and rental car companies.

Use an app to save money on last-minute accommodations.

- If you're far from being someone who plans in advance, there's a new feature as part of Priceline's app for Android and iOS that could save you up to 35 percent on hotel bookings that same night.

- The new Tonight-Only Deals feature is the latest addition to the free Priceline Negotiator app. Unlike the way Priceline normally works, you know the name of the hotel *before* you book. You can book anytime from 11 a.m. to 11 p.m. in more than thirty U.S. cities with a maximum stay of four nights.
- Another app that offers similar last-minute booking deals is called HotelTonight. Visit HotelTonight.com for more details.

FAMILY

. . . .

From weddings to nursing homes, from car pools to soccer games, family life presents us with opportunities to save money . . . and spend too much of it if we're not careful. In this chapter, we meet four families who are struggling with financial challenges common to modern American life. Read closely and you're likely to recognize yourself. I'll share tips to help you stretch your family budget and raise Clark Smart kids every step of the way.

FULL HOUSE

It's diapers to degrees for Scott and Jeannine, raising five kids from ten months to twenty-two years

THE ROAR OF GIRLS is overpowering at the Leopold home in Dayton, Ohio.

There's a *Hannah Montana* video on YouTube, and Cecilia, eleven, Myrna, nine, and Rhiannon, two, are singing along at the top of their lungs and dancing to the music. Meanwhile, forty-year-old Scott and his thirty-eight-year-old wife, Jeannine, are walking ten-month-old Bernadette around on wobbly legs like she's Bambi. But wait, what's that? Their son Vincent, twenty-two, is halfway out the door and it's slamming behind him. He's Jeannine's from a prior relationship and he's running off to catch the bus to class at a local community college.

Scott and Jeannine first met in 1991, just six weeks after Vincent was born. His buddy's girlfriend invited her out for the night, and Scott vividly recalls picking her up at her parents' home in his blue 1980 Chevette during a night out with friends.

"When Jeannine opened the car door, it was like a light went on—figuratively and literally, thanks to the dome light," Scott says. "I knew instantly that I'd be asking her to marry me at some point. To put this in a bit of context . . . being a teenage mother was much more scandalous then than it is now, and the thought of a young Catholic guy bringing a girl like that home to meet his family was unheard of."

The couple married in 1996, and had their first child together in 2001.

Today there are a total of seven people living in the Leopold household at a time when the average population per U.S. household is 2.55 persons, according to U.S. Census Bureau data.

Scott works as a situation manager for Hewlett-Packard, overseeing resolution efforts for any major issues that arise with clients. And Jeannine works part-time two nights a week providing in-home care for older women with disabilities.

Together they meet all the financial challenges of family life on a combined household income that ranges from $60,000 to $70,000 annually.

How do the Leopolds do it? How do they handle the expense of a baby in diapers while another pursues a degree—not to mention the costs associated with every age in between?

With a lot of thrift, a lot of planning, and, unfortunately, a good amount of debt.

"Diapers are probably the biggest expense," Scott tells me. "As a result we tend to only buy store-brand diapers. Our son works for Kroger so we get a discount on those, which helps immensely."

Over the past few years, the Leopolds experimented with old-fashioned cloth diapers, but they simply couldn't stay on top of all the additional laundry that was created every day.

"With seven people in the house, an extra load each day adds up, especially when you can't include anything else in that extra load and have to run them on a long cycle."

The family's formula bills are very low because Jeannine breastfeeds. When they do use formula, it's a brand name. That's in violation of one of my rules for young parents, though they break that rule for a very good reason, it turns out.

"We had some bad experiences in the past with generics and other brands so we stick with Similac, although we do use coupons for that."

When it comes to clothing and toys, thrift stores are a given for the family.

"We once bought two large bags of clothes, equaling nearly twenty complete outfits, for under $20. Thrift stores and consignment shops are also excellent for books and toys. Hand-me-downs are a way of life for our kids. We've been lucky enough that some articles of clothing have held up well enough to last through all four girls."

Vincent is the only one of their kids old enough to drive. But like many people his age, he's not getting a license.

He needs to be driven to work and community college, or else he bums rides with friends. And as he pursues a degree in law enforcement, he pays for tuition and books himself—though his parents have covered some of his school bills the last couple of semesters when he came up short. But no student loans, thankfully!

A recent study out of the University of Michigan found that only two-thirds of teens now have a license at nineteen. Perhaps the high cost of auto insurance, maintenance, and gasoline has something to do with it.

This whole mind-set is alien to me and probably to many older Americans as well. When I was a teen, I counted the days until I turned sixteen and could get a license! But the benefit to kids like Vincent and so many others who are choosing not to drive is that the longer young motorists wait to get behind the wheel, the safer they tend to be.

"We gave him our old Buick for when he finally does decide to start driving," Scott says. "Up until early last year I continued to pay all insurance and maintenance costs on it, but we transferred those costs to him, partly in the hope that it would motivate him to drive, and partly because I was frustrated covering the costs for a vehicle he refused to touch."

The Leopolds work hard to stick to a budget. They plan meals at home, use coupons, and check the circulars to see which stores have the best deals that week. Product substitution is a biggie for them to maximize their savings.

"One thing we've also done recently is to quit buying lunch meat. Just before Christmas I was excited to find roast beef on sale. After a coupon, it was $5.99 per pound. I then walked past the meat department and saw that Angus roasts were on sale for $3.49 per pound, while pork, turkey, and ham ranged from 99 cents to $1.49 per pound. It put the $5.99 for the roast beef in a different perspective."

During the summer, the family supplements its weekly shopping with fresh fruit and vegetables from their garden. They harvest gallons of raspberries and plentiful bunches of tomatoes, in addition to strawberries and asparagus.

Yet no matter how many corners they cut, the Leopolds define themselves as struggling. They're currently paying off $42,000 in credit card debt, which is down from $72,000 almost ten years ago. Their combined minimum payments to service that debt are around $1,100, which is a few hundred dollars less than it was a decade ago.

"Eliminating that is our primary focus, although we do put a small amount aside each month for both our retirement and the girls' college," Scott says.

A lot of their debt was charged up because of dying appliances, unexpected medical bills, and surprise car repairs. They take their tax return each year and sink it toward a bill, but often a major appliance will give up the ghost right around the time of their return . . . and there goes that money.

Just as a side note, I would prefer that you *don't* get a big refund. If you are getting one, it means that you've made an interest-free loan to the government and your money has been working for them all year long, not you. Try slowly reducing your withholding at work instead. You want to ideally be even-steven—no refund and no money owed—when tax time comes.

Scott is well aware of the cultural backlash against larger families. He says he doesn't see his lifestyle reflected positively in our nation's current cultural dialogue.

"I think the general portrayal of large families is negative, and there's a great deal of misinformation out there about the associated costs of raising children," Scott says. "I believe that a big motivation for this is to discourage larger families."

"You'll regularly see reports talking about how much it costs to raise a child. If any of these were accurate, we wouldn't have been able to afford our son, let alone the four girls."

Still, he and Jeannine are happy to have been blessed with a larger family.

"It can be difficult at times, but the good always outweighs the bad."

As for the thought of more children, Scott says, "I'm definitely open to the idea of another baby."

We'll have to see what Jeannine says about that!

If you have a larger family with kids of varying ages, what can you learn from the story of Scott and Jeannine?

Use generic brand diapers and formula.

- When you're in the young baby years, I strongly recommend generic formula and diapers. Generic formula is about half the price of the national brands and the Food and Drug Administration requires that it be nutritionally equal to brand names like Similac, Enfamil, and Good Start.

- Generic diapers, meanwhile, are available from supermarkets, warehouse club chains, pharmacy chains, and so many more places. They'll save you a ton over big brands like Pampers, Huggies, and Luvs.

- Scott and Jeannine tried everything from cloth diapers to mother's milk, which incidentally is the best food for infants if that's the choice for you. So above all else, be flexible. Some things will work and others won't. Keep what works in your life and keep looking for ways to trim costs.

Get thrifty buying and selling kids' clothes online.

- The Leopolds are thrift-store junkies and love their hand-me-downs. If that's you, I want to tell you about thredUP.com. It's a site that has given the idea of secondhand clothes and consignment shops an online makeover.

- As a seller, you order a bag online, stuff it full of your kids' gently used clothes, and ship it postage paid to the company. thredUP.com pays 20 to 40 percent of the retail value of what you've sent. *The New York Times* reports the average bag earns $25.
- As a buyer, you can purchase a wide spectrum of clothing starting from size 12 months at discounts of up to 80 percent off retail—all without leaving your home to go to a thrift shop!

Don't buy life insurance on kids to save for college.
- Beware of pitches from life insurance agents claiming that the absolute best way to save for your kid's college is to buy life insurance.
- The idea is to buy a policy on your kid and then they will have life insurance down the road in the event of their premature death. When they make it to college age, there's this wonderful tax loophole that allows you to borrow from the policy's cash value to pay for college.
- But the embedded costs in life insurance policies can be massive because they're padded with commissions for the salesperson. Plus, if you can't pay the premiums on a life insurance policy, the policy lapses and you're wiped out; there's no money there to tap for college.
- My preferred alternative for college savings? A 529 plan. (See pages 85–86 in my last book, *Living Large in Lean Times*, for more on 529 plans.)

Decide what you're going to do about allowances.
- I have a bias toward allowance as a paycheck that is earned for doing chores. The typical allowance for a kid is now $15 a week, though it's nowhere near that in my house.
- I give my kids a dollar a week multiplied by their grade level as long as they complete their chores. So a first grader gets $1 a week, a second grader $2 a week, and so on. The chores are detailed for them on a chore wheel so everybody knows what they've got to take care of in the house.
- When it comes to younger children understanding money, I love the three jars concept that came out of the Christian fundamentalist movement. Each jar is marked with a red, green, or yellow heart. One jar can be used to hold money for charity; another jar holds money for current spending; and the third has money for longer-term savings. This provides a very simple, clear, and tangible lesson for children.

THE GREAT AMERICAN
SANDWICH

*For Heather and Tim, taking care of two generations
meant major life changes*

HEATHER MCKUSICK IS JUST THIRTY YEARS OLD, but she's already struggling with an issue that many people don't run into until ten or fifteen years later.

Heather and her husband, Tim, also thirty, are part of the sandwich generation. That doesn't mean they like tuna salad on wheat bread. It means Heather and Tim are trying to take care of both their young children and their parents. That includes Heather's mother Barbara, fifty-six, and Tim's parents, Colleen and Martin, both fifty-three, who have struggled with financial and medical issues. Meanwhile, their sons, Tyler and Cody, are three years old and eight months old, respectively.

That's an awful lot to deal with for Heather, a third grade teacher in Warren, Massachusetts, a town of about five thousand that's big on young families, outstanding education, and a strong sense of community.

Tim is a full-time college student who also works in retail. They're former high school sweethearts.

"We both graduated high school in 2000 and he began going to college, but even at eighteen, he was responsible for helping his family with finances," Heather said. "After a semester, he decided to just pursue full-time work. We got our own apartment when we were nineteen and he maintained full-time work to support us while I went to college full-time and worked part-time about thirty hours a week."

The plan was for Heather to finish her bachelor's degree and start working. Then Tim would return to school, she would support the family, and he'd assume the part-time work and student role that Heather had.

"Unfortunately, we had accumulated significant credit card debt while I was a student—car repairs, books, classes, and of course we fell prey to the 'extras' that we also thought we needed but couldn't afford on our own. And my first teaching salary was $32,000 . . . with an automatic 11 percent taken off the top for my retirement/pension . . . and taxes . . . and health insurance. . . . I ended up making like $400 a week!"

That wasn't much money to cover rent, two car payments, a student loan she had taken to help cover expenses for a semester when she had to do her student teaching, and credit card bills in both their names, plus utilities and groceries.

So Tim ended up just returning to school part-time, one or two classes at a time, in order to continue working full-time. Along the way, he has had to take some semesters off, especially when Heather was pursuing her master's degree, which she had to get within five years to keep her job.

In 2007, Heather and Tim bought a duplex so they could stop paying rent and have a place to live. Tim's parents live in the other side of the duplex, and pay a discounted rent of $500 a month.

"We actually had bought our property because of my father-in-law's health," said Heather.

Her father-in-law developed an infection while he was in the hospital, and he and his wife ran into financial trouble. Heather and Tim were in the market for their first home, so they bought a house that would allow Martin to convalesce and focus on his health without having to worry about bills.

They're thinking about buying another house so Heather's mom could move into the duplex and they could have a space of their own. Barbara has also had medical issues, and has had several brain surgeries.

"Ultimately, I would like to provide for her," said Heather. "As a renter, she has some uncertainty—her landlord can increase her rent, she could be asked to leave so they could owner-occupy, etcetera. We also see the house we have as a potential investment to create a future income for our boys. So we want to keep the property for both reasons . . . provide for our parents in the near future and provide for our boys in many, many years."

In trying to care for kids and parents on a schoolteacher's salary, Heather and Tim have learned to be more frugal. As a college student, Heather developed a weekend shopping habit that almost did her in.

"I was essentially a kid, in college, working about thirty hours a week . . . and this is partially the root of my credit card debt and careless spending patterns, which earmarked my early twenties."

She and Tim, in struggling to pay their bills, ended up with $15,000 to $20,000 in credit card debt. Each had seven to ten credit cards.

"At one point, we were easily spending a quarter of our income on minimum payments!" she said.

Heather managed to refinance her car and consolidate her credit card debt with a local credit union, which improved her cash flow.

"It kept my head above water and probably saved my credit score because I was actually able to maintain the loans and pay them off."

Now they are reformed spenders.

"We pay cash. We are trying to build up savings. We think long and hard about financial decisions and are trying so very hard to pay off the credit card debt that practically drowned us! It is tough!"

They've been on only one real vacation in fourteen years and they paid cash for it.

"We are still paying for our mistakes with frugality and impulse control over a decade from when we first made them! We have learned!"

Being a member of the sandwich generation is hard for Heather and Tim, not just because of the financial or time stresses, but because they have to consider everyone's best interests and don't have the autonomy they would like.

"I'm not sure if this makes sense, but the whole notion of doing things for everyone and not for us is the hardest."

Fortunately, Heather loves her job.

"I am so fortunate to honestly be happy to go to work every single day! I truly feel as if teaching is a true vocation or calling to me. I work hard to 'pay it forward' and give back to the community and society."

She's grateful for what she has, and looking to build a stronger future for herself and her family.

Consider a long-term care insurance policy.

- If you are fifty or sixty, you're at the prime age to buy long-term care (LTC) insurance, a kind of policy that pays for care in a nursing home, an assisted living facility, or your own home as you age.
- Shopping for LTC insurance can be simplified by contacting an independent agent who can shop quotes from a variety of companies for you. Companies like AALTCI .org, LTCTree.com, and PrepSmart.com are all good starting points.
- When shopping for LTC insurance, look for a lifetime benefit—or at least five years' coverage if that's too costly. Also, be sure the policy adjusts for inflation so the benefit is not subpar when you need it.
- Finally, you only want to consider companies that have been rated "A++" (by A.M. Best), which means they are of the highest financial strength. Visit AMBest.com to search ratings. Free registration is required.

Get a will in place.

- If you have kids, you need a will for the simple fact that if you don't have one, the state will decide who raises your kids. That's the reality in the absence of any written direction from you. Some people use the excuse that doing a will is too complicated and too expensive for them to undertake. I don't buy that.
- It's true that if you have a complicated life—maybe you own your own business or have a blended family—you do need to go see a lawyer who specializes in wills, estates, and trusts.
- However, if you have a relatively simple situation like the McKusicks, I like the Will-Maker software that you can pay to use through Nolo.com. They do a great job of asking interactive questions to guide you through the will completion process.
- If you get confused along the way, stop and see a lawyer. Or push through and know that it is much cheaper to have a lawyer review the will you've self-prepared than to actually prepare one for you from scratch.

Get a durable power of attorney in place.

- A durable power of attorney (DPA) is a document that allows your parents (the "principal") to authorize you (the "attorney-in-fact") to make financial/legal decisions and to make financial transactions on their behalf.
- There are advantages to having a lawyer draft a DPA. First, an attorney-drafted DPA can be drafted to meet your individual needs. Although there are preprinted forms available, they are worded broadly and do not give you as much flexibility. Second, since DPAs are subject to abuse, it is a good idea to meet with an attorney to make sure both the principal and the attorney-in-fact understand the document and the attorney is assured of the principal's competency.

Protect your children's identities.

- It's an unfortunate fact that kids are targets for identity thieves. According to the 2012 Child Identity Theft Report, children are thirty-five times more likely to be subject to identity theft than adults are.
- Thankfully, AllClearID.com is now offering a new free service called ChildScan. The service combs through credit records, employment records, criminal records, and medical accounts to find out if a crook has been using your kid's Social Security number. Visit AllClearID.com/plans/child for more details.
- Crooks target kids because they're ideal candidates for identity theft—no credit history but a clean Social Security number. As a parent, you want to make sure nobody messes with your children. And the sooner you find out, the better, because if it goes on for a decade or more, it can take years to clean up.

BOOMERANG

Cesar is part of a generation of college grads moving back in with parents—even while making good money

IT'S SATURDAY MORNING at the Bonilla household in Glendale Heights, Illinois, and the TV is showing highlights from last night's soccer match between FC Barcelona and Real Madrid.

Maria Bonilla, fifty-one, is making scrambled eggs, toast, and quesadillas. Like many Mexican-American women her age, she's the foundation of her family, and she works tirelessly inside the home but never out of it.

Her husband, Eli, sixty, sits enjoying a plate of frijoles and Mexican rice along with his daily coffee before he's off to work. He recently retired from three decades as a construction worker pouring concrete. Now he works part-time at a Nissan dealership because he's too bored to just sit around, and who couldn't use the extra money?

Meanwhile, the couple's twenty-four-year-old son, Cesar, is enrapt in the game highlights.

Come Saturday night, Cesar will take the field himself at a nearby indoor soccer arena. He wears a turquoise blue jersey and squishes the synthetic turf beneath his cleats playing midfield for a local team modeled after Barcelona. It's one of several soccer clubs he's part of.

Soccer—or *fútbol*, as it's called by Spanish speakers—is the core of Cesar's weekends, and he's played since the age of seven. Because he lives at home, he's able to tow Mom and Dad to his games. His twenty-year-old sister, Jeanette, comes along too sometimes when she's home on the weekends from college.

"I usually have games Friday to Sunday," Cesar says. "By living at home, I'm able to bring my parents with me to my games and often go out to eat afterwards."

Cesar is among a generation of boomerang kids—adult children who go to college, graduate from school, and make a round-trip right back home, typically because they can't find a job. It's become a common phenomenon since the Great Recession.

Only in his case, Cesar isn't wanting for good work or good pay.

He graduated from Northern Illinois University (NIU) in May 2011 and began working five months later at public accounting firm PricewaterhouseCoopers in downtown Chicago.

While his father labored for decades with finishing trowels and premium high-strength alloy screeds to smooth poured concrete, the tools of Cesar's trade are Excel spreadsheets and ProSystem *fx* Tax software for CPAs.

Cesar earns about $60,000 doing tax compliance for corporations and wealthy individuals.

So why is he living at home? This is *not* a case of a failure to launch. Rather, it's smart and strategic planning, the kind of delayed gratification that can lead to scored goals on the soccer field or money in the bank.

"After graduating, I had about $50,000 in debt, so instead of moving to the city as many of my peers and coworkers did, I moved back home," he says. "By living at home, it lets me save money, pay down my debt, [and] gives me a chance to finally help out my parents by taking responsibility on a few bills after years of them taking care of me."

Cesar is responsible for household expenses like the cable and Internet ($175) and groceries for the family ($200 every couple of weeks). His other expenses include a $40 cell phone bill and a monthly car note (including insurance) of $333 for the 2006 Cadillac CTS that he bought used a few years ago.

The Bonillas live in a two-floor townhome with two bedrooms and two baths about forty minutes west of Chicago. On their walls, the sad eyes of La Morenita (Our Lady of Guadalupe) gaze toward a nearby picture of Santo Niño de Atocha—her baby-faced son dressed in pilgrim's clothes, his small child's arms offering bread to the world-weary and a guzzle of *agua* from a hollow gourd.

Like other Hispanic cultures, Mexicans are very big on family, and moving back home after college is quite typical, Cesar tells me.

"As children become young adults and are able to support themselves and contribute to the household, it shouldn't be a problem for a young adult to still live at home as long as they put in their fair share at home," he believes.

"With that said, this principle needs to be thought/communicated by the parents early on in order to avoid 'free riders' and lazy young adults, as many parents are afraid of their children turning into."

No threat of slacking on Cesar's part, though. He has a laser focus on his goals, which include paying down that $50,000 in student loan debt and saving up for a place of his own in about two years.

"I plan to save about 20 percent of my paycheck and use the rest for bills and my loans, which hopefully will knock out much of my current debt," he says. "When I'm finally ready to take the next step and live on my own, I want to make sure I have an emergency fund, additional savings, as well as a smaller debt burden.

"By living at home, I think I can accomplish these goals while I help out at the same time. At the end of the day, this will build a sound foundation that will help me for the rest of my life and will let me take care of my future adult responsibilities."

Like a lot of people his age, Cesar likes to enjoy himself when he's not doing serious accounting. Fortunately, he has a nice little accord with his folks in that respect.

"I feel like I have the liberty from my parents to party it up as much as I want and go out on the weekends. I believe since I have proven myself to be a responsible young adult, I have gained their trust to do as I wish and go out as much as I want, which is important while I enjoy my twenties," he says. "The benefits of living at home and building a financial future outweigh the cons of partying while living at home with parents."

His younger sister, Jeanette, is also attending NIU, just as he did, though she's pursuing a business degree.

"After living in the dorms her freshman year, she now rents an apartment on campus and is responsible for rent and utilities," Cesar says. "In order to pay her bills and have some money for herself, she comes back home on the weekends to work at her part-time job."

By the time Jeanette graduates, Cesar will be off on his own in his own place. And he'll have used his time wisely to take those first steps into adult responsibility by living at home.

Communicate and set up clear expectations.

- If you're a parent, any move by a grown child back into your home has to be prefaced by a lot of open communication. Will she pay rent or utilities? Who will pay for groceries? How long is she welcome to stay? The important thing is to have conversations routinely, not when something becomes a problem. In fact, a continuing series of conversations might be necessary.

Consider charging rent.

- Maria and Eli Bonilla are not charging Cesar any rent. That's a highly personal decision parents have to make on their own. In general, I like the idea of parents charging rent. But that's contingent on your grown child having gainful employment. Because if he doesn't have a job, it's not realistic to start expecting rent!
- Set a time line and let your child know how long he's welcome to stay. You might consider letting him live for free with you for twelve months, but anything longer than that, and you'll start charging the going market rate for rent.

Know the hotspots of cohabitating.

- In my experience, there are a few problem areas that crop up again and again when I talk to the parents of boomerang children.
- First up is food. Nobody likes a conflict over who ate what and when. So buy a small second refrigerator and let your grown child stock it with her own food.
- Laundry is another big point of contention. If your son or daughter were living on their own, you would not be doing their laundry, right? So don't do it when they boomerang back to you. Show them how to use the washer and the dryer and let them do it themselves.
- Finally, there's the question of whether your son or daughter can have a friend spend the night. Again, this is a highly individual choice that I can't advise you on; just know that the more you set the rules up front, the fewer headaches you'll have down the road.

Don't cosign a car loan for a grown child.

- Getting into debt over a car is a classic mistake many people make in their early twenties. With that first job comes the temptation to have a fancy ride. Not a good idea!

- If your grown child needs to buy a car while living at home, you can either lend her the money yourself or help her find the best deal on a car note. Credit unions are generally the best places to get a car loan. Have your son or daughter visit CUNA.org to find credit unions near you and see which ones they qualify for.

Get a first apartment the right way.

- Shared apartments are often the first exit strategy for boomerang kids ready to leave the nest. But apartment leases can be tricky.
- When you sign a lease with a roommate, be sure you can foot the entire rent in case the other person skips out. That's why I've said to consider a six-month lease instead of a twelve-month lease even if it's more expensive. (In most parts of the country, the supply of rental housing is rising dramatically, except in New York and San Francisco, where you might have a hard time doing this.)
- Let's say the living arrangement doesn't work out and somebody leaves. Whoever is left behind is then solely responsible for only two or three months of rent instead of seven or eight, if you've signed a six-month lease. Of course, it could be you who leaves to relocate for a job opportunity. That's why it's wise to negotiate a relocation clause. Try asking the landlord for a full lease termination in exchange for their keeping the security deposit should you get a job offer more than one hundred miles away.

MEET MR. MOM

Tony learned the hard way that his job was not recession-proof

Tony and Mary Tahkeal weren't prepared when he lost his job in late 2011. They had an emergency fund of $500 and even that was a struggle to scrape together. And they were dealing with credit card debt—much of it for groceries and lifestyle purchases like clothing—that at one point was $28,000.

Like most people, they didn't build up that kind of debt overnight. It really started back in the 1990s when Tony was "young and dumb," as he says.

"I was in college full-time and working full-time, but what did I do? I went and bought a car!"

Tony and Mary had just welcomed their little girl, Taylor, into the world to join their young son, Chris, when the suspension went out on their old vehicle. So rather than repair it, they went to a dealership and got a little Nissan Sentra.

But having two car seats in the back was tight, so they returned the car to the dealer after two or three days and explained they needed a bigger vehicle.

"We walked by a brand-new '95 Nissan Pathfinder, which was way out of our ballpark. Here I am with two kids, a job, and college, and I about fell over when we got approved [for the loan]. It was $500 a month," Tony recalls.

"We didn't drink our money away, we didn't smoke it away, and the only thing I can relate it back to was car payments. That led to credit card use for groceries and credit card use for clothes because all of our money went to paying credit cards. Because we were good at making our credit card payments, we got another credit card. Then three credit cards later, we were like, 'There's something wrong here!'"

Now they've given up the credit cards and have gone to a cash-only lifestyle. They're in the process of getting out of debt, doing what the economists call "deleveraging." But it's going to be a long climb out.

Tony is a member of a Native American tribe called the Yakama Nation. He grew up on a reservation in Yakima, Washington. Mary, meanwhile, is Caucasian.

In 2007, Tony and Mary left their hometown of Yakima so he could take a job as an X-ray technician at Memorial Hospital North in Colorado Springs, Colorado. The pay was in the mid-$50,000s and Tony thought the position was recession-proof.

Life was good at the base of the Rocky Mountains. The couple bought a home with a view of picturesque Pikes Peak—the mountain with the vista that inspired the lyrics to "America the Beautiful."

But in September 2011, the amber waves and purple mountains turned to pink as Tony received a layoff notice at work.

"The office I worked at was a small one-person diagnostic X-ray room, away from the [main] hospital. Working [there] meant I could clock out at five p.m., as opposed to the hospital, which never closes," Tony says.

"[But] X-ray departments don't make money with good old-fashioned diagnostic X-rays utilized by one person . . . so to lose my job was not a shocker by any means. In years past, the hospital could absorb that cost, but not when budgets aren't being met."

Fortunately, Mary became a licensed massage therapist in Colorado around this time. With her specialty in therapeutic postinjury medical massage, she was pulling in about $25 an hour doing massage work. But it wasn't steady income.

The anxiety of having a mortgage and no steady full-time work was a great burden on the family. Their debt level and lack of savings put them on the road to considering bankruptcy.

"Mary was losing sleep at night, worried about the finances, but I failed to notice. Hindsight is twenty-twenty. I saw signs of stress but didn't connect the dots," Tony says. "She felt responsible for our financial woes, and I couldn't relieve her guilt. I got a second job working part-time evenings [while still at the hospital], but our financial house of cards still came crashing down."

As their debt became more unmanageable, they bit the bullet and filed for bankruptcy. Tony and Mary initially thought they would at least be able to keep their home. But that wasn't how it would play out.

"We had to include our home, and add ourselves to the nation's foreclosure statistics. Then to add insult to injury, we had to wait about eight months for our bankruptcy hearing, due to the volume of bankruptcies at that time," Tony says. "It was like a lingering cloud hovering over us, reminding us of our financial failure. We just wanted to file and move on with our lives."

And that's exactly what they did. The Tahkeals made the decision to move back home to Washington to be near extended family.

In doing so, they had to make the difficult choice to move their daughter Taylor, now eighteen, during her scholastically and socially all-important senior year in high school. The couple's other child, twenty-year-old Chris, was already out on his own at the time.

Upon returning to Washington, the Tahkeals decided that Tony should stay home and run the household while Mary worked full-time at her newfound career.

Tony didn't appreciate how much goes into maintaining a home because his wife had done it since the birth of their children. His job was to earn the paycheck and bring it home during that time.

Thankfully, Michael Keaton and a certain touchstone 1983 comedy were there to help him through the transition.

"I rented *Mr. Mom* after being laid off. I figured I'd prepare myself for daily home life," Tony jokes. "I didn't feel like less of a man [for losing my job], but I did feel bad for moving my daughter during her senior year. Other than that, my self-worth wasn't affected."

A lot of guys really had a bull's-eye on their backs during the early days of the Great Recession. The *Financial Times* of London reported that men's jobs accounted for 80 percent of the jobs that were lost during the first two years of our nation's financial troubles beginning in 2007. That's because the recession really hit male-dominated sectors of the economy like construction and manufacturing.

While Tony was in the more female-leaning health care sector, he was not immune to job loss. And just like that, Tony became part of what the Census Bureau says is a growing group of 189,000 at-home fathers across the country.

What surprised him most about going from breadwinner to homemaker?

"I learned that the dishes are never done! I learned I'm a terrible cook. The house always needs something, be it laundry, lawn mowing, dog walking . . . fill in the blank here. When I clocked out at work, I was done. I'd go home. You can't clock out at home!"

Today Mary brings home an annual income of $35,000 doing therapeutic massage in Washington. That's roughly $20,000 less than the family lived on in Colorado, but the drop in income is offset by the lower costs of living in a single-wide mobile home.

I love Tony and Mary's story because it shows that families make changes as necessary to survive. The Tahkeals were able as a couple to figure out how to keep food on the table and a roof over their heads when times got tough.

If there's one thing Tony wants readers to take away from his story, it is that you can't underestimate the value of being financially prepared for the unknown. And that you can lose a job even in a supposedly recession-proof field like health care. Saving money today creates more breathing room in your life when the going gets tough.

Still, Tony feels blessed.

"I'd have to say we're fortunate. Fortunate that my job loss was cushioned by my wife's budding massage career. Fortunate enough to return home where we have extended family— extended family that we can rely on when needed [like for] auto repairs. Or vice versa, as I've become the family baby-sitter for my nieces and nephews."

> **The story of the Tahkeals is a very real and relatable one. What lessons can you take away from it?**

Prepare for a rainy day.

- If you unexpectedly faced a sudden expense of $2,000 in your life, could you handle it? A new study from the National Bureau of Economic Research found that right around 50 percent of Americans couldn't. They're like Wile E. Coyote in those old cartoons, out over the edge of the cliff and looking down.

- I know there are some circumstances that just blindside you financially in life. But let me ask you this: How much could you come up with per week? One dollar? Two? Ten dollars? Whatever it is, start taking it and stashing it away. I don't care if you put it in a jar in your house. Just start the process of building a reserve. If it's $10 a week, that becomes $500 over the course of a year.

- Maybe you can just take your change and throw it into a jar at the end of the day. Or take all your $1 bills out of your wallet each night and put them aside as a way of forced savings. Just do something. Start saving for a rainy day before the rainy day actually comes.

Go low-tech to manage your money.

- If you're having trouble managing your money, I want you to be like the Tahkeals and pay in cash for whatever you can. One of my favorite ways to do that is to use envelopes to divvy up your money and keep within a budget.
- If you've never done this before, you simply take envelopes and write "groceries" on one, "utilities" on another, "walking around money" on a third, whatever it is in your life that requires money. Then each payday, take out the dollar amount you need until next pay period and split it up among your envelopes. When one envelope empties, you either take money from another envelope or you do without until the next payday.
- I often tell couples to do this particular method of budgeting. I once sat down with a couple that had more than $30,000 in credit card debt. We came up with a thirty-month plan for them to get out of debt that involved the envelope method. They didn't think it would work, but they paid off their credit card debt in twenty-one months!

Or try a high-tech method.

- Imagine walking into a store and having your smartphone automatically tell you whether or not you have enough money in your account to make a purchase. That's the premise of a new app called Wink.
- This free mobile app uses your phone's GPS and geo-fencing technology to know immediately when you walk into a store. Once you're in the door, Wink will automatically pop up a message with your account balance so you can know at a glance how your finances stand. No need to fumble around pulling up your mobile banking app and entering your username and password to manually check your account balance.
- My hope is you'll never pay a $35 overdraft fee again thanks to this free app for iOS and Android. Visit IsMoreThan.com to sign up as a beta tester.

Find support if you're a stay-at-home dad.

- Men account for only 3.6 percent of all at-home parents, according to Census Bureau data. That means being a man at home with kids can be isolating. But it doesn't have to be. There's a national organization for men in this situation called the National At-Home Dad Network (AtHomeDad.org) that has an online list of dad groups throughout two dozen states and Canada.

• *The Wall Street Journal* ran a recent story on at-home dads and noted that local groups like the seven-hundred-member NYC Dads Group (NYCDadsGroup.com) arrange play dates for dudes with kids, "dad's night out" events at sports bars and pool halls, and even bracket betting pools. Who says March Madness is just for the office?

HEALTH CARE

Health care is the monster eating up American prosperity. We spend far more than any other wealthy country on health care and have shorter life spans to boot. We now consume more than one-seventh of the entire American economy paying for health care. That is almost double the share of national income that any other country spends. To add salt to the wounds, you or I could end up broke after an illness or an injury even with health insurance.

Navigating the health care jungle is like walking through pea-soup fog. I want to share with you the stories of five people who have had major financial and health hurdles and how they handled them. I am particularly excited about the story of one person who said no to the high cost of health care here and saved a fortune by getting care in another country. Plus, I will show you some practical ways to reduce your health care costs right here at home.

I have strong opinions about the right way to provide health care in America. Just search keyword "health care" at ClarkHoward.com and you can read my prescription.

CHRONIC ILLNESS AND NEVER-ENDING BILLS

*Heather looks on the bright side while dealing with
chronic illness and medical debt—the No. 1 credit score killer*

MEDICAL DEBT IS DAMAGING the credit of around 30 million people, according to the latest figures I've seen. You would expect damaged credit from medical bills to be a problem for the uninsured. But the untold story here is that people with insurance get their credit trashed because of both billing mix-ups and high debt-to-income ratios.

I spoke with Heather Christians of Kasson, Minnesota, who has seen firsthand how medical bills can compromise your financial future. Heather is a working mom who manages a chronic disease while serving as the primary breadwinner of her household right now.

Heather, forty-two, was diagnosed with scleroderma eleven years ago. It is an autoimmune disease in which, she tells me, "you turn to stone from the inside out" because of a hardening of connective tissue.

There is no known cure for scleroderma, but Heather doesn't let that get her down.

"I am forty-two years young [and] continue to work full-time with the support of my husband and son," she tells me. "I may have scleroderma, but I refuse to let it have me."

Heather has a position as a victim advocate on the county level in Minnesota.

"In a nutshell, my job is to advocate for a crime victim from the law enforcement interview stage all the way up through the sentencing process and beyond and help make sure their rights are protected and their voice is heard," she says.

"I have never hidden my disease from my coworkers and am so fortunate that I can do my job. Some days are tougher than others, particularly when the temperature doesn't even reach zero during the winter! I have a few accommodations, like a handicap parking sticker and the ability to remote in if I really have to. I work eight to five basically, but I also carry our on-call phone about eight weekends a year and one or two nights every couple of weeks."

Heather's husband, Eric, thirty-seven, lost his job about three years ago and now works at a local pizza place on evenings and weekends while going to school to complete a degree in elementary education. Together they have a nine-year-old named Ethan whom they adopted from Guatemala when he was only five months old.

When I spoke to Heather, she had just received a letter in the mail from her medical provider telling her that her balance is now due in full or she will be turned over to a collection agency.

"I laughed—because otherwise I will cry—and told my husband that I have a payment plan with them, and have for years, and I faithfully make my payment every month. But here comes their yearly letter telling me I will be turned over to a collection agency because I can't afford to pay in one large payment the costs of maintaining a chronic disease that I did absolutely nothing to bring on."

In addition, her debt level makes her an undesirable risk for lenders, as she found out recently when her car was totaled in a parking lot.

"We tried to be wise about what we purchased and look at what we could afford in conjunction with the insurance payout," Heather says. "Well, as you can imagine, we had to act quickly, and had about two weeks to make a decision. When we finally landed on one we were going to purchase, we were turned down by at least two banks but finally had one approve us; however, it was at a higher interest rate due to our debt."

In another example of how her financial outlook has been harmed by medical debt, Heather and Eric were practically rebuffed by their credit union when they tried to consolidate $29,000 in various lines of credit with high interest rates into one payment with a lower interest rate.

"The loan officer kept saying how she stuck her neck out for us to get approved and that with our debt it was not easy."

In order to do the consolidation, the credit union wanted to cancel two of their credit cards; charge them a fee to manage timely payments to the couple's creditors; force them into a secured credit card with a $500 limit; hold Eric's beat-up old car as collateral; and put them through mandatory budget counseling.

All for a consolidation that Heather estimates would have saved them $15 a month *and* actually extend their debt another two years versus the self-imposed budget plan they were currently on!

"I can only suspect that we would have had to jump through all their hoops because of our debt-to-income ratio, which encompasses my medical bills," Heather says. "Trust me, I wish I could pay off my debt faster, but we'll get there! Slow and steady."

Meanwhile, Heather considers herself one of the lucky ones—even though there is no known cause or cure for the illness she has.

"It has taught me to appreciate every day and to see the small things in life that are a gift. I may have to take the elevator up one flight of stairs because I have to conserve my energy, but I still get to get up, go to work every day, and *live!*" she says.

"Some people may curse me under their breath because I slow them down by making an elevator stop or not being able to walk fast enough in a crowd, but, hey, life does not pass me by. Scleroderma may have slowed me down, but it slowed me down to see all the blessings around me!"

What can you learn from Heather's story?

Know what bad marks are in your credit file.

- You can't address your medical debt without knowing what's in your credit report. As I described in "The Rising Star" profile of the Credit chapter, you can learn what's contained in your file for free by going to AnnualCreditReport.com. If you have to do a dispute based on what you learn, follow the procedure I outlined in that profile as well.

Consider small claims court if all else fails.

- If challenging an error on your credit report doesn't work, consider small claims court. File a suit in the county where the adversary lives or does business. Call the clerk of the court in the county where you'll be filing to learn that court's procedure. You'll pay a filing fee of generally less than $100 that is recoverable if you win.
- Small claims court is really best used as a tactic to call the errant party's bluff and get them to remove the bad mark on your credit. That's what you really want. But if you don't get your desired result once the medical provider is served notice of the suit, you want to appear well organized with strong documentation that shows how you've been harmed, why the person or company is responsible, and how much you're seeking in damages.

Find the right buttons to push.

- I recently heard from a caller to my show who was involved in a fee dispute with a dentist over the cost of services that had been rendered. She resolved her beef by appealing to the state insurance department.
- There's a teaching lesson here for everyone. You've got to push as many buttons as you can until you find the right one. The insurance commissioner's office in her state had no real jurisdiction over the dentist, but they used moral suasion to make things right for this consumer.
- If you have a fee dispute with a medical provider, you have options. If it's a dentist, the local chapter of the American Dental Association (ADA) usually will have some form of panel where you can file a fee dispute administratively just as the caller did with the state insurance department. For a doctor, check with the local affiliate of the American Medical Association (AMA) for the same procedure. Visit ADA.org and AMA-ASSN .org, respectively, for more info.

Never give up hope.

- Many of us face health difficulties in our life. But I want you to take a tip from Heather's playbook. Though she has a chronic disease, she doesn't sacrifice her life to it. Make no bones about it, her day-to-day existence is difficult. Yet she gets up and goes to work every day and refuses to let scleroderma get the best of her.
- Earlier in this book, I quoted Winston Churchill about never giving up. The British Bulldog also has another zinger that applies here: "If you're going through hell, keep going." Heather, your spirit of perseverance greatly impresses me and I hope it does the same for others! Keep on doing what you're doing!

FEET DON'T
FAIL ME NOW

*Even with health insurance, small business owner
Mimi struggles with medication costs*

PEOPLE AT HER RESTAURANT south of Atlanta say Mimi Gentilini never stops going. But about five times every day, Mimi interrupts what she's doing and begins to run around the block.

Mimi, fifty-seven, has Type 1 diabetes, but she doesn't take insulin, even though the U.S. National Library of Medicine states unequivocally on its website, "Everyone with Type 1 diabetes must take insulin every day."

While Mimi has health insurance, she's worried that if she becomes insulin-dependent, she will no longer be able to afford her coverage.

So instead of injecting herself, Mimi runs around the block, working the large muscle groups of her body to lower her blood sugar.

"I run or powerwalk to drop blood sugar levels when I notice them getting over approximately one-eighty, and yes, it does work," said Mimi. "I let the staff know that I will be right back."

Mimi is the owner of Mimi's Good Food in Peachtree City, Georgia, and has been in business since 1996. She pays nearly $1,000 a month for her health insurance, and her policy has a $6,000 deductible.

"If I change insurance companies, which I could do for half the premium, I would not be covered for many major events because of the pre-existing condition clause," she said.

Mimi's sister Joanna is six years older than her and has the same type of diabetes. But there's no running necessary for her.

"She has an insulin pump—and all the bells and whistles. She is married to a retired government employee with permanent benefits."

But Mimi, who was married for twenty-two years but divorced in 2003, has to rely on diligence and willpower to get her through.

"My greatest fear is that I will be priced out of insurance, even though I have never had a day in my life that I was uninsured. Right now I am doing a remarkable job managing this insidious disease, even to the point that people can't believe I have it."

Her hardest time of the day is in the morning.

"This is because I have been still all night not burning that sugar. Consequently, I hit the ground running in the morning. I'm up every day at four-thirty a.m. and at work by five forty-five. My doctors say that the day will come when insulin will become part of my daily life. As long as I monitor and do my labs every twelve weeks, I feel OK with it."

Mimi was born in New Jersey. She says she was "well raised" by a loving two-parent family in Medford Lakes, a rustic four-thousand-person town in the Pine Barrens that boasts on its website, "We don't have streets or roads, we have trails."

About eight years ago, she started feeling very tired, what she described as "lead blanket exhausted." A doctor said she was depressed, but she knew that wasn't right. Then she was diagnosed as a Type 2 diabetic.

"Three years ago, my blood sugar dropped suddenly to fifty. I was at work, incoherent, and getting worse by the minute. Thank God a physician friend of mine had stopped in for breakfast. She saw what was happening and started pouring OJ down my throat. Time to change doctors!"

Instead of Type 2 diabetes, Mimi had late-onset Type 1 diabetes.

"Since changing doctors, I have really regained a much better level of health. Actually, if you saw me, there would be guessing as to what is going on in my body. I'm five feet eight, one hundred thirty pounds—not bad for fifty-seven!"

Mimi is hoping in the near future to be able to shop for health insurance that she can afford and that will allow her to take the insulin she needs without jeopardizing her coverage.

Under the federal Patient Protection and Affordable Care Act, sometimes referred to as Obamacare, Mimi shouldn't have long to wait. Effective January 1, 2014, insurers will be prohibited from discriminating against people such as Mimi who have pre-existing medical conditions. They will not be able to deny coverage to them, nor charge more for coverage. Discrimination on the basis of gender also will be banned.

Until then, Mimi is keeping her running shoes nearby.

Check online for drug coupons.

- Some major pharmaceutical companies are now offering coupons to retain customers when their key brands start getting competition from generics.
- The drug makers typically post links announcing the coupons on their websites. Once you sign up, you get a downloadable coupon that offers a greatly reduced copayment at your favorite pharmacy.
- This is not for every brand name, just for those that face generic competition. Lipitor, Plavix, and Diovan are among the popular big-name drugs offering coupons at their sites as I write this. Note that these coupons won't work if you get your health care from the government or if you participate in a pharmacy benefit manager (PBM) program at work.

Pay cash for nonemergency medical needs.

- If you're looking to save money on medical bills, you might consider being a cash payer and shopping around for the lowest price on nonemergency medical procedures, completely circumventing your insurer in the process.
- The key is to make a deal up front with the billing department rather than after services have been rendered. I read an article in the *Los Angeles Times* that gave some concrete examples of how much money you can save doing this.
- In one case, a blood test that would have cost an insured patient $415 could be paid for in cash—after negotiating—for $95. In another case, one major insurer was charging a negotiated rate of $2,400 for a CAT scan at a Los Angeles–area hospital. But that was reduced to $250 when the reporter called to inquire about a cash price at the hospital.
- My editor on this book, Megan Newman, reminded me that every fee is negotiable. She told me the story of negotiating a fee with her doctor. When she learned what insurance would cover, Megan got her doctor to lower her surgical fee by close to $2,000! It can't hurt to ask. Of course, the key is to do it before you receive medical services, not after.

Look for charitable alternatives.

- What do you do if you have an illness that requires special medicine and you can't afford it despite having insurance? One pharmaceutical executive turned philanthropist has set up a charity called TheAssistanceFund.org to provide copay assistance that can make the difference between life and death for some patients. This nonprofit helps pay for some medications by footing a significant amount of the out-of-pocket expenses for insured patients. Best of all, TheAssistanceFund.org tries to approve people for assistance within twenty-four hours because they know time is of the essence.

Shop the lowest prescription prices from your smartphone.

- I talked in *Clark Howard's Living Large in Lean Times* about trying to lower the cost of your prescriptions by printing out the list of $4 generic meds from Kroger, Target, Walmart, and any of a number of other retailers. Take this list to your doctor and say, "Can you write my prescription from this list? This is what I can afford."
- Now there's a step you can take beyond that with the free smartphone app called LowestMed for both Android and iOS. With LowestMed, you just pop in the name of the medication you need and it will shop the marketplace and tell you who's got the best price in your area. Visit LowestMed.com for more details.
- A pharmaceutical company might have a deal with a particular pharmacy based on volume that could make your prescription a lot cheaper at one place versus the pharmacy where you normally go. This app gives you the opportunity to see the best deal on your medication.

YOU GOTTA HAVE HEART

At the crossroads of health care and bargain travel, Willy discovers medical tourism and pays pennies on the dollar

EVERYONE IS TALKING about the astronomical cost of health care. But major operations don't have to be financially unattainable in your life.

Just how affordable can health care be? To discover the answer, you might have to be like the nearly 1 million Americans who go overseas every year for radically discounted surgical procedures. They're part of an ongoing trend at the crossroads of health care and travel called "medical tourism."

According to Deloitte Center for Health Solutions, 875,000 Americans went abroad for procedures ranging from dentistry to elective hip replacement to bypass surgery in 2010. And that number was estimated to have increased to as much as 1.6 million in 2012.

Out of all those many Americans who opted for medical tourism, I want to tell you about just one of them. His name is Willy Bearden.

Willy is a sixty-two-year-old documentary filmmaker living in Memphis, Tennessee, whose arteries were clogged from decades of enjoying Southern cooking. "I've always had a soft spot for barbeque, tamales, cakes, and pies, and anything fried," he says.

Since 1988, he's owned and operated the William Bearden Company and makes a living doing corporate video for such clients as FedEx and Fred's Super Dollar Stores. He's also made documentary films like *Horn Island Journal*, *The Story of Cotton*, and *Visualizing the Blues*, among others.

Willy's documentaries air on local and regional PBS stations and he's become a Ken

Burns of the Deep South, telling the stories of both Memphis and the Mississippi Delta in a personal and revealing way.

It was on Horn Island back in 2008 that Willy first felt something might be wrong with his heart. He was unusually winded after hauling camping gear across the barrier island off the Mississippi Gulf coast but didn't make too much of it at the time.

This was right around when Willy made the reluctant decision to go without health insurance for himself, his wife, his twenty-year-old son, and his nineteen-year-old daughter. The cost of his health insurance was going up from $1,200 a month to $1,800. Sure, he could swing it because he was making more than $100,000 at the time, but he decided he didn't want to pay the increase.

Willy knew full well that he was taking a gamble if he ran into a catastrophic accident or illness. Over the next three years, he would continue to notice a strange tightness in his chest at times. But he learned to adjust to his health problems.

"I [remember I] was producing a corporate show in Long Beach, California. The walk from the hotel to the Long Beach Convention Center was about two blocks. Luckily it was downhill on the way there," Willy recalls.

"But the walk back was pretty miserable for me. I would have to stop every hundred feet or so, sometimes disguising my stop by taking a photo with my camera. I didn't feel that I could share with my coworkers just how much I was hurting. I knew they might freak out and call an ambulance, and I would be in a bad situation. My fear was that I would have to have emergency surgery, which would cost upwards of $200,000, and I would have to go bankrupt. It was all a very confusing and bizarre situation."

Eventually a friend convinced him to go see a cardiologist. Based on his persistent symptoms, the doctor believed Willy had clogged arteries and recommended a heart catheterization to confirm the blockage.

The price quote for a cash payer? More than $30,000 for the test that would give a definitive diagnosis; then another $60,000 to $80,000 for the arterial stents he'd likely need; and more—*much more*—if the situation was bad enough to warrant heart bypass surgery.

"The price I was quoted here was a nebulous '$150,000 to $300,000' figure [for the bypass]. That stopped me in my tracks and got me on the path of searching out alternatives," Willy says.

Within fourteen days, he used the research skills critical to documentary filmmaking to learn everything he could about medical tourism. He homed in on India mainly because of his wanderlust for a place he'd never been before.

Willy targeted a Fortis Hospital location in the bustling Indian city of Bangalore and read the bios of all their doctors online. He e-mailed a Dr. Vivek Jawali and got a response within a day.

He asked for a picture of the hospital rooms where patients stay—and they weren't what he imagined. "I was relieved to see a modern hospital room with a desktop computer, TV, and modern amenities. . . . It was simply the nicest hospital room I had ever seen," Willy says.

He probed for further info, such as the hospital's rate of staph infection and patient testimonials. Everything he read put his mind at ease. "I think we're all wired to think there's some gimmick, some catch, but there was none here. Admittedly, I took a huge risk, but I could see no other option."

On January 10, 2011, Willy started his trip to India. It was a Monday. When he arrived in Bangalore, hospital staffers were there to pick him up and help him settle into his hospital room. Everybody spoke English.

Willy told me he felt like these people genuinely cared about him—a feeling he had not necessarily gotten from the U.S. medical establishment. That's something money can't buy.

"The nurses and staff were so friendly and interested in me. I have always been a good judge of character, and have always prided myself in seeing beyond what is said. My dealings with the Indian people, whether the janitors or the X-ray technicians, were positive and very human. I felt the compassion and care from these former strangers at a very deep, very personal level."

The next day he had a heart catheterization and learned all four coronary arteries were blocked 70 to 90 percent. He was going to need bypass surgery.

At that point, reality set in. Here was Willy, a stranger in a strange land, 9,028 miles from home, needing to have his sternum sawn open and his heart dissected.

That was when he met Dr. Vivek Jawali in person for the first time. It was Friday.

"I had deluded myself, somewhat, by believing that mine would be an easy fix, and I was staring at the reality of having my chest cracked open and my heart completely replumbed. It was scary," Willy remembers. "After a while, I sat and talked with Dr. Jawali, who drew on a piece of paper exactly what he was going to do to my heart. I was so moved by his manner, his compassion, and his intelligence, that I was completely OK with going ahead with the surgery. That, and the fact that I probably would have been dead in six months if I hadn't had the surgery."

After their talk, the five-hour bypass surgery was scheduled for the following Monday.

It went off without a hitch. Willy's post-op care consisted of attentive nurses and regular visits from Dr. Jawali.

"[Following the surgery,] Dr. Jawali looked at me and said, 'You are just as important in this as I am. You have a huge role to play in your recovery, but I can tell from your face and your demeanor that you'll come through this just fine. In fact, you will be so surprised at how quickly you'll bounce back and be healthy again.'"

Two days later, Willy was up and ambling around the hallways.

"I had the surgery on a Monday, and by Friday I had been up walking around the hospital floor so much that I was feeling great. I decided to put my T-shirt and blue jeans on. The nurses were very concerned about this and wanted me to put my pajamas back on, but Dr. Jawali told them to let me do what I felt like doing. I think the act of putting my clothes on was a very important psychological step for me. I felt as if I had gone through this incredible journey and I was on the other side of it—alive."

Within a few days, Willy was able to check out of the hospital and into a four-star Bangalore hotel called the Woodrose for $100 a day, which included three vegetarian meals daily in the restaurant.

He had continuing checkups with Dr. Jawali, but the balance of the conversation switched to the doctor's curiosity about Willy's film work. That's when he knew he was fully on the mend.

After eighteen days in India, Willy got on a plane and made the long flight back to Memphis. Stateside, he gets free follow-up care from a friend who's a nurse practitioner, and his long-term post-op recovery is overseen virtually by Dr. Jawali. (Willy is now Facebook friends with Dr. Jawali!)

The total cost for the extensive medical care Willy received in India? $9,000. That is *not* a typo. That's *nine thousand dollars*. He paid for it on his debit card! His airfare, meanwhile, was $1,500 and his hotel stay cost him $500.

Willy has since become something of an ambassador for medical tourism. He's done interviews with local Memphis papers and appeared at the third annual India Summit at Atlanta's Emory University to share a patient's perspective on medical tourism.

Now he plans to pay it forward. Another friend of his is going to Bangalore for heart valve replacement surgery, so he'll pick up the tab for that friend's post-hospital hotel stay.

At the time I wrote this, Willy still did not have insurance. But he was planning to get it and to record his journey to reinstating his coverage in a documentary made with the help of a local doctor. Meanwhile, he's changed the way he eats to prevent future heart problems.

"I have been sticking to a diet low in sodium and high in fiber and whole foods for the past two years. I eat chicken and fish frequently but rarely eat red meat. I feel really good."

If you're thinking about medical tourism, here are some important things to keep in mind:

Check with your insurer first.
- Like all medicine, the path to medical tourism basically has two routes: You can either buy services at the going market rate and pay cash out-of-pocket, or you can run a procedure through your insurer if they allow it. Of course, not all insurers are onboard with medical tourism. But it's always worth calling your insurer during the planning stage and asking about your options.

Carefully vet all facilities and doctors.
- The Joint Commission International (JCI) is the top dog when it comes to inspecting medical sites around the world. At JointCommissionInternational.org, you can see if a facility you're considering has passed inspection and meets standards. Some 220 overseas medical sites are accredited by JCI. If the one you're considering isn't, I'd advise you to look at another one that is. You also want to be sure the doctors you're considering are trained or board certified in the United States or another First World country.
- Meanwhile, the American Medical Association also has its own succinct recommendations for patients and insurers interested in medical tourism. Do a Google or Bing search for "AMA medical tourism guidelines" to see them.

Make a plan for communicating with relatives back home.
- Willy used the desktop computer in his Bangalore hospital room to e-mail friends and family while he was on the mend. But smartphones also make it very easy to stay in touch thanks to free video chat options like Skype, Google Chat (for Android), and FaceTime (for Apple iOS).
- One word of warning, though: Never use your regular cell phone overseas. You'll generally have to buy an unlocked world phone and a SIM card for your country of destination to avoid getting hammered on the data rates from your U.S.-based wireless provider.

Know the downsides.

• While it has a lot of pluses, medical tourism is not for everybody. Knowing what to expect can help you make a decision about whether it's right for your life. Some of the criticisms of medical tourism include: fewer regulations in the industry; bringing malpractice litigation can be difficult; a lack of adequate follow-up care; and the culture shock and jet lag can sometimes be too much for patients.

THE YOUNG AND
THE RISKLESS

*Sara and Travis are young, healthy, and saving a boatload of
money on health care with a high-deductible health plan*

SARA SCHRYER WALKS TO A SHADY spot in the back corner of her garden in Jacksonville,
Florida, and just a few feet from her wooden stockade fence, reaches down for a closer look
at one of her year-old camellias. She's a bit concerned.

The variety, known as Colonel Fiery, can be spectacular, with an abundance of dark red
formal blooms and oval, glossy leaves. Because it flowers from mid- to late winter, it can be
a welcome addition to an otherwise colorless garden.

But camellias can drive a gardener to frustration. And Sara's, including her Colonel
Fiery, aren't in peak condition. Sara says they can be sensitive to cold, so you have to take
care to cover them during a frosty night.

"This is their first flowering season outside of a pot and so far they are not doing too
well. While I have a lot of buds, very few seem ready to open, and some of the flowers that
have bloomed have been small and messy."

Sara learned about camellias from her grandfather, John Bowen, who passed away
in 2009.

"They were a passion of my grandfather and he shared it with me," she said.

Bowen had a collection of camellias in his backyard that he trained into trees. He had
anywhere from twenty-five to forty different camellias at a time, and he was interested in
grafting together different varieties to see if a new hybrid could be made.

"He was lucky a few times and named a particularly delicate and beautiful camellia,
Lady Gwendolyn, after my grandmother. It was never formally registered so it cannot be

found if [you're] searching for one, but he did manage to make a few smaller cuttings and now my dad and uncle have a few Lady Gwendolyns blooming in their yard."

Sara travels a lot, both for her job, at CSX Transportation, and for leisure. When I spoke with her, she was recently back from Houston, and days away from a ski trip to Breckenridge, Colorado. Later in the year, she and her husband, Travis, are making their first trip to Italy, a two-week vacation with stops in Rome, Venice, Florence, and Sorrento.

"We love traveling," she says. "Every month we try to do an out-of-town trip."

But whether she's on a trip or out in the garden, she doesn't think much about visits to the doctor. She doesn't have to; she's healthy and has an advantageous health care plan I love called a "health savings account" (HSA).

I asked Sara if she would help me tell you about health savings accounts, which she and Travis have had for about six years and have been very happy with. And I'm happy to say that she agreed.

Sara, thirty, goes to the doctor three or four times a year. Travis, also thirty, goes once or twice. That means they don't spend a lot on medical care. So instead of paying a ton of money in premiums for a traditional health insurance plan, Sara has an HSA.

What exactly is a health savings account? It's a tax-free savings account that's generally paired with a high-deductible insurance policy to provide affordable health coverage.

Sara's HSA, which she gets through her employer, has a monthly premium of just $90 for both her and Travis.

"We are relatively young and healthy, and after costing out our various appointments needed during the year plus the cost of the plan, we found it to be the least expensive," Sara said. "I think the next plan up was around $160."

The downside to HSAs is the high-deductible insurance, which is intended primarily to protect people against the cost of catastrophic illnesses, like cancer, or injuries that might require surgery. So it doesn't cover routine doctor visits.

People with HSAs, like Sara and Travis, put the money they save on monthly premiums into a tax-free savings account, and use the money that builds up in the savings account to pay for the occasional doctor bill.

Sara's plan has a $3,800 deductible per year. That means insurance doesn't cover anything unless the couple's medical bills in a year top $3,800. After that, the insurance pays 85 percent of their medical costs. If their out-of-pocket costs hit $8,000, that's the limit. Everything else is covered at 100 percent for that year.

But the nice thing is that CSX softens the blow for Sara and Travis by depositing $2,400 in their HSA at the beginning of the year. So unless their medical bills top $2,400, they pay nothing.

Sara and Travis also put $250 a month into their HSA. That adds up to $3,000 a year, money they can use to pay medical bills and for which they get an income tax deduction. And the money is theirs, so it can grow over time into a nice investment account.

"The $250 a month is to build up money to pay for future health care and it is also an investment," Sara said. "We have roughly $7,000 in our account."

Sara also doesn't have to worry much about whether a doctor is in her network.

"We feel like it gives us more control in deciding which doctor we want to see and when. We don't need a referral to go see a dermatologist or podiatrist; we just research them online and go."

HSAs are not for everyone, but can work very, very well to hold down health costs, provide excellent coverage, and offer affordable premiums. I encourage you to give them some thought.

At CSX, Sara is responsible for overseeing the movement of coal to river terminals, where it is loaded onto barges. Once the coal is loaded, it can be delivered to a variety of places, such as steel mills, utility companies, and other smaller industrial companies, and for export.

When she's not traveling for work or leisure, or caring for her flowers, Sara enjoys watching football. She and Travis root for their hometown NFL team, the Jaguars, which is good because they have differing allegiances on the college football front.

Sara roots for her dad's school, the Florida State Seminoles. Travis, meanwhile, roots for the University of Florida Gators. In Florida, where college football rivalries are strong, that's a big deal.

"We love each other 365 days a year," says Sara, "but the day Florida and FSU play each other, we're not so friendly."

What should you keep in mind if you're thinking about getting involved with an HSA?

Understand the basics of HSAs.
- An HSA is basically a qualified high-deductible health plan with premiums that are lower per month than a traditional health plan. The cash you're saving with those lower

premiums goes into a tax-free savings account. You can then use it to pay for routine stuff or you can invest it for your future.

- HSAs are great for certain kinds of people. For example, if you're self-employed, you get a tax deduction for putting money in. Then the money grows and can be spent tax-free. It's such a great triple threat. You can contribute a maximum of $3,250 for a single person and $6,450 for a family.

- Where these kinds of plans really shine is for catastrophic things, not for when you have the sniffles and want to go to the doctor. If your health gets really bad, with many traditional health plans there could be more holes in your coverage than in Swiss cheese. Yet with an HSA, if something bad happens to you, you are covered to the max.

Pick the right investments for you.

- HSAAdministrators.info and HSAFinder.com both offer quotes and other info for individuals looking for HSAs and companies looking to start HSA enrollment for their employees.

- Health Savings Administrators is an affiliate of Vanguard and offers a full suite of twenty-two Vanguard no-load mutual funds. There's even a simple money market account available for those who like to take the conservative approach with their money.

- HSAs are not for everyone, but if you are in fairly good health and generally seek value in everything you purchase, this program probably will allow you to reduce health insurance costs and retain the savings.

Name your own price for health care.

- If you have an HSA and have to pay for routine procedures, you know that every dollar counts. Enter bidding for health care à la the Priceline model as a way to save money!

- BidonHealth.com lets you put out for bid the care you need from multiple providers who need to keep their lab techs busy during slow hours. The site claims it will save you 60 to 90 percent on labs, X-rays, mammograms, cancer screenings, ultrasounds, and more.

- *The Arizona Republic* reported that a woman who was on her husband's high-deductible health plan needed a spinal MRI and was quoted $3,200 at a nearby radiology office. So she went on BidonHealth.com and successfully bid $350 for the same procedure at a facility about 190 miles away. She had to drive about three hours to have the test, but what a savings!

HSAs are one answer to our health care quandary.

- Health care accounts for 20 cents of every dollar of economic output in the United States, with much of it coming from government and private employers.
- We all know this system lacks transparency and is anti-free market. So what would I do to fix the mess in Washington if I were in our nation's capital?
- I would take health care out of the hands of employers and the government. Each individual would be responsible for buying his or her own policy, if they wanted to. The elderly and those of low income would get a voucher to go shop for coverage on their own. That way, we would become consumers again, shopping for the best deals. HSAs go a long way toward achieving that goal.
- But since we're *not* doing it like this, we have removed capitalism from 20 percent of our economy . . . and that is not sustainable.

WORKING AND LEARNING

The Great Recession sent many an American back to college to learn new job skills, and re-emphasized to many the value of a college education in a tough economy. But the cost of college remains a huge challenge.

In this chapter, we meet people who have found creative ways to attend and pay for college, and those who have re-created themselves in an effort to survive and thrive in a world of fewer jobs. I'll also give you some tips on how to approach education, student loans, and the new job market.

CLARK SMART
CLASSROOM

With the cost of college a hardship for many,
Alex finds a way to pay the bills and hone his skills

GOING TO COLLEGE CAN BE STAGGERINGLY expensive, and over the years I've had a variety of advice to give students and parents on how to ease the cost. Rent textbooks rather than buy them. Attend community college for two years, then transfer to a four-year school.

But Alex Harker taught me one I hadn't considered.

Alex, now a graphic designer at a Washington, D.C., think tank, finished graduate school debt-free by working as a teaching assistant.

"I got a full tuition waiver and was paid a stipend of around $800 per month," Alex said. "I graduated in the spring of 2011 without taking on a dime of debt."

Alex, now twenty-six, learned about this method from his father, who is an anesthesiologist.

"I can remember a number of times hearing from my dad that he had done this and saved himself a significant amount that would have otherwise been taken out as loans. When I made the decision to go to grad school, seeking out an assistantship seemed like the natural route for me to take."

Alex actually applied for the position rather late in the game. He was about to graduate from Indiana Wesleyan University with a B.S. in media communication. He planned to attend grad school at Ball State University.

"I was sitting at one of the video editing stations at the TV outlet I worked for as an undergrad and it hit me that graduation was only about two months away. The first place I looked for prospective programs was the website for the state university closest to the private college I was attending. I was in the communication field already, so I looked at those programs first, saw one that fit my research interests and started gathering the required application material."

Alex says being a teaching assistant was a lot of work, but it was manageable. He taught during the day and took classes himself at night.

"The actual teaching was pretty easy, at least for me, but most of the work is in preparation and assessment of student work."

Alex taught public speaking, a subject he already had a basic level of familiarity with.

"I had taken entry-level public speaking as an undergrad, but teaching is completely different. In terms of theory, history, and structural models of speaking, there was a lot to learn."

Alex figures he earned about $35 an hour for his work as a teaching assistant. He says he made sure to tell others that it's a good way to pay your way through grad school.

He also liked the social aspects of it.

"It was great because nearly everyone in my program was in the same few courses for our master's work and nearly all of us were also assistants. We were able to work together on lessons for the courses we taught and were also able to assist each other with our own course work. It quickly became a very tight group."

But the work could be overwhelming at times, especially near the end of a semester.

"As a teaching assistant, this is multiplied by two because you're trying to finish your own work while also balancing increased grading loads from your own students finishing up their work as well. On top of this, students place increasing demands on your time as they start to feel the pressure from all of their work coming due. The last month of a semester is usually extremely demanding."

Alex grew up in the Midwest. His mom was a social worker who took early retirement when his dad finished medical school.

He learned to be frugal from his parents.

"They shop prices and wait for things to go on sale. If something is not in the budget, they wait until they know they can comfortably afford [it] before making large purchases."

Alex didn't start listening to me until he graduated. But he can relate to my oft-told advice about textbooks.

"As a student, I always spent a lot of time trying to get the best price on textbooks. This was difficult as an undergrad because the campus bookstore took a lot of measures to abuse its monopoly, to the extent that it would withhold ISBN numbers, titles, and authors. Many people would overpay for books at that store, but I would contact my new professors [for the list of required books] before the start of term or physically go into the store to get that information so I would have enough time to shop online."

Alex has always been interested in politics, and he loves working in the nation's capital. For now, he produces print publications, ranging from research papers to books, for the think tank where he works.

"Ultimately, I'd like to cover political topics, sports, or technology in some way through production of video, audio, or new media."

Wherever his career takes him, he has a huge advantage over other young people because he won't have a staggering debt load hanging over him—all because his dad taught him to work as a teaching assistant in graduate school.

What can you learn from Alex's story?

On-campus work can lower the cost of an education.

- Alex's story offers one way to reduce your out-of-pocket for tuition. Another possibility comes from Christa DiBiase, the executive producer of my radio show. She saved money on her education by serving as a resident assistant (RA) during her junior and senior years at Boston College.
- As an RA, Christa was in charge of the safety and well-being of students, making sure they were doing well socially and ultimately ensuring that campus rules weren't being broken.
- "It gave me a sense of responsibility and I made a lot of great friends doing it," she says. "I enjoyed it more than I imagined I would, and showing that level of responsibility was useful in obtaining my first job out of school."
- Perks of the job included free room and board in an on-campus dormitory and a free meal card.
- As Christa recalls, there was a pretty competitive application process that included an interview and a week of training simulations to see if candidates would make good RAs. Christa estimates she saved at least $12,000 per year serving from 1992–1994.
- If this sounds like something you'd consider, go to the residence life office at your school and ask about opportunities. You can't beat living for free on campus and a free meal card!

Pursue a $10,000 four-year degree.

- A number of states are coming up with ways to keep the cost of a college education down.

- The university system in the state of Texas has been deputized to deliver a standard four-year degree for a total cost of $10,000. Degree offerings will include information technology, business administration, organizational leadership, and more. Among the ten participating Texas colleges are Angelo State University, University of Texas at Arlington, and Texas A&M University–Commerce.

- Florida has its own way to reduce the cost of a degree. They've converted many of their two-year community colleges to offer four-year bachelor degree programs. Meanwhile, Georgia is also allowing a handful of its two-year community colleges to offer four-year degrees.

- Massachusetts has yet another idea. If resident students go to a Massachusetts community college for two years and maintain a 3.0 GPA or better, that qualifies them for free tuition during their junior and senior years at the University of Massachusetts at the Lowell or Amherst campuses.

Seek out unusual scholarships.

- If you're not excited about the community college route, why not check out some scholarship options? There are a number of bizarre scholarships available, including ones for being tall, for being left-handed, and even for drinking milk. (No, I am not making this stuff up!) Visit CollegeGold.com and search keyword "unusual scholarships" to see what I'm talking about. The really obscure ones are usually funded by someone who had to overcome some kind of disability in life.

Know the faculty and follow the money.

- If you are going to a private college, I recommend getting to know the dean, the department head, or a senior, tenured faculty member. That can dramatically open up paths to grant money, research money, and scholarship money that you might not otherwise know about. Perhaps there's a professor they know who needs research work done for a book. That's just one possible example out of many.

THE GRADUATE

*Kate finds a way to defuse her share of debt from the nation's
$1 trillion student loan time bomb before it blows*

KATE LECKONBY STANDS in a mobile trailer unit attached to Archdale-Trinity Middle School (ATMS) and looks like she's about to faint. A moment later, she's crumpled to the ground.

A quick check of her vital stats reveals normal blood pressure and heart rate. She shows no signs of exhaustion from hours of teaching Spanish to sixty students each day in her Archdale, North Carolina, school.

So what gives?

Kate is simply feigning collapse because a teeming trailer-load of seventh graders has butchered the pronunciation of a basic phrase like *¿Cómo te llamas?* again.

Until the kids can pronounce "ll" as a *y* sound, Kate had better get used to staying down. Because a day's lesson has culminated in "What's your name?" sounding like a Spanglish-ized inquiry about the South American relative of a camel.

"We joke a lot in my classroom. I let the kids tell me random funny stories where it's applicable. I fall on the floor pretending to faint when they make errors in Spanish that we have talked about one hundred times," she tells me. "They laugh. We have a great classroom atmosphere."

On one wall of her classroom trailer hangs a black sombrero accented with silver trim. Near it yellow cut-out letters reading *"¿Por qué aprendemos español?"* (Why are we learning Spanish?) spill out like a news crawl above a doorway. Another wall is plastered with color-ful student papers artfully arranged around the words *"Trabajo excelente"* (Excellent work).

Kate's done some excellent work of her own, chiefly in the way she's handling the student loan debt she amassed on the way to a master's degree in education.

"I went to a private school in New York State initially [for my bachelor's degree], but quickly transferred to a SUNY school [State University of New York] to save money. I was an RA in addition to playing college basketball and working constantly to try to cut housing costs," Kate says. "I was in that middle where my parents made enough that the government didn't write a check for my education. But my parents weren't able to help at that time."

For her master's, she went to the University of North Carolina at Greensboro part-time at night during her second and third years of teaching.

"I made so little that I had to take out enough loans to pay for books and my travel to and from [campus]," she says. "It was either that or not do it. . . . I know that it made me a better, more knowledgeable teacher."

The end result was graduating with $43,000 in federal student loans. Her current salary is $39,000.

Student loans are a backbreaking burden on many people in this country for both young and old. Collectively, borrowing in our country for education is nearing $1 trillion. I believe it's the next debt bubble to burst.

But Kate is hitting her little chunk of that $1 trillion with a one-two punch.

First, she's capping the amount she pays every month through an income-based repayment (IBR) plan. So while she was once paying $245 every month toward her education debt, she's now paying just $45 under the IBR plan.

Second, she's using the Public Service Loan Forgiveness (PSLF) program, which is open to a broad range of public service employees, not just teachers, to receive full loan forgiveness on any outstanding balance after making ten years of monthly payments on her loans.

By Kate's accounting, she'll pay somewhere around $5,000 over the next 120 months and have her loan balance of roughly $38,000 forgiven at that time. Those dollar figures could go up or down a bit over the next ten years based on family size and adjusted gross income, but you get the idea.

Trabajo excelente, indeed.

Kate's husband, Brian, is also a teacher at ATMS. He teaches history and is head coach of the school's football team. Together they have a two-year-old daughter, Lauren.

Like many teachers, Kate forms a deep bond with her students. It's one that's remembered years later on both sides.

"Just the other day, I went to the drugstore and the cashier was a student that I had four years ago. He is now a senior! His face lit up, as did mine, and he commented how much he always loved my class, that it was his favorite," Kate says. "Middle school kids don't often express their appreciation at age fourteen, so it's always neat to hear it—even if it is four years after the fact."

Kate says her personality as a teacher is hard to describe, though she's "very driven and detail-oriented."

When I spoke to her, she was looking forward to fun learning activities like siesta day, when the class would discuss the custom and its implications on society; and another day when they planned to make *churros*—a long, thin fried dough pastry sometimes called a Spanish doughnut.

Though both Brian and Kate love what they do, furloughs are a threat to their family budget. In 2009, North Carolina issued a furlough that amounted to a .5 percent cut to their salary.

"I think we got some workdays off in return, but no teacher can afford to take workdays off!" Kate says.

A teacher's salary tends to be laddered, with very few, if any, raises during the first three years and then bigger jumps in compensation during the fourth, fifth, and six years. But Brian and Kate were frozen just before they began their fourth year.

"[Living on] two North Carolina teacher salaries has been an incredible challenge—especially in trying to do more than just get by every month. Since 2008, we have not received any raises, not even cost of living. Brian and I make the same thing we made five years ago—probably a little less, actually."

In fact, the couple's health benefits have gotten worse and they've had to go from standard 80/20 coverage to a cheaper 70/30 plan.

"This year, they did give us a 1 percent raise, but then they raised dependent health coverage—which of course they didn't publicize—so anyone with kids didn't move forward at all."

Fortunately, Kate and Brian have been able to manage because, like many teachers, they work second jobs. Kate was a part-time instructor at a community college for a time. And Brian runs wrestling tournaments and is an umpire in the spring.

"We are grateful to have stayed employed during these tough economic times, but we worry about how much longer this will go and how it will affect our family's future. We love teaching and both got into it for all the right reasons, but unfortunately there is a sentiment that teachers shouldn't care about money [or] their paychecks. I think it's irresponsible for us not to."

Kate is originally from upstate New York and Brian is from the Canton, Ohio, area. She credits both of their parents for making them into people who can raise a family on teaching salaries.

In fact, Kate and Brian decided to go into a longer-term play for their financial future when they bought a condo in Myrtle Beach, South Carolina, with Kate's parents two years ago.

"We researched and shopped for two years, losing lots of properties in the process to people who had cash offers or who were just quicker than us. But we knew this was the time in history to make that investment. We finally fell upon the best deal we had seen in all of our searching."

Financing their share of the condo has been a big sacrifice that's required many cuts in other places.

"We don't own smartphones, we don't really take vacations, we have worked most summers since we started teaching, [and] we drive two paid-off cars," Kate says. "But we believe it will pay off, and [be] something we can enjoy with our daughter in the meantime."

If you're swimming in student loan debt, take heed of these tips:

See if you qualify for the Public Service Loan Forgiveness program.

- As per the PSLF program that Kate qualifies for, only federal Stafford, Grad PLUS, or consolidation loans in the Direct Loan program are eligible for forgiveness after ten years of on-time payments. Private loans are not eligible.
- Qualifying careers for the PSLF program include any job in government, military service, emergency management, public safety, law enforcement, public health, and public education, to name just a few. After 120 nonconsecutive months of on-time payment, the remainder of your student loan balance is forgiven when you're in this program.
- IBRInfo.org does a great job of explaining all the details of the PSLF in plain English.

Explore other student loan forgiveness and repayment options.

- Even if you don't qualify for the PSLF program, there is still help for you.
- Under the new Pay As You Earn repayment program, your monthly payments on federal loans will be capped at 10 percent of your income—regardless of your income. Outstanding debt is forgiven after twenty years of on-time payments. This new provision applies to federal student loans taken out after October 1, 2007; again, though, it does *not* apply to any private loans. See if you're eligible by visiting the Department of Education's website at StudentLoans.gov.
- For federal student loans taken out before October 1, 2007, you might qualify to have your payments capped at 15 percent of your income and outstanding debt forgiven after twenty-five years of on-time payments. This is part of the income-based repayment program I talked about on pages 13–14 of my last book, *Clark Howard's Living Large in Lean Times*. Visit IBRInfo.org for more info.
- If you have a mix of both federal and private student loans, pay as little as possible toward your federal loans with the help of one of these programs I've discussed, and then pour every dollar possible into your private student loans.

Get student loan forgiveness for homesteading.

- Like Kate and Brian, Americans have historically moved from where they were raised for opportunity. Today it's possible to do that and get your student loan debt forgiven if you know where to look.
- At least fifty counties in Kansas qualify as what are called "rural opportunity zones." In return for living in these communities, they'll absorb up to $15,000 of your student loan debt and exempt you from state income tax for five years. You don't have to be an existing resident of the state to qualify for this program.
- A similar program recently launched in Niagara Falls, New York, has been getting a lot of media attention. Niagara Falls is offering up to $3,500 a year in loan forgiveness if you rent and live there full-time or buy and occupy a home in the community as a full-time resident.
- Consider the pluses and minuses of the communities carefully before jumping at these opportunities. And be sure to contact the local governments in any of these places for more details.

Know the rules for student loan borrowing.

- I've long talked about some basic rules for student loan borrowing designed to keep you out of harm's way. Here's a quick reiteration of the fundamentals so you don't have to struggle with student loan debt in the first place.
- Borrow only what's available to you under the federal student loan program. Avoid private loans at all costs. Never take out more in loans for a four-year degree than your likely first year's earnings on the job that degree will get you. And start your degree out at a community college for two years before transferring to a four-year school where you plan to get your degree.

SEARCH AND EMPLOY

*Adrift in the age of the joblet, Jannet pieces together
opportunities to make ends meet*

It's been a rough few years for Jannet Walsh, but she's trying hard to get things turned around.

Jannet, forty-eight, was a photojournalist for ten years with the *Ocala Star-Banner*, a *New York Times*–owned newspaper in Ocala, Florida. She did digital still photography, videography editing, and production.

But in 2008, Jannet suffered a series of setbacks. In April of that year, her mother had a stroke. In October, she got laid off from the *Star-Banner*. And in December, her father died.

In May 2009, she got a job writing a column at an organization called Workforce Connection in Ocala.

"Yes, it is funny," said Jannet of the notion that she used to help people find work, and now is having trouble doing that herself.

"I was a columnist on workforce topics for job seekers and businesses. People would call me and write me about job searching."

Jannet resigned in August 2010 to be with her ailing mother and aunt back home in Minnesota. She got a job as a writer and photographer for the *West Central Tribune*, but was laid off, again, in August 2011. Her mom died a few months later, a week after Jannet hit a black bear with her car.

Now Jannet lives in her aunt's white wooden home in rural Murdock, Minnesota, population 278. Not 278,000—278 people. Her aunt, meanwhile, lives in a nursing home.

Jannet often walks her West Highland terrier to the edge of town to see the sun set, where a field of soybeans surrounds Sacred Heart Catholic Cemetery. She usually stops at her family's gravesite to pray.

Murdock is a farming community located on the railroad in Swift County, Minnesota. There's no bar in Murdock, no grocery store, no hair salon. The café closed years ago, although its sign still bears the traditional Irish shamrock.

You can buy a few items, such as eggs, sandwich meat, bread, cold drinks, pizza, and sandwiches at Dooley's, the town's only gas station, Jannet said. Travelers, locals, and tradesmen can be found eating at Dooley's executive-style boardroom table, even the local banker.

"I've been laid off twice," Jannet said, "and have no hope of finding a full-time job living in a rural area in an economy that has few jobs."

Still, she's earning a living—building a freelance writing, photography, and videography business while stitching together revenue from several other sources to make it work.

In 2011, she earned a little less than $21,000, including $5,100 in rental income from a local farm that has been in her family for generations. The 120-acre farm grows corn and soybeans. Her grandfather bought the farm, just south of Murdock in De Graff, Minnesota, on March 16, 1920. Her family was part of the Catholic colony in De Graff.

"Archbishop John Ireland formed the Catholic Colonization Bureau to help many Irish come to Minnesota, working with the railroad providing the land for farmers."

Jannet says not being able to find a full-time job has little to do with her talent or skills but with the state of the economy.

She recently completed Certified Life & Career Coach training, with Jay Block, a career coach and author. She thought it might help with future jobs, writing, or just getting her a job.

"My idea of the multiple flows of income came from my career coach training called Protean Careers, adjusting to opportunities and changes to the economy," Jannet said.

In an era of high unemployment, many are doing what Jannet is doing, piecing together several "joblets" rather than working at a single full-time job to make ends meet.

In the process, Jannet has developed a bit of a flair for promotion. In 2010, she was at Florida's Poynter Institute, a renowned educational institution for journalists, and someone suggested she post her videos in CNN's iReport.

"That's pretty cool, isn't it? It's a great place to post my videos while looking for work and promoting my business. CNN Radio visited me in July 2012 in Murdock!"

Being an iReporter helps Jannet.

"It's really more than I could have imagined living in tiny Murdock, needing any extra edge to find my way in a difficult and challenging economy."

Jannet says living in the age of the joblet is hard, "but until I find my way, that's all I have. My family might have been pioneers here, but I'm an outsider, as I spent most of my career working out of state."

Age might also be an issue, Jannet says.

"Out of college, newspapers would fly me to job interviews around the country as a newspaper photographer. That's all over. . . . Not sure if the problem is that I'm older, but there are fewer jobs in a bad economy, fewer jobs in a rural area."

The weakened state of the newspaper industry, which has been hurt by the Internet and the recession, has also hurt Jannet.

On the plus side, Jannet's efforts are for herself.

"I am working for me and my future, not promoting a company or corporation."

What lessons can you learn from Jannet's story of living in the age of the joblet?

You've got to change with the times.

- Jannet's years on the newspaper coincided with a time when technology caused great disruption across the entire media field. With the Internet and e-readers, people no longer subscribe to traditional print newspapers in the numbers they once did.

- That means you have to be willing to tear up the playbook and recognize how much things change. Today, education and training can never stop. What Jannet once did for print newspapers, she now does online in an effort to advertise her skills and secure a job.

- Just like Jannet, you've got to take off the blinders and look at alternative ways of doing things. Success today does not guarantee success tomorrow.

Education and training are the keys.

- When Jannet found herself with diminished job prospects, she went back for more training that she believed would be beneficial to her job hunt. That's exactly what you should be doing whether or not you find yourself painted into a corner in your career choice.

- For example, let's look at a different industry other than Jannet's. Did you know that at a time of high unemployment, America is returning as a manufacturing powerhouse?
- But here's the rub: Manufacturing is completely different now than it was twenty years ago. Today's manufacturing equipment is very often sophisticated and automated. So a factory in any given industry that might have required one thousand people in 1992 is able to put out the same amount of goods with only seventy-five people on staff today.
- There is opportunity, but you've got to be flexible. Get the training, skills, and education necessary to make the jobs that are available yours.

Relying on family can help.
- Like so many people, Jannet had family obligations that brought her to where she is today. She moved to Murdock to help care for her ailing mother and aunt. Throughout the Great Recession, as more and more families faced foreclosure, they too moved back in with relatives—whether they wanted to or not. Having family to rely on for a roof over your head is great solace in rough economic times. Don't overlook this important asset in your life.

Networking remains key to getting job offers.
- Living in Murdock presents one big-time challenge for Jannet. She has a very small pool of people to network with in a town of 278 people!
- Most jobs are filled by hirers who are likely to bring in someone they know or know of for an interview. A friend of a friend, a colleague of a colleague. People think that networking is passé. No way! Today, as the Great Recession marches on and headline unemployment rides high, the reality is that getting in the door is what counts.
- Nobody likes to be asked for a job, but everybody loves to give advice. So identify some key people in your industry who you can have a face-to-face meeting with and interview them for their career advice.
- Any method that gets you in front of people will work. What typically *doesn't* work is trying to apply for a job electronically to somebody who doesn't know you. Networking is core and key. That's how it gets done.

THE ICEMAN COMETH

Steven got laid off from an insurance giant and reinvented himself as the King of Pops in the frozen-treat business

OVER THE YEARS, I've met a number of people who've made dramatic changes in the middle of their careers, and I've wanted to bring that experience to life for you.

There was the financial analyst who worked on Wall Street for twenty years, lost his job in the Great Recession, then went back to school and emerged as a pharmacy technician. There was the fellow who managed restaurants for fifteen years, reached his stress limit, then decided he wanted to drive a taxi.

But the person whose story I'm choosing to tell you about now is Steven Carse, who got laid off in 2009 from the notoriously troubled insurance giant AIG and ended up founding King of Pops, one of a handful of companies across the United States that sells high-quality frozen ice pops.

That's right. He went from insurance to ice pops, about as radical a career change as you can make.

And he told me about it after he got back from "ice cream school" in Pennsylvania.

Steven, still just twenty-nine, actually got the idea for King of Pops in 2005, two years before he started at AIG. He was with his two older brothers, Nick and Ashley, at a beach in Puerto Escondido, Mexico. They were eating *paletas*, which are ice pops, common in Latin America, that are usually made from fresh fruit.

"We had been discussing how amazing these *paletas* were, and how much fun it would be to have a place back home, and at this moment—for the first time—it seemed like something that could really happen."

Steven said it actually took some time on that monthlong 2005 trip to fall in love with the Latin treat.

"While there are a lot of amazing *paleta* producers in Latin America, there are a lot that seem to freeze sugar and water," he said. "We did our best to find the artisan variety. I had some of the best and worst desserts of my life on that trip."

In 2005, Steven was just about to finish college and head to Idaho to work at a small newspaper. After another year, he came back home, to Atlanta, to take a higher paying job at AIG.

When he got laid off from the $50,000-a-year insurance job, Steven realized it was time to start his business.

"I felt like it was now or never. I had nothing holding me back, very little obligation. The time was just right."

The first task was figuring out how to make great-tasting ice pops.

"It was more or less trial and error," he said. "I spent the winter forcing medicine cups full of frozen fruit down my friends' throats. I also sent out a bunch of letters to people around the country asking if I could come work for free. People's Pops in New York was nice enough to let me come and check out their operation. More than anything I saw the amount of energy operating a small business takes, but also the amount of enthusiasm a loyal excited customer base can bring."

So what's the difference between King of Pops' gourmet pops and the ones you can buy in the supermarket?

"There is really no comparison," Steven said. "I just finished the Ice Cream School at Penn State. Most of the classes were about how to make those products that you see in the store. The ones that are $2.50 for twelve—ours are $2.50 for one."

The difference starts with the ingredients. Steven says King of Pops uses fresh, organic, local fruit.

"Next, we try to be creative. We make straightforward flavors like Strawberry Lemonade, but we also have a lot of fun incorporating flavors people might not expect—like Tangerine Basil."

The company's best-sellers are Chocolate Sea Salt, Banana Puddin, Key Lime Pie, Raspberry Lime, Grapefruit Mint, Fresh Georgia Peach, the previously mentioned Tangerine Basil, and Coconut Lemongrass.

"Our product is our primary concern, and we spend a lot of money to make sure it is good. The big brands are more concerned with operating at the lowest cost they can. They are concerned with distribution, and have to pack their product full of artificial ingredients so it can go across the country, sit on a shelf for a year, and still taste like they want."

Steven's first day in business was April 1, 2010. After running into some roadblocks opening a small storefront location on an Atlanta street corner, he asked the property owners if he could set up a cart on their property.

He sold about twenty ice pops on the first day.

"It is all relative. I was pretty excited from the response. I was living on my brother's couch. He wasn't charging me, and I had a little bit of rent at a shared kitchen to cover. . . . My cart wasn't branded yet, and I really had no idea what I was doing. A lot of people agonize over the perfect grand opening. I wasn't ready, but I was just ready to get started."

He realized he had a hit when he set up shop at a local festival called May Day.

Steven's brother Ashley was in town, and he and brother Nick, who had been helping from the beginning, were working at the original cart location.

Steven sold all the ice pops he had brought to the festival and went to celebrate with a beer.

"It had already been my best day yet. And I felt like all was right with the world. On my way home I called to see how my brothers were doing. They said they had run out very quickly. They had brought some of the masses back to our kitchen to give them whatever spares we could find laying around. From then on I think we were making pops until two a.m. nearly every weekday."

Steven says those sessions are about what you'd expect, with one stainless-steel table, a blender, and some food containers, with the new team learning as they went and "balancing our perfectionist tendencies with a need to have product for the next day."

Steven gives a lot of credit to his girlfriend, Gabriella Oviedo, whom he met at his first location and started dating. She was working at a nearby barbeque restaurant, and after her own long shifts at work, she would come in and help him finish up and clean the kitchen.

"She basically kept me sane that first year," Steven says.

Today, King of Pops sells a couple thousand pops from its carts on a summer Saturday. On a dreary Monday, he says, it might be one hundred.

"The process is the same, just scaled up. We have a bigger freezing machine, more tables, more knives, more blenders."

The company sold 600,000 pops last year, a remarkable total for a young company.

It has four locations every day, plus dozens of street food, farmers market, and weekly event locations.

"We have sixteen carts in Atlanta, so we have the ability to go to a bunch of places."

Geographic expansion has already begun. The company opened in Athens, Georgia, and Charleston, South Carolina, two years ago. In 2013, it planned to open in Richmond, Virginia, Charlotte, North Carolina, and Chattanooga, Tennessee.

Like many of the people you'll meet in this book, Steven had good role models growing up.

He was born in Austin, Minnesota, to Jim Carse, now sixty-four, and Lib Carse, sixty-two, both from southwest Nebraska. Jim was raised on a farm and later worked for Hormel, a job that sent him around the country. Steven moved to Omaha, Nebraska, as a child, and ended up in Atlanta by kindergarten.

Lib's father was the town lawyer of Benkelman, Nebraska.

"I think my mom has always been great at budgeting. I can remember when I was eleven or twelve, my mom had us write a proposal for our monthly allowance. We had to take everything into consideration, school lunch, haircuts, and fun stuff too, like movies, baseball cards, etcetera. I remember after that day I shaved my head because I used my money to buy a pair of shears and kept collecting my $11.99 per month that I had budgeted for haircuts."

He says his father is an amazing salesman. "Everyone likes him, and he works very hard. It was a good combination."

As for Steven, he's happier today, after his dramatic career switch, than when he worked for AIG. But there is a cost.

"I'm a lot busier," he said. "I could check out when I finished work at AIG. My mind rarely stops thinking about business now."

Steven has a fascinating story. What can you learn from it?

Anticipate double duty when changing careers.

- When Steven transitioned from AIG to launching King of Pops, he didn't have any financial obligations holding him back. Nor did he have much experience in doing what he wanted to do!

- If you're eyeing a career change and have an entrepreneurial bent like Steven, I want you to smooth the transition by starting to work in your new field part-time while keeping your current steady job.
- *Money* magazine reports that 70 percent of men and 50 percent of women maintain full-time jobs while starting a new business. That's the smart way to do it. Of course, that means that you're working your tail off both day and night. But it also lowers the risk should your new career change or business venture fail.

Seek out continual re-education and training.

- Steven spoke with me as he was returning from Penn State's College of Agricultural Sciences and its famed Ice Cream Short Course—a program dating back to 1892 believed to be the first continuing education course in the United States.
- The King of Pops was seeking to learn more about ice cream production techniques as he continues his rise to the top of the frozen confections world. (Being a lifelong ice cream lover, that's some curriculum I'd like to sink my teeth into too!)
- But here's the message: You can never stop learning, particularly if you're a career changer. Technology changes so fast that what you're doing today in any given field could be obsolete in five years or less. Don't go through life with blinders on. Look for the wider changes in an industry and figure out how to adapt. Be ready to reinvent yourself for success.

Get upskilled.

- An estimated three million jobs go unfilled every month because employers can't find people with the right skills. That's led some employers to partner with philanthropies, governments, and community colleges to educate existing employees so they can fill those openings. That kind of promoting within is now being called "upskilling."
- Imagine going from moving furniture as a hospital maintenance worker to a highly paid nursing position in the same hospital. That's what happened to a man named Roddale Smith I read about in *Business Week*. His employer funded his nursing school education at night while he continued doing maintenance work by day at a Cincinnati hospital. Now he's graduated and doubled his pay as a skilled nurse.
- If you're stuck in low-wage work, there could be an opportunity for you to get some free training and move to a highly paid career, particularly in the manufacturing fields. The key is to find an employer willing to upskill you. A good starting point is the National Fund for Workforce Solutions website (nfwsolutions.org) and their list of regional collaboratives in twenty-four states.

Take time away to germinate ideas.

- Inspiration for a career change or a new business can strike in the unlikeliest of places. For Steven, his life-altering moment came on the sandy beaches of Puerto Escondido as he enjoyed *paletas* with his brothers. Who knows where the inspiration to change careers or launch a new business will start for you?

- You never know what else is out there unless you challenge the way you see yourself and reinvent yourself in a new mold. You don't have to be stuck in a rut. If you pursue what you love, the money you need to survive will generally follow.

THE EMPOWERED CONSUMER

Too often I hear from people who feel beaten down by a business they have a gripe with even though they're actually in control—only they don't know it. In this chapter, we'll take a look at how social media has leveled the playing field between consumers and businesses. We'll also meet someone who makes her point by lower-tech means, and another who can tell you how to get a fair shake when you're dealing with an insurance company.

GOING SOCIAL

Megan uses technology to help other consumers spar with misbehaving businesses

I'VE HELPED A LOT OF PEOPLE with customer service issues in the more than twenty-five years I've been on the radio and TV, and even more with the Consumer Action Center I set up years back, through which volunteers take off-air calls and help resolve problems.

But I believe Megan Smith is the first person who has ever created a company, inspired by what I do, to help people deal with uncooperative companies.

Megan said she heard me helping people and thought, "I can do that!"

"I was hearing story after story of people having problems with service issues," Megan said, "but they didn't have the tools to help themselves. I decided to start a little company that could help those who didn't know what to do but who wanted to fight back. After I helped myself a few times and knew the ins and outs, helping others got easier and easier."

Megan, forty-two, works as a professional extra in Frisco, Texas, a fast-growing city north of Dallas. She's been a background extra in movies like *Any Given Sunday*, *Hall Pass*, and *The Odd Life of Timothy Green*, and on TV dramas like FOX's *The Following*, starring Kevin Bacon. It's work that doesn't pay much—$8 an hour for twelve-to-fourteen-hour days—but she enjoys it.

"You have to go in knowing it's a long day for little pay. I just like seeing how it's all done and getting to be so close to some big names."

Her quest to curb poor customer service doesn't pay a lot, either, but she didn't start her company to make a lot of money. She gives a free consultation, and if she thinks she can help, charges a one-time fee of $50.

"I am very flexible on that fee, though," Megan said. "I am a softy when it comes to the elderly or those in need, so once I talk to them on the phone and get a feel for them, I might lower or waive the fee altogether. For me, it really isn't about the money, it's about helping people."

Megan has had success in dealing with what I call "customer no-service." For example, she helped a gentleman who, after planning a trip, was told his frequent flier miles had expired.

"I knew I would get nowhere with a supervisor over the phone, so I went directly to e-mailing their corporate office. I explained that this individual had flown for many years with their airline and accumulated many miles in doing so. I also stated that he had spoken to an agent just before his miles disappeared, and she had said nothing to him about their expiration date closing in, which seemed a little shady and definitely not what I would expect of a company such as theirs. Within twelve hours, I received a response with a heartfelt apology and a reinstatement of his miles."

Another client was a woman who had trouble with her dentist. She had gone in for a crown, and while it was being positioned in her mouth but before it was cemented in place, the dental assistant left the room.

"She was extremely lucky that she did not swallow that thing. Afterwards, she explained that she did not want to pay the $1,000 because of what happened. The front desk attendant explained that it was not in her control and demanded payment. Of course my client paid, because that is what most honest people do. She did have to go back two more times because they had not placed the crown right, and each time she was told there was nothing they could do about the original payment of $1,000. That is when she contacted me. I contacted their office manager and her check was mailed within the week."

Megan's philosophy is to be nice, not angry, when she approaches a company.

"Everyone knows the saying 'You get more flies with honey than with vinegar,' and that is the absolute truth when dealing with customer no-service. If you come to the company blazing mad, yelling, calling them names, and telling them everything they've done wrong, their first instinct will be to defend themselves and fight back. You probably won't get very far, you definitely won't get results, and you'll walk away angrier than when you started."

Instead, she says, "kindly state your problem, let them know you respect them as a company, and tell them you are sure they will handle your matter appropriately because of their excellent reputation. Nine times out of ten, they will want to live up to your expectations and they will take care of you. In the rare instances that they don't help on first contact, I then use the tiny threat of social media and let them know it would be in their best interest to resolve the issue as quickly as possible."

Megan does hold out the threat of using social media against a company, but that isn't a tool she goes to frequently.

"In my opinion, social media isn't taken too seriously when it comes to business matters. If you want to get your return accepted or get your frequent flyer miles returned, posting on a company's Facebook page isn't the way to go."

But social media can get results. One of my all-time favorite examples of how it works is the case of Canadian musician Dave Carroll.

Dave was flying from his home in Halifax, Nova Scotia, Canada, to Nebraska, via Chicago, on United Airlines when airline baggage handlers broke his expensive Taylor guitar.

In nine months, Dave got nowhere getting the airline to replace the guitar, until, being a musician, he decided to express his feelings in a song.

As his website recounts, "His 2009 YouTube music video 'United Breaks Guitars' became a worldwide sensation." Dave's video showed actors portraying United baggage handlers gleefully tossing his guitar around and showing "complete indifference." His musician friends appeared in the video wearing sombreros and fake mustaches.

The parody went mega-viral, and United was cowed. It made Dave a pioneer in using social media to bring a corporate giant to its knees.

A year later, Dave was speaking at Columbia Business School, telling the story of making the video with volunteers and friends and then realizing it was attracting an audience.

First there was a local newspaper story, then one in the *Los Angeles Times*.

He was talking about the incident on a regional Canadian TV show when the cohost told him during a commercial that his story was on CNN's *The Situation Room with Wolf Blitzer*.

Dave watched the story that night.

"It was just too bizarre. It was surreal," he told the crowd at Columbia. "I saw a story on Barack Obama and the pope, and there in the middle of this were my friends, the Three Amigos, singing their guts out with their sombreros on."

Dave's website says, "His creative use of social media to share that message has reached over 150 million people. 'United Breaks Guitars' was named one of the five most important videos in Google's history."

Dave wrote a book, *United Breaks Guitars: The Power of One Voice in the Age of Social Media*, is a sought-after speaker, and also helps others fight customer no-service.

Another example I love of fighting back via social media is Arijit Guha, a PhD student at Arizona State University, who was able to use Twitter as a bully pulpit to get Aetna insurance to pay for his medical bills.

According to *The Arizona Republic*, Arijit, who passed away on March 22, 2013, at thirty-two, had Stage 4 colorectal cancer, but his health insurance policy, which he had through Aetna as part of a co-op deal with ASU, had a $300,000 lifetime cap. Arijit blew through that in no time, leaving him in a battle to secure the treatment that could keep him alive.

Arijit took to Twitter and started tweeting at the CEO of Aetna, Mark T. Bertolini, when he was getting the runaround from regular Aetna customer service channels. The CEO is a Twitter guy (@mtbert) and started tweeting back, even admitting, "The system is broken, and I am committed to fixing it."

The insurer agreed to pay his medical bills. Arijit, in the meantime, had raised $100,000 on his own, and with Aetna paying for his care, he decided to donate the money to cancer research.

Megan Smith thinks companies are improving in their handling of customer complaints.

"I think it varies with the company, but for the most part they're getting better. Most companies are aware of the impact social media has on consumerism and are more likely to do what they can to please customers because of that."

She said people should watch out, though, for stock answers.

"These show up mostly on online chat sessions or [coming from] outsourced call centers. They pick keywords out of what you are saying and read back a response that might help you. It just shows that they aren't listening to you, and that to me is a prime example of customer no-service."

She recently complained to a major hardware chain regarding dogs in their stores. She was OK with stores allowing pets inside but got upset when she stepped in some dog waste.

The manager apologized but said even though they have a sign stating no pets allowed, the store allowed them anyway. She contacted corporate, but all she got was a stock response saying some stores allow pets and sorry for your trouble.

"I was disappointed but decided the battle wasn't worth my time. I just decided not to frequent their store anymore, and now I go to their competitor for my home improvement needs."

And that's the ultimate power any consumer has in the free market.

Enlist some outside firepower.

- In a post–"United Breaks Guitars" world, the use of Facebook and Twitter to complain is routine. Now a new site called Groubal.com is trying to organize all the social media gripes and says it will take your complaint to the company and demand an answer. Groubal even compiles its own customer satisfaction index on companies. It's like social networking for complaining, as people look for more and more effective ways to be heard in a busy world. Meanwhile, Dave Carroll has co-founded a site called GripeVine .com that puts the focus on effective problem-solving, providing a forum for customers and businesses to work out their differences.

Identify your targets.

- Arijit Guha had spectacular success using Twitter to address his grievance with Aetna, and it began by targeting tweets to Aetna's Twitter account. But sometimes you might have to penetrate deeper into a company's social media sphere of influence than just their public Twitter account. If that's the case, I recommend you go to the company's website and read press releases in the investor relations section. Look for the names of both the top company brass and the lower-level executives. Then go on Twitter and do a search to determine if any of those individuals have private Twitter accounts. When you find a match, start tweeting away at them.

Use humor as a weapon.

- Particularly if you're doing a YouTube video to spotlight your gripes with a company, you want to do it with an element of humor. Take a cue from Dave Carroll, who softened his blows against United by dressing up with guys in sombreros and fake mustaches. Remember the old saying, "You get more flies with honey than with vinegar." Because no one likes it when somebody just posts an angry rant!

Gripe when you're on the go.

- It was only a matter of time before griping went mobile. ComplainApp is a free app for Android and iOS that gives you one-click access to send a complaint to a company's Twitter, Facebook, LinkedIn, and Google accounts. The app will even help you craft an effective complaint and help you find other users who have complaints for the same company. Just search "ComplainApp" wherever you download apps to see if it can help you.

OLD SCHOOL

....

*Polite persistence and a pen that's mightier than a sword
allow Betty to enjoy customer satisfaction*

(WHILE ALL THE PEOPLE *in this book are real, several did not want me to use their real names
or locations. That's the case here. All the other details of Betty's story are true to life.)*

It was a sunny day in Grand Junction, Colorado, when Betty Elizabeth went to the attorney's office to close on a small home for her retirement years.

The sixty-five-year-old widow was buying a 1,100-square footer for $90,000 at a very competitive 3 percent interest rate in March 2008. She got that fantastic rate through an affordable housing organization in her state.

Though she was assured everything would go smoothly with the closing, there were inevitably some bumps in the road that day. The lender questioned her debt-to-income ratio and pulled a surprise debt pay-down request on Betty.

"One hour prior to closing, they made me pay off my $10,000 car note, which was at 0 percent interest, and a Discover card that had a $250 balance," Betty tells me. "I suspect they thought I could not do this at the last minute, but I cashed in a 6 percent CD in order to get this great rate."

So there she was, scrambling across town to her bank to do an early CD withdrawal as the close of business approached. Thankfully she arrived in time to cash out the CD and run back across town to close the deal.

"I had to fight for that rate, but I got it," she says.

The next day or so after closing, Betty knew that what happened wasn't right. Her lender was trying to pull a fast one on her, and the $10,000 CD she cashed out had been earmarked as her burial money. So she contacted her congressman's office.

Betty met with the congressman's secretary, who told her to write down the details of her complaint in a letter. The secretary then took her letter and wrote a more formal one on her behalf that got things straightened out. Ultimately, Betty was able to recoup the lost interest and penalty she had to pay to cash out the CD before its term, plus some extra money to compensate for the trying experience.

"I was very frustrated but proud of myself for fighting this rip-off and so happy I did all this to get my house," Betty says.

This story shows two important things. First, elected officials are attuned to their constituents' needs—particularly when they're up for re-election. Second, there's a lot of power in the written word, specifically in the letter.

Today, Betty spends April through August in Colorado and snowbirds in Florida to be near her daughter. Her monthly mortgage payment in Grand Junction, including insurance and taxes, is $483.

Down in northern Florida, she found a two-bedroom duplex about one mile from her daughter and sixty feet from the beach. She rents it completely furnished for $437 a month, including utilities.

"I reside there from September through March each year and can only do this because of my low housing payment back in Colorado and this good deal down in Florida," she says.

Betty's monthly income includes about $1,500 from Social Security and $98 from an annuity, plus quarterly payments of $262 from another annuity. (I am generally not a fan of annuities. Visit ClarkHoward.com and search the keyword "annuities" to read why I think they stink.)

I like Betty's story because it shows how you as the little guy can take on big companies and win with surprisingly little technology. It's the David versus Goliath tale in modern American business.

The mortgage episode wasn't the first time Betty used the power of the written word to get satisfaction when she felt she'd been wronged by a company.

Just two years before that incident, Betty went to buy a new car by herself. She spent hours at the dealership and got worked over by the salesperson during "the grind" and then worked over again by the F&I (finance and insurance) man when it was time to finalize the deal.

"I was told everything I was paying for [at the closing table] was necessary. But then I reviewed the contract when I got home and saw I was paying $500 for LoJack and even more for an extended warranty!" she says.

Betty got so fired up that she wrote a letter warning people away from the dealership. She intended to circulate it among friends. But before she did that, Betty wanted to give the dealership a chance to make things right. "I went back the next morning to the dealership at eight a.m. with twenty copies of the letter in hand before I mailed it to my friends," she recalls.

She got a meeting with upper management. Having the letter in hand gave her some leverage. When the dealership read what she'd written, she was offered a refund of part of her money for the LoJack and extended warranty—both of which were *not* necessary purchases, by the way!

The lesson learned? "Don't ever go by yourself to a car dealership if you're a senior citizen," Betty says.

What can you take away from Betty's story?

Don't overlook low-tech approaches to issue resolution.

- There's an old saying, "The pen is mightier than the sword." We tend to forget that in an era of tweets and Facebook posts. But that fact isn't lost on Betty, who comes from a generation that's not shy about putting pen to paper.

- If you want to try this old-school approach, begin by writing a letter with three pieces of information: an explanation of your problem and who you spoke to about it; what attempts you've made to solve it; and what action you want to resolve it. Be sure to name a reasonable time frame for any resolution to take place.

- Make the tone positive and friendly. But above all, be brief in what you write! Your letter should be short and to the point. The longer you write, the less someone reads.

- If you don't get a response, send a second letter with a copy of the first attached. Always keeps a copy of your letters. If you are repeatedly ignored, then try sending it one last time by certified mail.

- Failing that, you might have to take the matter to small claims court. See the tips after the profile titled "Chronic Illness and Never-Ending Bills" in the Health Care chapter for more advice on going the small claims court route.

Contact your government representative.
- Many elected officials have constituent services people whose sole job is to handle complaints from voters. But you have to be sure to contact your representative at the right level.
- If you have a problem with your city water bill, contact your city councilperson. If it's about your county property taxes, contact your county commissioner. If it's about your state-issued driver's license, contact your state representative or state senator. If it's a federal issue, contact the office of your congressman or U.S. senator.
- The first job of every politician is to get re-elected, regardless of what political party they're affiliated with. So that's a key point to remember when you have an issue that you can't seem to get resolved on your own.

Try picketing in front of an offending business.
- Disgruntled customers seeking satisfaction from business owners used to picket outside the business. That approach has largely been supplanted by virtual griping online in this digital era. Still, it's worth remembering how people used to do things and seeing if it makes sense for your life today.
- Historically, I've had four pieces of advice for picketers: First, check with local authorities for rules governing a picket line in your town. Second, stick strictly to the facts with your complaint when you actually picket; say nothing about the character of the person who wronged you. Third, pick the busiest day of the week for your protest. For many businesses, that's typically a Saturday. Finally, get your children out there picketing—or borrow a friend's kids! Nothing else has the same impact as a nice family picket outside a business.

Use polite persistence.
- Polite persistence is the key to so many things in life. Some five years ago, my wife, Lane, was involved in an auto accident. While everybody involved was OK, we were having problems with the other driver's insurance company. They didn't want to pay for damage to my wife's car and kept pushing us to file a claim with our own insurer—a process known as subrogation.
- The problem with subrogation is that two insurers can cut a deal, leaving each driver with an at-fault accident on their driving record. In this particular case, there was no question that the other driver was the one who hit Lane.

- While the insurance struggles were going on, we were able to use a spare vehicle to get around. The insurers like to play a waiting game because they know that not everyone has more than one vehicle. So most people eventually roll over and just go the subrogation route. But instead I was politely persistent. I got on a first-name basis with the investigator and called every single day. On the eighth day, the other person's insurer agreed to pay for damage to Lane's car.

- And that's the message: Be patient and be nice. Demanding anything rarely works.

EXPERT ADVICE

*Anita shows why sometimes calling in outside firepower is
the best way to handle an insurance dispute*

It's May in Grand Teton National Park in Wyoming and the weather is unusually warm.

Anita Taff is strapped into a hang-gliding kite, preparing to soar above one of the most beautiful places on Earth. She begins to run across the snow, and the wind catches the kite. Instantly, she is floating, a sense of peace and tranquillity moving over her.

Four thousand feet above the jagged edges of the Tetons, the view is breathtaking. She glides over the snowcapped mountains and looks down to see wild rabbits and foxes, and then a big-horned sheep. She is literally flying alongside eagles.

Then she hits a heat thermal, and up she goes, swirling higher and higher. She sees buffalo grazing in a valley off in the distance. She's delighted that the updraft has treated her to a longer flight, allowing her to glide weightlessly back and forth over the mountains. But soon, the ground draws closer and her exhilarating ride is coming to an end. The green grass comes up quickly, and she's back on the ground, surrounded by mountains and the meadow.

"It is definitely not an ordinary day in the office!" says Anita, fifty-two, who makes her living in insurance. "You only live once and I believe in living life to the fullest!"

Anita traces her love of high-adventure sports, such as hang gliding, skydiving, zip lining, snowshoeing, and skiing, back to her first ride on the back of her brother's dirt bike.

"It was exciting and scary at the same time, but I always arrived at the end safe!"

Her day-to-day thrills consist of helping her clients stay safe in the confusing world of insurance claims. For twenty years, Anita and her husband, Foy, have owned and operated Taff Claims Services, which represents people whose homes have been destroyed by fire, flood, tornadoes, and other calamities.

Anita started on the other side, as an adjuster with St. Paul Insurance Companies, dealing with all types of insurance claims, including property, automobile, bodily injury, and workers compensation. She moved to Chubb Group of Insurance Companies to specialize in high-valued property insurance, handling claims from a few thousand dollars to multimillion-dollar losses.

She's managed and trained independent and staff adjusters for daily and catastrophe claim handling. She's traveled the country handling commercial and homeowners hurricane, tornado, hail, and crop damage claims. She's investigated and handled all types of claims insured by commercial and homeowners policies, among them movie set/equipment damage, boiler and machinery breakdown, ocean cargo/motor truck cargo loss, employee dishonesty/theft/embezzlement, and robbery and burglary.

After more than a decade in the industry, she switched sides and became a public adjuster.

"In the early 1990s, I noticed that the focus of the insurance industry, along with many other industries, transferred from customer service to stockholder satisfaction. This meant cost-cutting measures that reduced claim settlements to policyholders. I saw this as an opportunity to use my experience to help those with an overwhelming loss navigate their recovery and extract the maximum financial benefit the insurance policy offers."

Anita says that an insurance company will be real nice to you when you've had a $1,500 car accident but very tough when your house burns down.

"The goal of every business is to be profitable," she explained. "If you've been paying $1,000 a year for insurance and have a loss that costs a small amount, you may have already paid enough to cover the loss. Therefore, the insurance company may not lose money on you for a small loss."

However, you could pay $1,000 a year for homeowners insurance for thirty years, a total of $30,000. But if you have a fire in your home, it could cost several hundred thousand dollars.

"The insurance company will never recoup its expenses from you, so the incentive to pay you the maximum benefits of your policy isn't there. The goal of an adjuster is to minimize or completely eliminate the insurance company's loss as much as possible."

What kinds of things can an insurance company do that can be costly to a consumer? Anita says delaying payments has become a very popular method of reducing claims.

"The longer an insurance company delays a payment, the more [the company] makes in interest, and the more people give up and go away or take reduced payments just to move on."

Anita says insurance companies are denying a higher number of claims than ever before. That often forces consumers to hire an attorney, which is very costly.

Instead, some hire public adjusters like Anita, who knows the tricks insurance companies try to use and works hard to make sure they get a fair shake.

How fair? Anita represented one client who had a water line burst in his $3 million home, flooding the finished basement and also damaging the foundation. The insurance adjuster offered $50,000 to repair the house.

"The homeowners knew it would cost more than that but didn't know how much. After evaluating and documenting all the damage to the three-story home, we settled the claim in excess of $500,000."

In another case, a small business owner suffered a total loss due to fire.

"He was so overwhelmed he had to be hospitalized and called us from his hospital bed," Anita said. "He lost the building, inventory, income, and his employees were out of work. We provided the guidance and peace of mind by analyzing his policy, documenting his loss, and providing information to help with his decisions while he planned the grand reopening of his store."

And there was the woman whose home was destroyed by a fire set deliberately by her husband—who canceled the insurance policy before he set the fire.

The insurance company denied her claim.

"We were able to prove that the policy had been improperly canceled and had the decision reversed, and settled the claim for her financial interest. She went from being totally hopeless to having enough money to rebuild a smaller home and furnish it."

In the interest of full disclosure, I should mention that Anita also represented my coauthor, Mark Meltzer, when his house was destroyed by a fire in 2006. She earned him a settlement of several hundred thousand dollars.

Anita was born and raised in Milwaukee, Wisconsin, with four siblings. Her parents divorced when she was young, and her mother worked very hard to provide the basic necessities.

"I realized early that if I wanted anything more I would have to work for it," she said. "At the age of ten, I began earning my own spending money by helping neighbors with snow shoveling, yard work, maintenance projects, and baby-sitting. Those people admired my strong work ethic, so I decided young that I would have my own business."

She graduated high school a year early while working three part-time jobs, and she worked full-time while attending college.

Anita also helps those who are less fortunate than her. Every summer, she participates in the fund-raising project for the March of Dimes and its twenty-mile walkathon.

Her major role model, not surprisingly, was her mother.

"She was a very strong, tireless, determined woman. She loved her children unconditionally yet didn't tolerate excuses or laziness," Anita said.

A few words of her mother's advice stay with Anita in everything she does:

- Education, honesty, and integrity are things no one can take away from you.
- Live your life so the preacher doesn't have to lie at your funeral.
- You'll be surprised how much you will learn if you just listen, and . . .
- Read, read, read.

Sometimes it's necessary to call in outside firepower like a public adjuster to avoid being shortchanged on insurance payouts. What should you keep in mind when you're trying to get a fair shake from your insurer?

Protect yourself at home with diligent documentation.
- Anita has some good advice to protect yourself if you ever have to make a claim against your homeowners insurance.
- She says to keep receipts and photos, off premises, of all unusual or expensive items you purchase. Add an annual reminder to your calendar to take photos of your entire house, whether it's doing it all at once or one room a week. Open drawers and doors to show the items inside—they add up and are easy to forget!
- After a loss, she says, take a ridiculous number of photographs. Keep a detailed journal of names, dates, and activities of the claim process. Document all damage in writing and all receipts. And be sure to protect your property from further damage or the additional damage won't be covered.

Know when a rider is necessary.

- *Real Simple* magazine recently ran a story about what's possibly not covered by insurance and might require you to buy an additional rider. Their list included cameras, china, silver, crystal, collectibles, fine art, furs, jewelry, musical instruments, and sports memorabilia. (For my money, I'd advise you to skip the rider on cameras unless you have professional equipment.) Here's the sticky thing, though. You can buy a rider, but you might also need to go one more step and have an appraisal. That's very common when you're talking about collectibles and jewelry.

Be sure you have enough coverage.

- If you've been in a house for five years or longer, chances are you might be grossly underinsured for homeowners coverage. In fact, you'll only discover it after a catastrophic loss, when it's too late.

- So you must read the coverage limits when your policy comes up for renewal every year. Let your insurer know if there's no way you could rebuild your house for the specified amount. Note the name of the rep you speak to and the date/time of the call. That way if your insurer refuses to raise your limits and a catastrophic loss happens, you've already begun building a case against them.

- My insurer would not raise my limits, so I triggered a clause in my contract and got a third-party appraiser to look at my home. The insurer accepted the appraisal and then complied by raising my coverage.

- There's a corollary to this tip: Don't make a claim unless you have a major loss. The home insurance industry is such a tight business that it's called "use it and lose it" insurance by the industry itself. Having the highest deductible allowed will prevent you from making small claims.

Learn how to counter lowball offers from auto insurers.

- Auto insurance adjusters use an industry database that's stacked against the consumer and tends to value cars at 70 cents on the dollar—a whopping 30 percent less than what your car is really worth!

- If you feel an insurer is trying to cheat you on the value of a vehicle that is totaled or stolen, here's what I want you to do. First, develop an average value for your vehicle, adjusting for mileage and condition, on KBB.com, Edmunds.com, and NADA.com. You'll want to look for the retail value numbers, not the trade-in value, because those numbers are a joke.

- Second, write a letter to your insurer stating these are the values you found. Ask to meet with your adjuster's supervisor if the adjuster is not cooperative. If the supervisor isn't having it, tell him you want to invoke the appraisal clause of your contract. That's when you involve an independent appraiser who develops the value for your vehicle. That's the best way I know to deal with lowball offers.

CONCLUSION

In this book, we've met dozens of people whose approach to their financial life made them interesting to me, and I hope to you. So what did we learn from them? And how can we use those lessons not just to "Live Large in Lean Times," the theme of my last book, but to live large for the long haul in the decades that will follow the Great Recession?

I want to leave you with some rules to live by, some guidelines to firm up your finances for the future.

1. You have to save money. It's tempting to want to spend everything you earn, but that's not the way to build a sound future. It's critical to save. The earlier you start, the better, but it's never too late. The money you set aside will give you more freedom to make choices, like taking a lesser-paying job because you love the work or starting a business.

2. Invest for the long haul. Sometimes people are afraid to buy stocks because they see them as too risky, but you need your money to grow faster than inflation to build your buying power. Or people sell their mutual fund shares when the market is down. If you buy regularly, such as through a 401(k) plan, and keep doing so whether the market is up or down, you'll build wealth over time. The markets might have a bad year or two, but they invariably rise over the decades.

3. Keep debt to a minimum. When you owe money on your credit cards or on an expensive car loan, you're a financial prisoner, giving your hard-earned money to a lender every

month to pay interest. Pay your credit cards off every month and keep your debt to the bare minimum, and you'll have more to save or to spend on the things you really want.

4. Buy a house. Despite the postrecession housing crash, buying a house remains an excellent way to build wealth over time. In fact, with house prices still down and interest rates still low, housing is incredibly affordable. Paying rent puts money in someone else's pocket. Buying a house means paying down your mortgage balance a little bit every month and seeing the value of your house grow over time, with the ever-widening gap between the two—equity—being yours to keep.

5. Keep your cars for a long time. Cars are expensive, and they lose value over time. So they are an expense, not an investment. If you buy or lease a new car every few years, you'll never stop making payments. If you buy a sensible used car, pay it off, and keep it for years after the loan is done, you'll keep the monthly payments for yourself. You can even save them and either pay cash for your next car or make a huge down payment and take a tiny loan.

6. Keep a good credit rating. Nothing good comes from having a bad credit rating. It will be harder to get a mortgage or a car loan, and you'll have to pay a higher interest rate if you do. Pay your bills on time and don't use too much of your available credit, and check your credit report for free at least once a year.

7. Spend your money wisely. Shop for good prices on the things you have to buy and don't waste your money on things you don't, from $6 cups of coffee to cutting-edge electronics, and you'll be way ahead of the game. Keep a budget and use a free online program like Mint.com to track your spending and make adjustments when you slip.

8. Travel smartly. Traveling is one of the great joys of life, and you can do it without going to the poorhouse. Look for airfare, hotel, and car rental specials, and try to be as flexible as possible in your travel dates and where you choose to go. Buy what's on sale and save, just like at the supermarket. And you don't have to eat in a fancy restaurant every day you're on the road. Rent a condo with a kitchen and cook for yourself, or grab a sandwich at a deli and have a picnic.

9. Don't let companies take advantage of you. Persistence is the key when you have a consumer problem. People who are persistent usually win. People who give up in frustration generally miss the chance to have the problem resolved to their satisfaction.

10. You don't have to change your financial habits all at once. Each year, make more good decisions and fewer bad ones, and over the years you can steer your finances into calmer, warmer waters.

ACKNOWLEDGMENTS

Writing any book involves the help of many great people, and that is especially true of this book. First and foremost, I want to thank the fifty-plus people whose life stories make up the bulk of *Living Large for the Long Haul*. I asked them some very personal questions to get the details we needed to tell their stories, and they answered with candor and courage. I am immensely grateful for that.

Next, I want to thank my book agent, Laurie Liss of Sterling Lord Literistic, who has represented me with integrity and tenacity for a dozen years.

Thanks also to our wonderful friends at Avery Books, including publisher William Shinker, associate publisher Lisa Johnson, our editor, Megan Newman, editorial assistant Gigi Campo, publicists Casey Maloney and Lindsay Gordon, and copyeditor Janice Kurzius. They've been a pleasure to work with and took my last book to number 1 on the *New York Times* Best-Seller List. Who could ask for anything more?

I'm so grateful to the team at HLN, which has supported my books with tremendous enthusiasm. Thanks to Dave Siff, Mike Kane, and Tim Mallon.

And finally, thanks to my radio team, led by my remarkable executive producer, Christa DiBiase. Christa spent many hours helping my co-authors and me plan and create this book, and her insights were, as always, invaluable.

INDEX

flexibility on dates and
    destinations,
    203, 306
free attractions, 214
hotels, 204, 207, 208–9,
    212, 214–15
interstate bus service, 59
medical tourism, 251–56
reward credit cards, 207,
    208–9
staycations, 211–14
travel websites, 203–4
vacation time off from
    work, 213–14
world travel for free,
    201–3
TravelDK.com, 207
Travelocity.com, 204
Traxo.com, 209
TrueCar.com, 145
Twitter. *See* social media

ultra-light start-ups, 191–93
upskilling, 283
Us.SunPowerCorp.com, 150

vacation rental property
    Airbnb.com, 42–44,
        45–46
    covenants and legal
        restrictions, 41,
        42, 45
    insurance, 45
    pricing and income, 42
    taxes, 46
    valuables and sensitive
        information, 42,
        45–46
vacations. *See* travel
Vanguard, 122, 126, 127, 129,
    132, 198, 260
vehicle sharing, 59
virtual hiring halls, 192

Walsh, Jannet, 275–77
warranties, third-party, 63
water usage, 158
Web. *See* Internet
websites for businesses, 192
Wigge, Michael, 201–3
wills, 227
window caulking, 158
Wink bank balance app, 238
work. *See* employment;
    entrepreneurship
work-at-home businesses, 23

Yelp.com, 63, 207
YoBucko.com, 99
YouTube, consumer
    complaints via,
    289, 291

Zaccardi, Mike, 118–20
ZipCar.com, 59

ABOUT THE AUTHOR

Clark Howard is a nationally syndicated consumer expert who advises consumers on how to save money, spend less, and avoid getting ripped off. His radio show is heard every day on more than 200 radio stations throughout North America.

Mark Meltzer is executive editor at *Atlanta Business Chronicle* and lives in Atlanta.

Theo Thimou is director of content for ClarkHoward.com and lives in Atlanta.

Also by Clark Howard

The ultimate guide to saving money, covering everything from cell phones to student loans, coupon websites to mortgages, investing to electric bills, and beyond.